SCRIPT CONFERENCE WITH GOD

Nathan peered over the top of his knees. He was in Plastic Tolstoy's study, seated on quite the softest, lowest couch he had ever encountered. On the table in front of him stood a glass of fizzy water, but he could not reach it, not without a rope to haul him out of the couch.

"Uhm . . . hic . . . do you think perhaps, hic, we might show something of the little girl's fate, but tastefully? . . ." Nathan began.

"Do I think perhaps hic!" Plastic quoted Nathan with such withering sarcasm that all the potted plants died. "Do *I* think. *I'm* not the damn writer. I'm just the moron who *pays* the damn writer."

Nathan hiccuped miserably.

"You think I'm being hard on you, don't you? You think I'm being unnecessarily negative. You want to see negative!" barked Plastic. "This is negative."

Suddenly Plastic pulled open a drawer of his mighty desk and took out a gun. Nathan could not have moved had he wanted to, being stuck in a couch as he was, but there was no time anyway. It was over in a second. Plastic took two steps toward him, pointed the gun into Nathan's astonished face and fired. Three shots, point-blank range. The gun flashed, the noise in the confined space was deafening, and the glass rattled as acrid smoke filled the room.

"Have they gone?" Plastic inquired mildly.

Nathan could not reply; you cannot talk when your heart is in your mouth.

"The hiccups, have they gone? . . ."

Also by Ben Elton

Stark
Gridlock
Gasping *(stage play)*
Silly Cow *(stage play)*

This Other Eden

Ben Elton

POCKET BOOKS

New York   London   Toronto   Sydney   Tokyo   Singapore

This book is a work of fiction. Names, characters, places and incidents are products of the author's imagination or are used fictitiously. Any resemblance to actual events or locales or persons, living or dead, is entirely coincidental.

An *Original* Publication of POCKET BOOKS

POCKET BOOKS, a division of Simon & Schuster Inc.
1230 Avenue of the Americas, New York, NY 10020

Copyright © 1993 by Stand Up Limited

First published in Great Britain by Simon & Schuster Ltd.

ISBN: 0-671-89702-0

First Pocket Books trade paperback printing May 1995

10 9 8 7 6 5 4 3 2 1

POCKET and colophon are registered trademarks of Simon & Schuster Inc.

Cover design by Matt Galemmo
Cover art by Lee MacLeod

Printed in the U.S.A.

For Sophie

This Other Eden

1

In which a much-loved man pursues the elusive green light

A rat's tale.

A RAT FEEDS GREEDILY ON ROTTEN MEAT. . . .

A rat feeds greedily on rotten *human* meat. A rotting human limb, attached to a living body.

The desperate man knows it will be easier to detach the limb from the body than the rat from the limb. The diner is stronger than the dinner, for the diner has no drug to numb its pain. The rat's head is buried deep in the silver-green flesh, its claws hidden beneath the blackened skin. Only its plump body and twitching rump can be seen as it pushes deeper and deeper into the decaying muscle. The desperate man knows that the hungry rat will never let go. Yet if it remains, how long before it or its friends and relations discover the living meat beyond the putrid thigh? Not very long, surely, and even a rat must prefer fresh meat to foul.

If one is to die, then there are better ways than being eaten alive by enormous flea-ridden rats; even in his weary, drifting state, the man can see that. Swallowing two sparkling capsules, the only bright thing in his dull world, the man waits for the drugs to rush his brain and then takes up his big knife. The knife is blunt, but the flesh is rotten and falls apart before the blade, as if it has been braised. In a moment, man and leg are parted. His mind on other things, he pulls himself away, leaving the rat to its refreshment.

This is how it will be in the century to come. No savage biker tribes, no lone still-human heroes, no Mad Max millennium, only ill, old people and large, hungry rats eating them.

Those who love you hurt you most.

Nathan knew it was good; it was the best work he'd ever done. That was why he so desperately wanted the job. This was more than just a bit of seriously good copy. This was prophecy, this was the truth.

But telling the truth is never easy. Nathan was drained. The night Los Angeles reignited, as it did at regular intervals these days, he had been a prisoner in his hotel room for a week. Held captive not by a gunman or a sex criminal or even the fantastical illusion that the room service he had ordered in a previous life might one day arrive, but by a great and terrible desire to please.

There were people in that town who loved Nathan, and he had to justify that love. He knew they loved him, for they had told him so many times, and they had also sent a limousine to collect him at the airport, when they might easily have suggested that he take a cab and keep the receipt. For a man used, as Nathan was, to the finances of British radio, this was big love indeed.

Sometimes though, mere love is not enough. In Hollywood you can be embraced and rejected with equal fervor and integrity by the same people and at the same time. This, over the years, had led to movie people getting something of a reputation for craven hypocrisy. But there is nothing disingenuous about combining love with rejection. It is quite possible, and indeed reasonable, to like and admire, yes, even love somebody without wishing to commit hundreds of millions of dollars on the strength of their script.

Every day, all over town, writers faced producers, producers faced bigger producers, bigger producers faced studio heads, and the same tortured mantra was heard: "You are a great artist and we all love you. Speaking personally, yours is the kind of talent that was the reason I came into this business in the first place. Will we be picking up your project? No, I don't think so, but that's about us, it isn't about you."

Nathan understood his position. They loved him, but he frustrated them for, try as he might, Nathan had so far been unable to produce a treatment in which the plot *curved* sufficiently or in which the characters possessed heart, moral worth, and, above all, warmth.

"It's no good this guy dying, one-legged in a polluted world," the men who loved Nathan would tell him, "if we don't *care* that he dies."

Nathan understood what was required of him. He returned to his room and tried to make the people who loved him care; for if they cared, then so would Mr. and Ms. America, and if Mr. and Ms. America cared, then it was a reasonable presumption that the whole world would care. That was Nathan's brief, to make the whole world care. If he could achieve that then he would truly have justified the faith that Plastic Tolstoy had placed in him. With this thought Nathan turned wearily back to his computer. For when Plastic Tolstoy placed faith in you, it was wise to justify that faith. For Plastic Tolstoy was the most important man in the whole communications industry. It was his job to market the end of the world.

Everything is fascinating when you should be working.

All week Nathan had moped from his bed to his desk to his bathroom and back to his bed. Trying to think of ways to make those who loved him, Mr. and Ms. America, the world in general, and above all, Plastic Tolstoy, care. But everything is fascinating when you should be working, and Nathan had also spent his week fighting the desire to stare out of the window, leafing through magazines, and flicking through the endless permutations available on the in-room entertainment system.

The Hitler trial was reaching its climax. That sad, gray monster stood before the cameras every day, his shocked and baffled face devoid of any real understanding of the crimes they told him he had committed. Under normal circumstances DNA cloning was banned; the world was overcrowded enough without people regrowing the dead. However, when a lock of Hitler's hair had been unearthed, the World Court ruled that an exception might be made, the general feeling being that Hitler was one villain for whom being dead should not prevent justice being done. Besides, the United Nations was always hugely in debt, and the TV rights to the trial were worth a fortune.

Nathan carried on through the news channels. They were all pretty similar, which, considering they were all owned by the same company (Plastic Tolstoy Communications System), was hardly surprising. The daughter of the British king had been videotaped turning tricks in Piccadilly, although a lot of people said it was just a clever hologram. Jurgen Thor was to address the European parliament yet again, on the subject of banning or at least massively taxing Claustrospheres. A new fish had been developed that was capable of surviving in the dead waters of the Atlantic, a fish that had the added advantage of being so radioactive it could cook itself while the busy house-spouse prepared a salad.

Under normal circumstances Nathan would not have

dreamed of watching a news item about marine research. Nor would he have allowed himself to get sucked into a public forum-style talk show, where victims of pedestrian-dog feces encounters were brought together with dog owners, in order to come to terms with their anger. But everything is fascinating when you should be working.

Making them care.

Nathan snapped the TV off, as he had done a hundred times that week. He dragged his hand angrily from deep within the great plastic bag of Bacon Cheezos on his lap. He resisted the colossal temptation to spend twenty minutes staring at the wall and scratching his balls. He avoided the Virtual Reality helmet beckoning him from the coffee table. He must concentrate, he must focus. He had to make those who loved him care.

"What I need," Nathan mused to himself, "is a kid . . . a cute kid who is in some way relying on the dying man who chops off his leg. . . ."

Nathan grabbed his Voice to Screen DictaType Transmitter. Suddenly, after all the waiting and procrastinating, inspiration struck. The words tumbled out.

"All right, so the man has a child . . . a tiny little girl who peeks out from her hiding place amid the mountain of rotten garbage . . . rotten, *stinking, putrid* garbage. . . . Um . . . she's dirty and thin . . . but cute, very cute . . . the dying world has yet to dull her bonny beauty . . . nice sentence, *good* sentence. . . . Okay, so somehow we know that the half-dead man with the big knife is the little girl's father . . . a signet ring? Maybe the same haircut? . . . Or else we see her mouth the word *Daddy* . . . yes, that's it, she mouths the word *Daddy* so we know he is her father, her last chance, her only protector. Then we see him drug himself into oblivion and cut off his own leg . . . beautiful, that is *great*. . . . So the gorgeous little girl knows that she is now in deep doo doo . . . Um . . . her sparkling eyes fade to dull despair as her dad . . . no, as her *last best hope* drags himself away to die. . . . Then what happens? What's the punch?''

Nathan paused for a moment, willing his little flight of fancy to see him through to some stunning conclusion. Yes! He had it. Breathlessly he spoke again into the Dicta-Type microphone: "The little girl retreats back into the rotting garbage, which provides the only warmth available to her now . . . and the rat is left on its own, eating her dad's leg . . . great image, hold on that a moment. . . . Then the rat's head emerges from the severed leg . . . its snout all twitching and gruesome . . . um . . . The white fangs show amid the soft, maggoty meat bulging in its mouth . . . good sentence, good sentence, keep that. . . . So why has the rat stopped eating? Because it's *heard something,* that's why! . . . Something tempting . . . something exciting. The evil rat turns and stares toward the place in the garbage where the tiny child is hiding. Freeze-frame. . . . Cue voice-over. . . . Doesn't your child deserve a better tomorrow? Invest in Claustrosphere today.''

Nathan turned off his DictaType machine.

"It's good," he told himself. "They've *got* to pick it up."

And as the flames that a few hours earlier had burned only in the hearts of an angry people began yet again to engulf large sections of one of the world's premier cities, Nathan sat, hand clamped unconsciously on his crotch, hoping that those who loved him, who had failed to care about a dying man, might now care about a threatened little girl. Hoping that his assuredly fine treatment for a Claustrosphere commercial, his unquestionably brilliant vision, would also now have that all-important factor, "warmth." That those who loved him might love him all the more, love him, perhaps, even enough to suggest to Plastic Tolstoy that his project be green-lighted.

Nathan did not resent the compliant, entirely reactive nature of his creative endeavors. That was the town, he thought, and indeed, as the flames danced outside his window, he was right.

If I should get lost in development, think only this of me. That there is some corner of the U.S. entertainment industry that is forever England.

Nathan was British, but despite this, he did not suffer from that terrible anger that many Brit artists who visit Hollywood feel. That private shame that comes from the knowledge that *you* have come to *them*. That, for all your babble about seeking a more vibrant culture, about fleeing the anally-retentive, small-minded snobberies one encounters at home, they know and you know that the only reason you have come is because they have more money. Much, much more money.

Brits in Hollywood divide largely into two categories: the ones who are living there and the ones who would like to live there. The ones who are living there tend to be aggressively Yankophile, partly taking on the characteristics and language of the town. They wear loafers, or smart deck shoes, sometimes without socks, and drink Lite beer and dry martinis, ordering them by brand name. "Get me a Beefeater martini and a twist, please."

The visitors, on the other hand, affect an exaggerated Britishness as a defense against the obvious fact that they are on the make. They ask for tea and are gently amused when it arrives with the tea bag still in the cup. They order obscure malt whiskies, secretly hoping that the bar won't stock them. They tell their hosts that the thing they like most about L.A. is the paper toilet-seat covers. When they get home to Britain they speak wittily of toothy but empty smiles and glib, automatic admonishments to "enjoy." They claim firmly that it is a fine place to visit but they could never live there, which translates, of course, as nobody has asked them to.

7

Nathan made no such pretense at indulgent distaste. He thought California was lovely. He enjoyed the toothy smiles. He thought it was nice to be greeted cheerfully.

"But for God's sake, they don't *mean* it," a disaffected independent producer from Fulham had said over an Isle of Locharno McClaymore, the Bonny single malt in the hotel bar. "They don't care if you live or die."

"Since when have good manners been a matter of sincerity?" Nathan replied. "You wish me 'all the best' every time I see you, but you wouldn't lift a finger to make it happen."

"Look, I was taught good manners, not vacuous hypocrisy," snapped the producer, who had that day failed even to be loved very much, let alone green-lighted.

"Exactly," said Nathan. "You were *taught* to say please and thank you, not because anyone wished to indoctrinate you with a false sense of goodwill, but simply because it is important to show consideration. Is the Californian 'have a nice day, enjoy your life, die happy and come back as something wonderful' any different?"

The producer from Fulham moodily ordered another drink. He thought that Nathan would sing a different tune when Plastic Tolstoy's people rejected his Claustrosphere ad and put him straight on a suborbital back to dirty old England. Then he'd be bad-mouthing the Yanks along with all the other unloved Brits.

But Nathan had no intention of getting rejected; he was going to be green-lighted. Because he was prepared to bet that, with the addition of the scared little girl, his description of the end of the world would be the warmest description of the end of the world that Plastic Tolstoy's people would have seen all week.

An idea whose time has come.

Everybody was talking about the end of the world these days. It was a very big subject, not perhaps quite as big as sports, or the love-lives of the British royal family, but nonetheless very big. Some people, like Plastic Tolstoy, were trying to market it. Others, like Jurgen Thor, the Great Green Warrior, were trying to prevent it. Some people were, of course, causing it. Whether by accident or design, every day countless incidents, both large and small, were hastening the Earth's untimely demise. One such event, a rather large one as it happened, was shortly to occur off the coast of Alaska. There, while Nathan awaited the studio's reaction to his heartwarming vision of catastrophe, would be found images of Earth death every bit as chilling as those he had invented. Not *quite* as chilling, perhaps, for in real life the plot rarely curves and people are often less inclined to care.

2

A *loose-fitting coffin in a watery grave*

A view from a cliff.

THE MESS WAS INDESCRIBABLE. YET IT WOULD HAVE TO BE DE-scribed, as always, described in yet another of the pointless reports that had to be written. No report could ever adequately convey what a mess it really was, though. As Judy, the investigating officer on the scene, often said, you had to be there.

"You know how, with babies," Judy would say, "you can never quite believe what a state they can get things into, until you find out for yourself? Well, it's the same with supertankers."

Everything was as it always was on these occasions. Judy sometimes wondered why anybody bothered turning up at all. As far as the eye could see, the boiling ocean was black. The cliffs and rocks were black. The dead creatures were black. The emergency operations personnel were black from head to foot, as they got their emergency operation underway in the usual totally inadequate manner.

"Tanker disasters are like the first snows of winter," Judy would explain to friends. "You remember how we used to have snow? Well, year in, year out the stuff would fall, and every time it was like the first time, it was like nobody had ever had to deal with snow before. The roads would get clogged up, the trains would stop, the pipes would burst. Nothing was ever ready. Well, it's the same when a billion quarts of crude hits a coastline. People think the authorities know what to do. They don't. We all just shrug our shoulders and get down there with a shovel and a bucket like we always do."

Judy was standing on the highest cliff overlooking the disaster with the coast guard people and a couple of local cops.

"Well, guess we'd better go get the captain. I hear he's drunk," said the chief coastguardsman with the weary sigh of a man who had left a good dinner to come and bear witness to an event that would follow its tragic course, whether he was there to watch it or not.

"Are you going down onto the bridge?" Judy inquired.

The coastguardsman turned disdainfully to look at Judy.

"I don't see any reason to discuss my plans with you, nerd," he said.

A boy named Judy.

Judy was a man even though he had a woman's name. He was called Judy because he had been unfortunate enough to be born during the time of the great gender realignment. A period when it was a commonly held belief in the university common rooms of the world that all single-sex imagery was oppressive. This was a time when men were strongly encouraged not to grow beards, which were seen as visual assertions of gender, whereas it became fashion-

11

able for women to be as hairy as possible, in order to blur the margins. The idea was that if everyone could pretend to be exactly the same, then no one could be held back by being different, and hence, it was argued, the individual would be in a position to prosper.

That was how Judy came to be called Judy. One morning before he was born, as his father waxed his face and his mother applied mascara to her legs and upper lip, it was decided.

"If it's a boy we'll call it Judy," they said, "and if it's a girl we'll call it Hercules." In this manner the margins were not blurred, and Judy got hounded every day at school for sixteen years.

When Judy reached his majority he astonished those who knew him by not changing his name. He had, of course, always intended to do so the moment he got the chance; but when that chance finally came around, he had suffered so much at the hands of bullies that there seemed little point in bothering. Children are much crueler than adults, Judy reasoned, so he had already weathered the worst of it. He was, of course, wrong. At college, the coarser element laughed at him and pushed him around every day, and as an adult he rarely turned his back without hearing a snigger.

It was not just that Judy was a boy with a girl's name; his problems were further compounded by the fact that he was the least prepossessing of men. He had one leg slightly shorter than the other and something of a stoop. His glasses were thick and his hair always greasy. He was a textbook nerd. It was almost as if he had been deliberately designed that way. In terms of appearance there was literally nothing about him that was not nerdy. If they gave out frequent-flier miles for looking ineffectual and inadequate, Judy could have been the first man on Mars.

If he had been a stupid nerd Judy might simply have been ignored, but he wasn't: he was a smart nerd, very smart indeed, which was of course something of a red flag to the bullies. It was bad enough, the bullies reasoned, putting up with someone who was such a dork, without that dork having the gall to be smarter than they were.

Occasionally, in his younger days, Judy had considered having a physical rebuild, or at the very least getting his face done. But as he grew up he came to resent the idea of paying a surgeon to attack his body simply because people did not find it attractive. Besides which, he could not have afforded a really good operation. The cosmetic surgery industry had become fearful of creating a world filled with semi-identical, plasticized, doll-like figures. They had therefore introduced a system that they called "financial discrimination," which meant that only very rich people could turn themselves into semi-identical, plasticized, doll-like figures.

Therefore Judy remained as nerdy as the day he was born and suffered the consequences. It was probably because of this discrimination that a clear sense of what was right grew strong in Judy's heart, and he determined that he would spend his life fighting intolerance and injustice. To this end, he employed his considerable intellect to win himself a place with the FBI, reasoning that he would certainly find plenty of intolerance and injustice in the FBI.

He was right. Nothing changed. Judy irritated the nastier element among his new colleagues no less than he had irritated the bullies at school and college. He continued to look stupid and talk smart, a combination almost guaranteed to bring out the bully in anyone who was even remotely so disposed. During his training the oafs and toughs continued to beat him up as they had always done. He was shouldered aside on the firing range and wet-toweled in the showers. Many of his colleagues were, of course, nice to him, but a kind smile does little to mitigate the pain of being held down and given a Chinese burn, or of having a Magnum .44 suspended by a piece of string from your scrotum.

The passage of years had not tempered Judy's sense of

injustice, and the resentment he felt at being constantly dismissed remained undiminished. Therefore, when the coastguardsman on the polluted cliff top called him a nerd, he drew himself up to his full height, which was either five-five, or five-five and a half, depending on which leg he put his weight on, and prepared to confront yet another nerdist.

"My name is Judy Schwartz," he said. "I am an FBI agent, and I demand that you take me with you onto the bridge of this stricken tanker. Otherwise I shall devote the rest of my life to finding out who your mistress is and then revealing her identity to your wife."

Dead hand at the tiller.

The little coast guard helicopter stood with its engine idling on the roof of the ship's bridge, while Judy, two coastguardsmen, and the local chief of police went inside and surveyed the scene.

"Well, he sure saved us a lot of trouble," said the police chief.

"Did the decent thing, I reckon," a coastguardsman added.

They were referring to the captain of the stricken tanker, who was dead, killed, apparently, by his own hand. There he sat, slumped across his bloodied charts, a bottle in one hand, a revolver in the other, and his brains in the wastepaper basket on the other side of the room.

It was déjà vu for Judy. He had seen this scene before, on another bridge in another storm. In the midst of a different disaster he had seen a ship's master dead over his charts. Dead before he could explain why he had allowed his ship to get so close to shore in such inclement circumstances.

Outside on the enormous deck, which was listing at an angle that made standing up extremely difficult, the crew were being winched to safety. Apart, that is, from the captain, who was dead, and the second-in-command, a competent-looking woman named Jackson. She was standing near the bridge, awaiting any further instructions from the coast guard before following the crew off the ship. Judy wandered outside into the gale and spoke to her, shouting, to be heard above the wind and the rain.

"Did you order the abandon ship, Ms. . . . ?" he asked.

"Jackson. Barbara Jackson. No, I did not, sir. The captain ordered abandon ship and most of the crew got away in the boats before the situation deteriorated to necessitate coast guard helicopters."

"So the captain discharged his duties and then killed himself?"

"That is the case."

"Was that like him?" Judy asked.

"Was what? Discharging his duties or killing himself?"

"Killing himself."

"Well, he didn't make a habit of it," Jackson responded angrily. "But then he didn't make a habit of losing ships. Certainly not like this. We went down like a stone, holed both sides. The captain would have known what the consequences of that would be. This coast's finished for three hundred miles, the fishing, the wildlife, everything. Would you want that on your conscience? He was a decent man. I reckon he'd have been dead inside before he pulled the trigger."

"Holed both sides, you say?" Judy inquired. "Seems rather unusual, doesn't it? The rocky coast is only on the one side."

"There's plenty of channels, we must have got caught in one."

"And yet the captain was a good seaman?"

"As good as I've sailed with. . . . They say he'd been drinking."

"Did he often drink on duty?"

Jackson hesitated. She was a loyal crew member, but did not wish to lie to the FBI.

"He may have touched it. But, as I say, he was a good seaman. I never saw him even remotely drunk on watch."

Judy was lost in thought for a moment. The captain was a drinker, that much was clear, which could certainly make him the culprit . . . but it could also make him a very convenient scapegoat.

"Do you think he got drunk and ran the ship aground?" he asked Jackson.

"I suppose he must have," she replied.

Inside, the coast guard and police chief, having completed their perfunctory investigation, were preparing to leave.

"Can I see where the ship's ruptured?" Judy asked hurriedly.

"Sure, if you're a fish, they're both below the waterline," Jackson replied.

"But the ship's listing, eventually the port-side rupture will emerge."

"It might," Jackson conceded, "if the ship hasn't broken up by then, which it probably will have, the way this storm's blowing."

But Judy was insistent; he wanted to see the hole in the side of the ship. The coast guard people were astonished, and informed him that if he wished to risk his neck on damn fool errands he could do it alone. Then they left in their helicopter without him. Jackson, despite Judy's protestations, elected to stay, arguing that Judy would have no hope whatsoever of finding his way into the ship's hold without guidance.

Judy thanked her and radioed the helicopter, which had by now winched the crew aboard, requesting it to stand by overhead. The pilot was not overjoyed.

"Lieutenant Schwartz!" the pilot called back. "We're getting blown all over the damn sky! What the hell are you *doing* down there?"

Judy replied that he was conducting the fullest investiga-tion possible into the source of a major environmental catastrophe before the principal piece of evidence was lost to the elements.

"Something," Judy added angrily, "which the coast guard has signally failed to do. Now shut your face and do your job or I'll give your address to the Mormons."

Hidden depths.

With one side of the ship shuddering slowly upward and every inch of the vehicle screaming and groaning and loudly announcing its imminent breakup, Judy and Jackson edged their way below. It is not easy trying to descend a ship's stairway at the best of times, but when those stairs are leaning over at an angle of forty-five degrees it is very nearly impossible. Particularly if you are extremely conscious of the fact that at any moment the entire million-ton ship is going to snap in two and hurl you into a freezing vortex of oil, rock, and toxic seawater. It was also pitch-black, of course, the ship's emergency lights having given up at the first sign of an emergency. Jackson led the way with a flashlight.

They found the breach in a vast container dock still half-filled with oil and water. There was no way they could actually reach the great tear in the side of the ship, because the flood stood between them and it. Judy played the flashlight around the edges of the rupture.

"Notice anything strange about this hole?" he inquired, shouting himself hoarse above the crashing of the sea outside and the huge booming and creaking of the ship itself.

"Only that it's pretty big. I didn't think we'd done that much damage. If the hole on the other side is as drastic, we'd better get out now. I don't give this hulk five more minutes." But Judy continued to play the light around the edges of the hole, or at least those parts that the flashlight beam could reach.

"It is strange, though, isn't it?" he said, almost to himself.

"I can't hear you," Jackson shouted. "Give me the flashlight. We have to leave!"

Judy took no notice. He was still thinking, his mind elsewhere. His body was in danger of being elsewhere shortly too. The ship was shuddering its last, and it was a question of get out now or go down with it. Fortunately for Judy, Jackson was much stronger than he was. As he mused, she wrenched the flashlight from his grasp and let them both out of the huge quarter-mile chamber that could so nearly have become a rather loose-fitting coffin.

As they ascended the stairs, Judy could not resist taking one last look back despite the danger.

"It *is* strange, though, don't you think?" he said.

But Jackson was way ahead of him.

3

On a drive through Hollywood

The city that Liz built.

BEFORE YOU CAN BE GREEN-LIGHTED OR REJECTED, YOU HAVE TO make a pitch, and it was Nathan's day to pitch. The biggest day of his life.

The riots were dying down as he drove his rental car through Century City, the city, legend had it, that Liz Taylor built. Nathan had heard the story a number of times in various versions. The facts seemed to be that the whole area had once been the back lot of Twentieth Century Fox. It was here that in another, more innocent age they had reenacted great wagon trains, built medieval castles, and refought the Pacific battles of the U.S. marines.

Anyway, the story went that Fox lost so much money on Liz Taylor's movie *Cleopatra* that they had to sell most of the backlot to real estate developers. This debacle was a direct result of the curious Hollywood belief that equates gossip column inches with potential ticket revenue. The extraordinary idea that just because the public is interested in whom some celebrity is screwing, it will go and see them in a movie is a delusion that nearly cripples the industry regularly.

So Fox sold their back lot, and a mighty city of steel and glass skyscrapers grew up, and was subsequently burned down as a result of the civil unrest that became part of day-to-day life in the L.A. area. It was through this urban strife that Liz's city gained a far more significant claim to fame than as a mere monument to the fiction of the star system. For it was here that pollution was first used as a means to facilitate social engineering.

Environmental protection.

The problem was a serious one. Every time the city was rebuilt, the disaffected have-nots would come up from the badlands to loot it and burn it down again. This, obviously, was a source of considerable irritation to the civic authorities. Even more galling, though, was the fact that these regular acts of vandalism were perpetrated under the protection of top-quality filtered sun and the very cleanest air, for which the victims of the attacks were paying.

Century City, by dint of its great wealth, boasted a state-of-the-art municipal ecodefense system. Its sun was UV-filtered by the satellite method, whereby a solar screen was placed in orbit over the city. The air was kept reasonable by the simple blow system, where huge fans prevented smog from gathering by blowing it away into other parts of the city.

All this safe sun and clean air made life in Century City very pleasant. Unfortunately, it was as pleasant for the visiting vandals as for the legitimate residents. The outrageous fact was that honest citizens were paying local taxes so that the people who robbed them might be protected from skin cancer and lung disease. Something had to be done.

Something was. The world's first pollution-based security system was installed. The orbital sun-shield was sent
spinning away to join the ever-growing slicks of debris
caught in the gravitational pull of other planets, and the
giant fans were silenced. The sunscreen was replaced by
a solar cell intensifier, which acted in the manner of a vast
UV magnifying glass. A deal was done with the electricity
people, who stopped pumping their exhaust out over the
Pacific and let it out on the Avenue of the Stars instead.
Parking lots were connected to buildings via Bio Tube, so
that the legitimate citizen could step from the safety of his
or her car directly into a sealed environment. Anybody
without BioTube access was in big trouble.

The effect was dramatic. Signs went up on the freeways
entering the district: "WARNING. This Area Is Environmentally Protected!! Even short-term exposure to the Century City environment will result in serious illness leading
to death! Stay in your car and keep moving unless you
have access to a BioTube."

By this simple method, unfiltered sunlight and industrial smog were transformed from problems into solutions.
Pollution became a salable commodity.

Fame is the spur.

Nathan eased his car to a halt. He lowered his windows
only very slightly because the atmosphere outside was
pretty foul. He would have liked to have dealt with the
guards via his car-roof air-lock, but that might have appeared furtive, and the last thing you did with the Beverly
Hills Perimeter Private Police Force was appear in any
way furtive.

Looking furtive was crazy behavior, and as far as the
Beverly Hills Perimeter Private Police Force was concerned, crazies were the principal targets of their profession. Beverly Hills was the home of the stars and hence

attracted crazies like bees to honey. Crazies would stand in line to get a chance to try and murder the object of their love and admiration. There were hot-dog vendors and cheap hotels all over the surrounding area, set up purely to cater to the number of unbalanced losers who flocked to Hollywood in pursuit of this vicarious and violent brush with celebrity.

How Hollywood had changed. There had been a time when every bus that pulled into L.A. had ten kids on it all desperate to be a star. Suddenly it was ten kids all desperate to kill one.

The problem, as always, was one of celebrity. Just about everybody seemed to want it, but not everybody could have it. Celebrity could be achieved by becoming a star, but that was a very tough call. The crazies had discovered an easier way. Why, they argued, spend years going to acting and improv classes, exhaust yourself moonlighting as bartenders and waiters, suffer the endless auditioning for commercials and pleading for bit parts in exploitative cheapo videos, torture your conscience wondering whether to sleep with producers or not, generally fritter your life away looking for that million-to-one break that would make you a star? Why do all that when you could get just as famous by finding some idiot who had already done it, and shooting them?

It was this kind of remorseless logic that had led some people to ask themselves who were the crazies.

Agencies had sprung up to deal with what had become a major part of the industry. The life of a star-killer was big news; there were the book rights, the movie rights, the exclusive interviews, the exclusive photos. These things needed careful handling.

"Lock up your past," was the first thing agents would tell a hopeful young crazy who approached them for representation. "If you get lucky and waste a biggy, every childhood photo of you becomes a goldmine. Believe me, the press will have stripped your ol' mama's home clean before the gunshots die away. You have to have every document, every picture relating to you hidden away, ready for me to sell the first day you go on trial. We need to do exclusive interview deals with all your old pals and schoolteachers *before* you kill your star. Believe me, even your own family will start seeing dollar signs once they realize what you're going to be worth."

By the time Nathan arrived in Hollywood, the worst excesses of stardom via murder were over. At its height, though, people were walking out of prison straight into talk show host jobs and six-picture deals. A vicious circle developed. Scarcely would the ex-murderer have time to adjust to his or her newfound celebrity when he or she would be shot, and so the dreadful cycle continued.

Some agencies who represented both genuine stars and crazy stars (and of course crazy stars who had become genuine stars) even discussed the possibilities of mutually profitable deals between both parties, whereby a star who was in big financial trouble might do a deal with a crazy, whereby the crazy only wounded the star and they split all revenues that ensued. These deals never really took off. For one thing, there was a distinct whiff of insider trading about the whole thing. Besides which, in the midst of all the wheeling and dealing, it was easy to forget that the crazies involved were, by the very nature of their profession, crazy, and could rarely bring themselves merely to wound a target.

All in all, the Beverly Hills security guys had reason to be nervous. Being a mad gunman was one of the best-paid jobs a talentless nobody would ever get, and fame is universally recognized as the spur. Certainly, in order to get the fame, you had to be caught and imprisoned, but then the objects of your murderous careerism were also forced into prison, living as they did behind wire and guns and leather-clad security men. Yes, their prisons were more comfortable, but they were prisons nonetheless.

The market force.

Nathan could see that the private cops thought he was a crazy.

"I'm not a crazy," he said, "I'm a British writer named Nathan Hoddy."

The cops' demeanor stiffened noticeably. They fingered their armaments conspicuously. If crazies were a little crazy, writers were dangerous lunatics, embittered socially dysfunctional grudge-carriers who had spent so long in development that they had come to believe that they and their scripts were the only real things in the world and that everything else was irrelevant fantasy. The private cops had lost count of the number of writers who had come their way, armed to the teeth, having decided that the only way to get their projects through development was to shoot any reader, editor, or producer who stood between them and a green light.

"A writer, huh?" the first guard sneered. "Ain't no casual labor hired here, son. I believe they're hiring pump attendants at the gas station 'bout a mile back."

The guards sniggered at the joke. It is a curious facet of the Hollywood obsession with success and pecking orders that literally everybody in the town, from studio head to studio cleaner, harbors the same snobberies and prejudices.

"I hear Hank Wank's new picture didn't open," one tramp will remark to another. "Overspent and overblown, the studio lost its shirt."

"What a schmuck," the other tramp will reply. "Always had that guy picked for a loser."

Nathan hastened to establish his legitimacy.

"Yes, all right, I'm a bloody writer, but I am a writer who has an appointment with Plastic Tolstoy."

Nathan could not help but be pleased as the guards' manner changed yet again. A crazy was just a crazy, and a writer was of course something that you scraped off your

THIS OTHER EDEN

shoes, but Plastic Tolstoy was a man of stratospheric importance. If, as is said, power is the ultimate aphrodisiac, Plastic Tolstoy could have teased an erection out of a concrete monk. The man was an industry legend. Not only did he own a large percentage of the global media, but his company held the Claustrosphere account and had since almost the very beginning. Claustrosphere was the world's biggest industry, and it was Plastic Tolstoy who had made it so. Through ruthless, attrition marketing, he had made hermetically sealed BioSphere environments the biggest single consumer durable of all time. Bigger than cars, bigger than hamburgers, bigger even than wars. Because every time Plastic Tolstoy made a sale, he sold a whole world— only a little one—but a world nonetheless. A world that some lucky group or individual could forever call their own.

Plastic Tolstoy marketed the future, which, of course, made him the enemy of the present. He was PR man for history's most irresponsible idea. The idea that it was possible to survive the end of the world.

4

The life of a salesman

Communication breakdown.

THE STRICKEN TANKER STORY WAS ON THE NEWS. NATHAN HAD
heard it on his car radio as he drove up toward Beverly
Hills. Plastic Tolstoy saw it fifteen times all at once, standing before the vast fiber-optically fed information wall that
he had had built in his kitchen.

First the news, then the commercials. Plastic sipped his
coffee and watched.

The first ad was for snack food: "You know that feeling
when you're hungry as a horse but you're also fat as a
pig? Donut Heaven understands, which is why we're
now offering free, on-the-spot liposuction to any customer who eats twenty Donuts or more, plus extra frost-
ings! So if you're feeling hungry *and* fat, why not get
down to Donut Heaven. . . . You fill your face, we'll suck
your butt."

Plastic Tolstoy was watching one of the channels on his
own Plastic Tolstoy Communications System. Despite this,
his grim, angry expression suggested that the thing that he
had hoped to see had not materialized. Long before the

Donut commercial was over, Plastic Tolstoy had patched a multicall through to his media coordinators and program controllers.

"What, in the name of my mother, is happening, excuse me!" he barked. "An oil tanker has sunk, and what do I see first up on the break? On one of my own damn networks, no less! Donut ads and liposuction! After an *oil tanker has sunk!* You're supposed to be ready for this kind of thing!"

What Tolstoy was upset about was the failure of a classic piece of cross-promotion. Tolstoy marketed Claustrosphere, and he had a policy that whenever there was an environmental disaster, the news would instantly trigger a buying program within his own media mainframe. The theory behind this shameless abuse of influence was this: Whenever planet death lurched a small step closer, the vast Tolstoy worldwide audience would be instantly hit with Claustrosphere commercials playing in heavy rotation. That was the theory; it appeared not to have worked.

"We're up next break, Plastic," an anguished employee spluttered over the line. "The Donut people had the space booked and threatened to sue if we shifted them. They think the end of the world will make people reach for comfort food."

Plastic Tolstoy looked back at the screens. Sure enough, the current Claustrosphere campaign was now showing. A gorgeous sun rising over a geodesic dome and the simple slogan: "Claustrosphere. Who are you to deny your kids a future?"

"You see, Chief! You see," the anguished employee pleaded. "Right there, second slot. Personally, I think that's a better placing. More impact."

"Listen, man with no brain, shortly to become man with no job," Plastic shouted, "when there's a disaster, we take first slot, okay! Not second, not third, ever. First. Donuts, for chrissakes! I'm selling people the future here!"

Tomorrow's man.

It wasn't a new idea, the Rat Run mentality with which the human race ushered in the third millennium and that Plastic Tolstoy marketed with such enthusiasm. It was not the first time people had taken a good square look at Armageddon and decided that they would prefer it to happen to somebody else. Ever since Noah built the Ark, the seductive notion that it is possible to opt out, to stand on the sidelines while global cataclysm passes you by, has exercised a strong pull. Prior to the First Great Green Scare of the 1980s, it had been nuclear war that seemed most likely to carry off the human race. Then, people had built fallout shelters, as they now built Claustrospheres. Although admittedly, not on quite the same scale.

It was Jurgen Thor, the man whom many people considered to be the last sane person on Earth, who had coined the phrase the "Rat Run" to describe that hypothetical time when people would take refuge in their Claustrospheres. He had appeared on numerous TV talk shows, condemning the very idea of Armageddon survival. Sitting on couches wedged between pop singers and popular authors plugging their books, he would thunder that Claustrosphere was a terrifyingly dangerous illusion, a kind of global death-wish madness. He, in his capacity as head of Natura, the World Environmental Party, had taken a civil action against Claustrosphere all the way to the United States Supreme Court, attempting to question the very legality of marketing a product that, he claimed, encouraged planet death. It was then that Plastic Tolstoy and Jurgen Thor had first crossed swords. Jurgen Thor had called Plastic Tolstoy a salesman of doom. Plastic Tolstoy had told Jurgen Thor to lighten up.

"Hey, survival is a commodity," Tolstoy had said. "People should be allowed to buy it just like anything else."

Claustrosphere won the case.

Plastic's mother.

Plastic Tolstoy was named Plastic by his mother, who thought that plastic was the most beautiful material on Earth.

"Wood will always be wood, and stone will always be stone," she would say. "But plastic can be anything, anytime, anywhere."

"It's cheap and it's common," grumbled her husband.

"So am I," Mrs. Tolstoy would reply. "So is rock 'n' roll." Then she would peer down at her son, asleep in his crib, and say again, as she always did, "Plastic can be anything, anytime, anywhere, my darling. And so can you."

Mrs. Tolstoy was Professor of Popular Culture at the University of Disney World in Florida. It was there that she had developed the thesis for her best-selling book *The King Is Not Dead,* which demonstrated conclusively that Elvis did not die. He could not have died, Mrs. Tolstoy asserted, because he had in fact never existed. The meticulous detail with which she documented and then disproved every single sighting of the King between the years 1935 and 1977 (the period of his supposed "life") obsessed the nation for nearly a whole morning.

Mrs. Tolstoy used the revenue from her book to set up a school of modern art, dedicated to the principle that the Barbie doll was greater sculpture than the Venus de Milo, and that a reproduction of a great painting was of more value than the original. As she explained, with an original all you got was a painting, whereas a reproduction could also be a tablecloth, an apron, indeed, anything one cared to print it on.

Don't judge a book by its contents.

Plastic was his mother's son, but his eye was better than hers. While she worshipped populism via its products, he saw that the real beauty lay in that which surrounds the products, the marketing. It was a lesson he learned early on, as he often explained to the numerous documentary filmmakers who were endlessly doing films about his life.

"I was at this kid's party, you know? With the clown and cakes and the abuse therapist and stuff. Anyway, we all got a present of a toy gun. Brand-new, still in the box, right? Well, let me tell you, those boxes were big! And the picture on them? Wow! A marine blasting away with an M-16! We were in heaven. So we open the boxes, right? And of course there's this tiny, shitty little toy inside, and all the other kids think they've been ripped off. But not me, I didn't think so. All I could think of was how beautiful that box was! It looked so big and exciting, it had fooled us all. I lost the toy that same day, but I kept the box a long time."

Plastic had realized the great truth. A truth he would later embody in his First Law of Attrition Marketing. That law said that almost everything anybody ever buys is crap: instant noodles, four-wheel-drive trucks with huge wheels, vaginal deodorants. Anyone can produce any amount of crap, Tolstoy would later explain, in his famous educational video entitled *Selling: My Soul;* the clever part is to get someone to buy it.

"Listen," the video explained, "the world is one big marketplace full of people buying and selling useless, shitty stuff that nobody ever dreamed they wanted. So why do they buy it? Because while the product may be ugly, the marketing is beautiful. You don't believe me? Turn it around, consider trying to sell a truly great product, but with useless, shitty marketing. You couldn't do it, right? The message is the only thing that counts."

At the age of twelve Plastic Tolstoy made his first million. He had been pondering the delight with which his friends searched for the little snap-together toys hidden in their cereal boxes.

"Toys in cereals, that's great," the boy Plastic thought, "but timid."

So he wrote to the manufacturers, suggesting that they reverse the ratio and market boxes full of snap-together plastic toys with a free cornflake hidden among them. Kids went crazy for it.

Plastic always considered himself fortunate to have been young and impressionable when the great cola wars of the 1990s erupted on screens and in shopping malls. He watched with childish wonder as two nearly identical drinks made of carbonated water and flavored with vegetable extracts indulged in a worldwide orgy of aggressive saturation marketing that became *in itself* a multibillion-dollar industry. The name was sold, the image was sold, the history was sold. Eventually, people actually began to forget about the drink because *the marketing had become the product.* Young Plastic watched in starstruck awe as Pepsi and Coke actually marketed their own marketing. It was beautiful.

The only thing that could be more beautiful, the boy Plastic thought, was if both companies were owned by the same people.

It would be well into the twenty-first century before the truth about that emerged.

Advertainment.

All kids love TV, but it irritated young Plastic intensely. Years later, in *Selling: My Soul,* he would recall his youthful anger.

"I kept wondering why there had to be commercial breaks. You know? Insulting little ghettos where the marketing got crammed in any old how? As if the commercials were some kind of embarrassing necessity, instead of the very thing that was paying everybody's damn wages! And I'm thinking, one day I'm going to change all that. But I knew even then that, to do it, I'd have to control not just the imagery but also the *means of communication.* I vowed then on my mother's memory—except, of course, at the time she wasn't dead—that one day I would own a network, and on that network the insulting division between entertainment and commercials would be banished forever. The shows, the ads, even the news would all be mutually complementary. Sure, everybody knows that now, but one time I was a pioneer! I conquered an American frontier, I'm the guy who invented Advertainment."

Often when *Selling: My Soul* was being screened at marketing seminars, the eager young salesmen and women would burst into spontaneous applause at this point, such was the passion and conviction of Tolstoy's message.

"Let me remind you of something incredible," the video Plastic would pontificate with evangelical zeal. "There was a time when they made films just so that people might watch and enjoy them. You hear what I'm saying! Then gape in awe, why don't you? Let your jaws drop in disbelief. For decades, Hollywood created entertainment from which the only source of revenue was the price people paid to see it! You got millions of people sitting silently in cinemas, their attention completely focused, and *not being sold anything!* A hundred million Americans went to the cinema every week, and what did they see? A stupid movie! A story, nothing else! No subliminals, no product identification, nothing! People actually went to all the trouble of telling a story simply in order to tell a story! It makes me sick to my stomach."

Even the most committed students of marketing were sometimes a little surprised at the passion with which Tolstoy spoke of his contempt for the likes of *Gone With the Wind, The Grapes of Wrath,* and *Casablanca.* To Plastic these were not classic works of art, they were sterile self-indulgences. Pointless, egotistical displays of imaginative power and technical skill, nothing more.

"It's like a tennis player without a sponsor," he would

say. "Take the brand name plugs off the guy's shirt, and what have you got? Some rich brat hitting a ball around with a bat, and that's *all* you've got. Which is nothing."

Of course, even in Plastic's childhood, things were changing. He well remembered and spoke glowingly of seeing *Batman* as a tiny child, and noting with great satisfaction the extent to which the film was in fact a colossal commercial for the spin-off paraphernalia that accompanied it. But the product still followed the story: The film came first, and the marketing developed out of that. It was Plastic who finally put things in their proper order.

"The Second Law, boys and girls, is that the marketing is the product, and vice versa."

Selling the future.

Some people say that the hour produces the man.

"That's bullshit," Plastic Tolstoy would answer. "You have to make your own history in this world, ain't nobody going to make it for you."

Perhaps the truth lies somewhere in the middle. Certainly Tolstoy was no scientist, and he never designed a Claustrosphere. On the other hand, by his late twenties he had built up a communications empire that put him in a position to pitch for what would become the biggest sales campaign in history. When it began to dawn on people that the Earth was dying, Plastic Tolstoy was perfectly placed to take up the portfolio.

The Second Great Green Scare was sparked off when it was revealed that the governments of the world were using BioSphere technology (i.e., the research into self-contained, self-supporting environments) to construct boltholes to be used in the event of the Earth's becoming unable to support life. The powers that be had recognized that planet death was a possibility, and they had begun to sink bunkers from which they might administer the world's death throes. The argument was the same as had been used during the Cold War. The responsibilities of the civil authorities remain unaffected by global catastrophe. Though the public might be dead, their interests would not go unrepresented.

Concerned individuals the world over reacted in horror to this revelation. If those in power were actively anticipating and preparing for life after ecodeath, then the situation was clearly horribly serious. Even the most complacent began to realize that the Earth was in terrible danger, and a vast and furious groundswell of public opinion grew up. The immorality of those in power, preparing to survive ecodeath rather than prevent it, was clear to all. The fact that BioSpheres cost millions of dollars to construct, hence placing them beyond the reach of all but governments and the most stupidly rich, fueled righteous indignation.

This was the chance the environmentalists had been looking for: clear proof that those in control accepted the reality of the approaching catastrophe.

"When the rats prepare to leave, you can be sure the ship is sinking," thundered a very young Jurgen Thor in his first appearance as leader of Natura. It was a speech that rang around the world.

"These despicable individuals are preparing their escape! Their rat runs!" the big Norwegian declaimed. "Having first destroyed the Earth by their greed and irresponsibility, these human rodents seek to escape the dreadful consequences of their actions."

Such was the horror this idea engendered that people finally began to demand real action on the environment. Sustainable development became politically fashionable, and for a time it seemed that out of evil (the BioSphere alternative) had come forth good, that the craven self-interest of the few had spurred the many to action.

Then the price of BioSphere technology began to drop.

It always happens. Pocket calculators started off as luxury items; a decade later they were giving them away with gasoline. One day, the first backyard Claustrosphere went on the market, and the Earth was in big trouble. At first the threat seemed small. The unit was still pretty pricey and its life-support systems basic and uninviting. It required a quarter of an acre of good firm land under a two-hundred-foot geodesic dome. It could provide water and air and recycle human waste, but that was all. It didn't offer a night and day cycle, and nothing could be grown. The food supply was just a hundred years of military C rations. Hardly an appetizing prospect.

It didn't take long though.

Techno-research that had been sold to the public as pertaining to some future trip to Mars was employed on Earth. A five-year secret development was undertaken in the Arizona desert. When the pioneers emerged from their exile with a tray of hot muffins freshly baked from BioDough, raised within the dome, the first true Claustrosphere was ready to market.

Plastic Tolstoy called it Eden One.

The initial ads were a teaser campaign. They featured Rodin's "Thinker" pondering an apple, and the caption was a simple, bald statement: "Think about it."

Plastic loved an enigmatic little come-on.

"Think about the Earth, think about the apple, think about Eden, think about the future. It's all there in the one image. It's brilliant, if I do say so myself."

Next came an apple that was also a globe. "The Earth is in danger!" screamed the caption. "Recycle! Join Greenpeace! Buy a Claustrosphere!" That had been Plastic's strategy in the early days, to equate Claustrosphere with the concerned individual. One percent of the cover price of an Eden One went directly to the Worldwide Fund for Nature.

All that had been nearly forty years ago. Now, both Claustrosphere and Plastic Tolstoy were huge on a scale that the multinationalists and media moguls of the twentieth century could only have imagined. Tolstoy had fulfilled his dream, and he owned the very news and entertainment services that delivered his messages.

At heart, though, he was still just a salesman. Which is why, big though he was, he was standing in his kitchen, watching a stricken oil tanker on the news and personally bawling out his staff for allowing some donut commercial to get between him and the proper exploitation of an environmental disaster.

5

A spy unmasked

The man who talked too much.

JUDY WAS BEING HOISTED OFF THE STRICKEN TANKER. NATHAN
was stuck with the private cops outside the Beverly Hills
Fortified Village. Plastic Tolstoy was in his kitchen, giving
his people hell. And Rosalie Connolly, a Mother Earth unit
leader, or terrorist, as Tolstoy would have called her, was
standing in a California desert.

An Irish girl of twenty-five, she carried great responsibilities
on her young shoulders, for it was her job to save the world.
Not on her own, of course. Mother Earth was a large organization, and despite being a unit leader, Rosalie was by no means
particularly senior. Nonetheless, saving the world is a big job,
even if you have help, and the romantic, slightly mystical girl
who had joined Youth Natura at the age of ten had grown into
a tough and cynical individual. Tougher and more cynical than
she would have liked to be, had the world been different.

But the world, of course, is never different. Nothing ever
is, and Rosalie had a nasty little job to do before she and
her team could depart in the large personnel-carrying helicopter that stood waiting for them.

Shackleton, her tough ex-marine second-in-command, was priming the charges on the detonators when Rosalie approached him.

He nodded at her, she nodded at him, there was a pause, then she put a gun to his temple.

"Mr. Shackleton, I believe you are an FBI spook, and I think I may have to kill you."

Rosalie was right. The man was an agent, although in a very different mold from Judy Schwartz. This man's name was Cruise, and he was tall and tough and rugged and handsome. He was also one of the bullies who had tormented Judy, having been in the same training team. Cruise and the guys had regularly given Judy and the other nerds surreptitious pummelings during forensics classes and compared their dick sizes unfavorably with a .22 slug from a ladies' handgun.

Rosalie, of course, knew nothing of this, but if she had, she would have liked Cruise even less, which was saying something because she did not like him at all. She had suspected him from the day he had joined them, ostensibly fresh from service against loggers in South America. The man had just talked too bloody green.

"Sometimes I think it's my own environmental impotence that makes me most angry," Shackleton (or Cruise) would say as they sat around the fire at night, while everyone else was trying to talk about sports or sex.

"I mean, the logging is ten times worse than the press admit, and the defoliants are so deep into the water table they're never going to come out. . . ."

The man was a complete bore. Greener than green, whiter than white, and holier than thou. It was like he'd found God, started therapy, and given up smoking all on the same day; he just wouldn't shut up.

"God, Shackleton goes on, doesn't he?" other members of the team would remark to one another. "I don't think I can stand it much longer, let's turn him in to the Feds."

But Rosalie was beginning to fear that Mr. Dull *was* a Fed.

Most Mother Earth activists had been in environmental politics so long they never discussed it. What was the point of talking about planet death? It was too depressing, and everybody felt the same way about it anyway, so why go on? There was nothing worse than a bunch of self-righteous zealots sitting around the bean casserole, all nodding in agreement and going, "Yeah, doesn't it make you so angry? I mean it's just *unbelievable!* Don't you think?"

At one point, the problem of endless talking about the environment had actually begun to have a seriously destructive effect on the whole Environmental Movement. People were forever getting trapped into spending entire evenings agreeing with each other. It had begun to affect recruitment. The syndrome became known as "green discussion fatigue" and so many potential fighters had drifted away as a result of it that eventually it became an unwritten rule within the environmental movement that you did not discuss the environment. Therefore, when an ostensibly experienced activist turned up in her unit, stating the bloody obvious about eco-Armageddon over and over again, Rosalie was immediately suspicious.

And then there was Shackleton's endless references to Mother Earth funding. Of course, everybody would love to know who was putting up the cash, but it had been a secret for thirty years and was certain to remain so. Rosalie herself had been an activist since leaving college. She was moderately well advanced in the movement, yet completely ignorant about the greater part of Mother Earth's financial affairs. The FBI, and indeed every other law enforcement agency in the world, were endlessly probing and investigating, trying to get to the heart of it. But they never would. It was the big secret, and had Shackleton been the experienced fighter he pretended to be, he would have known not to mention it.

The clincher came when Shackleton got on to the subject

of Jurgen Thor. He professed to worship the man, quoting that old chestnut about his being called the last sane person on Earth. That did it for Rosalie. Nobody who had been around Mother Earth long thought Jurgen Thor was sane, and nobody worshipped him. The people who dodged the bullets did not have much time for a personality cult egomaniac who would try to screw a tree if it had a dress on. Jurgen Thor was immensely talented, hugely charismatic, and absolutely crucial as a spokesperson to the wider world. Where the fighting was done, however, the general impression was that he was a bit of a big hairy jerk.

Rosalie began to investigate the history of the man who called himself Shackleton.

On the surface it all looked fine. An American named Shackleton had been assigned to join her active service unit after seeing action under cover in Argentina. But anyone could switch a body, Rosalie thought. She had the Mother Earth database modem her up a photo of the real Shackleton. That checked out too, but since, if you had the money, you could get a temporary cosmetic rebuild done in an afternoon, that was also inconclusive. Eventually Rosalie took a scroll of the man's fingerprints from an organic carrot juice container that he was carrying around until he could find somewhere to recycle it.

The result was great news. Shackleton was a spook. Nobody would have to listen to him whine on about the environment ever again.

Rosalie continued to hold the gun to his head.

"What did you do with our man?" she inquired. "The real Shackleton."

"We've got him, that's all, he isn't hurt," replied Cruise. "How did you see through me?"

"You just didn't talk about the environment enough," replied Rosalie. "It just didn't seem like you cared at all."

Cruise was mortified. He had studied so hard, he had felt he could spout green crap in his sleep. He had got the majority of his environmental bilge from that asshole nerd Judy Schwartz. Cruise made a mental note to kill Judy at the next reunion.

"Where's your tracer implant?" asked Rosalie. The spy glanced down at his arm. "Do you want us to cut it out, or do you want to do it yourself?"

"Hey, listen . . . ," Cruise protested nervously. No matter how tough you are, you still don't relish having a hole cut in your arm.

"Oh, come on! You know all about today's hit," snapped Rosalie impatiently. "If we leave you wired up, you'll send out an alarm. Your pals will come and get you, you'll tell them where we are, and we'll be blown out of the sky. Now you know very well that we either have to shoot you or cut out your tracer, so which is it to be?"

Reluctantly the FBI man offered his forearm. Rosalie drew her Swiss Army knife. There was a brief hiatus while she tried to find a blade. She searched through the scissors, the toothpick, the digital video camera, the miniaturized two-way communications system, the BioShield umbrella, the thing for getting stones out of horses' hooves. . . .

"Christmas present," Rosalie said apologetically. "Stupid, really. I never use any of these things." Finally she found the knife, only the little one, but it would do. She advanced upon a rather scared Cruise.

"Now you might feel a bit of a prick," said Rosalie. And she was right, he did.

6

When two stars collide

Fortune's child.

IT WAS STILL THE SAME MORNING. NATHAN WAS NEGOTIATING with the thugs at the Beverly Hills Fortified Village. Plastic was in his kitchen, watching Judy and Jackson get winched off the stricken tanker on fifteen different screens. Rosalie was in a helicopter with the Mother Earth direct action team, heading for a spot of terrorism, and back in the desert, Cruise, who has little further to do with this story, was nursing a bleeding arm.

Max had problems too. Problems, that is, in addition to his usual one, which was that of being a screwup. Admittedly, at present he was a rich and famous mess, a colossally popular mess. The mess, in fact, of the moment. But Hollywood is a place where the distance between being a celebrated mess and a despised, pitied casualty doing underwear ads is a short one. Something in the very back of Max's addled brain was telling him that the time was coming to pull himself together. At twenty-six he had been a very big star for over eight years. A celebrated "brat," to be found drinking, partying, and getting into fights all over town. What's more, he was the real thing, a genuinely naughty boy. Not one of the amorphous mass of pouting pretty things who got puke-drunk once on their eighteenth birthday and spent the next five years telling *People* magazine how they kicked their booze hell. Max was adored not only for the wild, confused characters that he played on screen and inside Virtual Reality helmets, but also for the wild, confused character that he clearly was.

The Good Fairies that had attended Max's birth were many and generous. They gave him great charm, tremendous acting talent, and a fine, powerful, if rather small, physique. They gave him wonderful looks, which included ice blue eyes set against dark Mediterranean coloring. Also, and perhaps most importantly of all, they gave him James Dean eyebrows that slanted upward in a sad, little-boy-lost manner whenever he frowned. All this did the Good Fairies give to the baby Max, who laughed and gurgled as befitted the carefree, devil-may-care, sunny personality that was also their bequest to him. The Bad Fairy, on the other hand, gave Max only one gift, but it nearly killed him. For the Bad Fairy decreed that at the age of seventeen, Max would, without any warning or preparation, become hugely famous as the supercool teenager in a Levi's ad.

Some high school kids, faced with suddenly becoming the most celebrated and drooled-over adolescent on the planet, might have handled it with calm detachment and genteel reserve. Max was not such a kid.

"Max, last week you were shooting hoops with your pals in Burbank, now you're on the cover of every magazine in the store. Do you worry about what you will do when the adoration ends?" a motherly talk show host had asked Max in one of his very first celebrity interviews.

"No way, little lady dude, babe," young Max had replied. "For I hereby vow to party myself to death while I'm still on top."

The commercial that shot Max to superstardom was a cosponsorship deal between Levi's and Claustrosphere. It was set in the future, on the day of the Rat Run. Ecodeath had ostensibly arrived, and everyone was fleeing in terror for their Claustrospheres. Max's character, the cool teen, refuses to join his fleeing, terrified family until his jeans come out of the tumble dryer. The memorable caption being: "Without your Levi's, eternity will seem like a very long time."

Ever since that famous last shot, when Max had set a billion hearts fluttering as he rushed toward the Claustrosphere's closing door, pulling on his faded jeans while his mother screamed, Max had been front-page news. He still was, but behavior that is cute in a lad of twenty is a bit pathetic in a man of thirty. Max was twenty-six and getting rather bored with himself. It would not be long, he reasoned in his occasional lucid moments, before he began to bore everyone else. Someday soon, he kept promising himself, maybe not today, but someday soon, he would get himself together.

Morning head.

There were, however, more immediate things to consider. Where was he, and what time was it?

It was, in fact, nearly time to meet Rosalie and for his life to change forever, but of course he did not know this. What he did know was that he had a mouthful of carpet. By this he deduced that it must be morning. He always started a day like that. Of course, it wasn't always carpet; sometimes it was asphalt, or concrete, garbage quite often, occasionally even a pillow. Max slept facedown and breathed through his mouth, so whatever he collapsed into the night before was what he would find his tongue stuck to when he woke up in the morning. He could generally tell where he was without opening his eyes.

Carpet, thought Max, not bad. Things were looking up already. Police cells did not have carpets, nor did streets.

Max reasoned from this that he was neither under arrest nor in immediate danger of being so. The carpet was also clean, that was a surprise. Max could not remember the last time he had tasted a clean carpet, but this seemed to be one. He could detect no booze nor vomit beyond that which traditionally adorned his person when he awoke in the morning. Where was he? They had carpets in whore houses and cheap bars, but you tended to stick to those carpets, and this one was definitely nonadhesive. Max wondered whether maybe he had made it home. It seemed unlikely; he had never made it home before. As a matter of fact, Max was only vaguely aware of where his home was. On the morning of his mother's latest marriage, he had woken up in the surf on Malibu. He had had to buy a tourist map of where the stars lived, just so he could get home to have half an hour on his bathroom stomach pump and grab a change of clothes. Max never went home unless he absolutely had to. Home was dull, and Max was wild.

Max decided he did not care where he was. Whatever, wherever, it was okay by him. The carpet tasted good. This would be a good day. Max could not see how being crashed out in some place with a nice clean carpet could get him into trouble. It was not worth a spread in the tabloids, it was unlikely to land him in court, and it would not give his mother an excuse to get back on the talk show circuit claiming that she blamed herself.

Cautiously he opened his eyes and raised his head a little. It took a moment or two to focus, and maybe another half a moment for all the vague confidence he had been feeling about the clean carpet to evaporate before his bloodshot eyes. He had made an asshole of himself again. Stretched out on the carpet before him was a naked woman. A gorgeous naked woman. The sort of woman who looked great on the front of scandal magazines.

Even in repose her natural instinct to adopt the position of a centerfold had not deserted her. She lay on her back, slightly propped up against a few silk pillows, one arm

45

thrust gently behind her neck, supporting her head, the other soft against her belly. A knee was slightly raised, exposing a firm, flawless thigh, while the other leg stretched long across the floor, culminating in a ballet dancer's point, the delicate toes so close to Max's head that it might easily have been the foot rather than the carpet that he had found in his mouth that morning.

What a magnificent creature she was! Mother Nature and plastic surgeon working together in perfect harmony! Her breasts stood out firm and separate against her taut body. Despite their generous size and obvious weight, they still pointed defiantly heavenward, as if invisible threads tethered her nipples to the ceiling. The woman's crotch had been waxed by a fanatic. It was virtually bald. Smooth and shiny as a car hood, almost as if it had been laminated. There was one tiny fringe of pale, soft hair hovering above the cleft. This was a vagina with a mohawk.

Max felt depressed. How had he ever allowed his life to arrive at a point where such a gorgeous woman could be a problem to him? Yet she was a problem. The problem being that Max was married. Very publicly and very recently married to a fellow movie star. Max was a man of certain principles. He valued his honor. Certainly he fought and he drank, that was fine; what he did not do was publicly humiliate his wife.

Irresponsible use of drugs.

Fidelity, or at least a decent pretense at such, was a major pose on the coast; it had been for years. The place was stuffed with megastars assuring journalists that they had found true bliss in marriage and that their hell-raising days were over.

AIDS was still around. There was still no cure and no vaccine, no vaccine available to the public, that is. It had, in fact, been possible to immunize people against the disease for many years, but the drug had been suppressed. The reason for this being that the vast chemical conglomerate that had isolated the vaccine had found to its dismay that it was extremely easy to copy and reproduce, a simple compound, made from the cheapest and most basic ingredients. Ingredients that a child could reconstruct from a junior chemistry kit and a bag of household groceries. The conglomerate concerned realized that, were it to market its new drug, its secret would instantly be wrested from it. That done, in defiance of copyright, the recipe would be published in every scabrous, alternative publication in the world. Faced with this wholly unacceptable prospect, the vast chemical conglomerate had taken the only course open to it. This was, after all, business. There was no point in its developing a drug from which it was impossible to profit. It had therefore decided to withhold the drug until such time as its chemists had been able to develop a sufficiently complex molecular disguise. It would secrete its simple little miracle drug deep within some intricate atomic structure that was fantastically difficult to break down, and near impossible to reproduce. This way its patent would be protected and a reasonable price could be charged.

Expensive bodywork.

Max looked at the slumbering woman. How the hell had this happened? How had he ended up crashed out on a carpet with a naked woman? He wasn't even the sleep-around type. What Max liked to do was get shit-faced, act like a rich asshole, and fall over. Certainly he liked to flirt, but screwing around was stupid. Getting caught was stupider. Could he get away with this? Not easily, he thought, and certainly not cheaply. The woman stretched out before him had not spent the countless dollars she clearly had spent getting a body like that in order to hand it out gratis. That body was a career move.

It was too perfect, too calculated, not one inch of it had been left to chance. This was a body that would almost certainly be featuring in next year's Coscars (Cosmetic Surgery Awards). Max searched in vain for signs of human frailty. Just one dimple of cellulite on the extraordinary limb stretched out before him might have given him hope that here was a straight shooter. A woman who would wake up and say, "Wow! That was fun and so unlike me, now you go back to your life, and I'll go back to mine." But there were no dimples of cellulite, not the tiniest stretch mark, hair, or crease to suggest that this was a real human being.

The leg pointing at Max seemed to be singling him out, accusing him: "There's the jerk," its stern posture seemed to say. "There's the guy I'm going to be talking about on every talk show for the next ten years. The asshole who's going to make me a celebrity."

Max never understood why he got married. His wife, Krystal, herself a huge star, was no clearer about her own motives. It was almost as if they'd been forced into it to feed the Max and Krystal industry that had grown up around them. Like a king, Max lived in a world where everything he did was deemed to be important. If he got drunk it was important. If he hit a journalist it was important. His notorious decision to have a penis *reduction* ("I owe it to the women I sleep with") had made the cover of *Premiere* and been the number one news item on MTV. This, despite the fact that MTV now had a core audience in its fifties, twice Max's age.

The problem was that, like most kings, Max began to believe that what he did was important. There are few people in the entertainment industry with the strength of character to turn their face against the tide of popular obsession and say, "I am not even one millionth as interesting a person as I'm cracked up to be." Certainly, Max could not resist the endless seduction of self-importance. It was a short step from throwing up on request to getting married on request.

Since then, both Krystal and he had assured the world that they had been tamed by love and that their hell-raising days were over. But they weren't. Krystal had continued to paint the town at night and have her body reconstructed in the morning, while Max had kept right on drinking, punching people, getting punched, and waking up face-down, not knowing where he was. Now it seemed he'd got sufficiently shit-faced to make a real idiot of himself. Max did not love Krystal, but he had no desire to insult and embarrass her on the front page of the *National Enquirer*.

The woman stirred.

"Max, I want a divorce," she said.

Max was surprised. He squinted his aching eyes to focus.

"Krystal?" he said.

"What?" she replied.

Max fell silent. He felt ashamed. It was all very well being a complete mess, but not recognizing your own wife was just gross. Certainly she had had a number of faces since he married her, but a husband is supposed to keep track of these things.

"I want a divorce, Max. Last night at Simone's we got treated like yesterday's news. I felt like an old married lady. Well I'm not an old lady; I'm just twenty-four, and I want a divorce."

"Okay," said Max.

"Don't you have anything else to say?" Krystal asked.

"Well ..." Max thought for a moment. This was his wife, and yet he scarcely knew her. This beautiful woman was a stranger to him. The aimlessness of his existence swept over him. For a moment he saw himself clearly, and he saw nothing, for there was nothing to see. His whole life was a pointless charade. Fortunately for Max introspection was a passing thing.

"Any chance of a final jump?" he said.

Krystal never could resist a bit of romance.

"Oh, all right, go ahead."

Max crawled forward across the carpet and up along Krystal's astonishing body.

"I don't think my breath's too sweet," he confessed. "You didn't see anyone take a leak in my mouth last night, did you?"

Krystal always had her disinfectant at hand. She sprayed Max's mouth and then her own, for she had dined on pepper vodka and garlic corn chips the previous evening. Stretching across to her handbag she produced an altogether more formidable-looking aerosol.

"Okay. Stand up and drop them," she said. "You may be my husband, but I don't know where you've been."

"I don't think I can stand up, Krystal. Going anything higher than carpet before I've had some coffee gives me vertigo."

"Stand up and show, Max, or you can whistle for a wriggle," said Krystal, who had very strict views when it came to sexual hygiene. Max knew that nothing blew a screw quicker than resisting the precautions, so he staggered to his feet and dropped his jeans. Krystal sprayed his crotch, coating his dick in spermicidal stretch laminate.

"The spray-on condom has to be the greatest invention since inflatable handguns," said Krystal as she blew on it to help it dry.

"I like this part," said Max. "I hope you have some solvent, though."

Max spoke from painful experience. The spray-on condom was a triumph of synthetic fiber engineering. It could be applied to a flaccid member and would then stretch and move like a second skin. Obviously, with a conventional condom there is a teat on the end that provides somewhere for the ejaculation to go. With spray-on jobs the laminate simply stretched to accommodate whatever was necessary. It would stretch, but it would not break, ever. This was fine for the containment of a bit of sexual effluvia, but less convenient if you needed a wee, and you had no solvent.

Max, like most men, had experienced the pain and embarrassment of driving to the drugstore with a big balloon of piss hanging off the end of his dong.

Krystal drew Max down on top of her. They embraced, and she kissed him long and hard. In a town where good kissing was the norm, Krystal was a star. It was said that if you had had a cosmetic lift you should not kiss Krystal for at least six months, because she would suck your face right off. This rumor began when Krystal was just sixteen. She had been a child star, and having been through sex, drugs, college, and fully diagnosed media dependency, she had married an aging star, a man with the career of a seventy-year-old and the face of a thirty-five-year-old. At least, he had the face of a thirty-five-year-old until his wedding night with young Krystal. Loud screams were heard from their hotel suite in Aspen, Colorado. A paramedic Cosmetic Surgical Rapid Response unit was scrambled from Cedars Hospital, L.A., and the aging star was not seen in public for four months.

"Ate the old boy's face right off," the gossips assured each other.

"I heard they had to cut his teeth out of the back of her throat. That little girl nearly choked on her old man's dentures."

Krystal was now giving Max the benefit of her plungerlike skills, but despite administering a kiss that could have unblocked a drain, she could feel that the fire was not getting lit.

"I'm not stretching your laminate, am I, honey?" she inquired gently.

"It isn't you, Krystal, it's just early, you know? I had a gutful of booze last night and . . ."

"Hangover hanging over, is it?" she said. "Let me show you something I had fitted last week."

Krystal rose to her feet and glided across the room. It was a walk that had made a hundred million Virtual Reality helmets steam. Crossing to her dressing table and perching herself gently against it, she looked down at the prostrate Max.

"Like what you see?" she inquired, and Max would have had to be made out of granite to demur. What's more, it would have had to be granite that was probably gay, anyway. Krystal was an extraordinary vision of market-research-generated design perfection. She looked as if a Japanese porn artist had just created her from computer graphics. Certainly it was a little soulless, but as her body sculptor often said, "Krystal, there are tits men, and there are ass men; the only soul men I ever knew were musicians."

"You think this is good, huh?" Krystal pouted. "Watch."

She took up a thin tube that was attached to a little cylinder in her vanity case. Max watched in astonishment as she removed what he had imagined was a tiny mole deep within her cleavage. She attached the tube to the spot where the mole had been, there was a hiss, and Krystal's already generous bosom began to expand. Max gaped, he had never seen anything like it. Krystal laughed at his confusion.

"Neat, huh? It cost an awful lot," she said. "Great for the career, though, so it should pay for itself. You see, now I can do big girl parts and little girl parts. Versatility is so important for a serious actress, don't you think? I've had the skin elasticized so it won't stretch, either, and they go down after a couple of hours. You like?"

Well, as it happened, Max wasn't particularly into big ones, but it seemed churlish to say so when a woman had just gone to the trouble of inflating her body for his benefit. Besides, Max's libido was finally beginning to struggle through the fog of stale booze and old smokes that had so far kept it down, and Krystal was a woman who would look good in any proportions. He definitely wanted to get horizontal with her. The problem was getting the message through downstairs.

Max had had trouble with hard-ons for years. It was that

age-old problem, erection awareness. The minute he started thinking about them, poof! they were gone. It was not a physical thing, it was purely mental. As every man knows, the penis is a paranoid portion. If it knows you're worrying about it, it heads south. Fortunately there is a solution. It is a matter of getting one's mind off the subject. Max's method was to indulge in a discreet fantasy, in order to transport his libido away from the current pressurized circumstance.

However, Krystal would not have felt put out had she been a party to Max's secret thoughts, for it was not other women he thought of, but himself. Not sexually, but professionally. Max was an actor, and the most exciting thing in the world to him was just how *fucking good* he was. He thought of the triumphs, the tears, the quirky little workshop productions he still got involved in because, despite being a megastar, he was first and foremost an artist. He thought about how great he looked warming up in leg warmers and an old torn T-shirt . . . and there it was, a great big proud upstander, all present, correct, and ready for action.

Krystal was pleased. As far as she was concerned, her inflatable tits had worked their magic.

"So you do like," she purred, giving them a jiggle.

"Sure I like, Krystal," Max said. "Just so long as they don't go pop, and you end up being blown all around the room like a balloon."

Raunchy sex scene.

Max had already dropped his jeans and underpants in order to receive the laminate. Now he kicked off his moccasins, advanced across the room, and stood before her, smoldering for a moment. Without taking his eyes off hers, he pulled off his T-shirt to reveal the taut, tanned torso beneath. He was naked, and looking great.

Apart from his socks.

Socks are terrible things. There is no way you can take them off in a sexually charged manner. Shoes, you can kick . . . T-shirts, you can pull . . . underwear you can drop. . . . But socks, you have to hop around on one leg, tugging at. A few years previously, someone had attempted to market socks that dissolved under the heat of passion, but since the temperature of most people's feet drops by about forty degrees the moment they get into bed with anyone, the idea was a flop.

Having disposed of his socks as quickly as possible, Max gathered Krystal up in his arms and carried her to the bed. Max was a small man, but he was strong and wiry, and at just twenty-six the booze and smokes had yet to reduce his strength. They fell upon the bed together with the usual, slightly ungainly thud and tangle of arms and legs that traditionally accompanies this move. They both laughed a little, as if to acknowledge the moment, then they clinched into an embrace.

It is an irony that only movie stars can truly appreciate that sex is not like in the movies. Here were two international icons of popular entertainment, who had delivered more sensational sauce in their time than Mr. Heinz, and yet, when it came to actually getting it on for real, they were as inept as anybody else.

"Your arm's on my hair," Krystal said gently. "It's pulling my hair."

Max whispered an apology and shifted, making them both yelp loudly because their skin had got stuck together, and it hurt when Max moved his arm. Returning to the business at hand, Max placed his mouth gently on Krystal's and began to tease her tongue with his. Moments later, like all couples, they had to stop for a moment to fish the hair out of their mouths.

In all the countless shows that Max had starred in—movies, Virtual Reality Reactive Scenarios, Direct Input home entertainments—all the times he had been called upon to plant huge sloppy kisses on flaxen-haired beauties, never once had he fished a hair out of his mouth.

He and Krystal returned to their embrace. There was another yelp.

"Do you think perhaps you could take your watch off?" Krystal inquired. "It's in danger of amputating one of my buttocks."

Max's watch was a fully equipped home entertainment center with a library of ballgame minivideos and a six-pack of Dehydrated Budweiser. He took it off.

"Thanks," said Krystal.

"No, I should have remembered," said Max, smiling his sweetest smile.

"Oh, my God," Krystal said, "what's happened to your mouth? . . . Oh no, hang on, it's just my lipstick."

On-screen, of course, Krystal spent almost entire shows with her gums around some guy's plums and still had impeccable lip gloss when she came up for air. Off-screen, however, like any other woman she could smudge it eating a banana.

Slowly the romance returned, and the two lovers began to work their bodies against each other until Krystal opened her thighs and allowed Max to slip between them.

"For old times' sake, huh?" she whispered.

Max could not actually recall any old times, but he was happy to believe there had been some, and with one smooth, gentle motion, he entered her.

Except, of course, he didn't. That was what he did in the movies. In the movies, one lover can gently enter another without so much as a guiding hand; without even breaking the embrace, they just slide in. This is, of course, virtually impossible. For a penis to simply glide into a vagina, while the lovers involved continue a passionate embrace, would actually require a funnel. In real life, people have to probe a bit.

"Almost?" Krystal breathed. "Down a bit, that's it,

nearly, no, up a little, yes, a little more, almost . . . No! Not there! Get out of there!"

Max jerked back like a startled rabbit.

"Sorry, sorry, sorry, sorry!" he gasped.

The misunderstanding over, Krystal guided Max to the correct orifice, and they began, finally, to make love. And it was good. She gasped, he gasped, they both gasped. Then they squelched.

It was the old problem. When a man is on top of a woman and the sweat begins to flow, the woman's cleavage will often start to blow raspberries. It never happened in movies, of course. Max had pumped his body up and down on top of countless gorgeous actresses, Krystal had gasped and sweated beneath numerous pieces of thespian beefcake. Yet never once had a single cleavage so much as squeaked. In the real world, however, it was a noise that had intruded on many an ecstatic moment. It's always a difficult decision, whether to refer to it or not. Krystal always did.

"Your chest is making my tits fart," she said.

"Yeah, I know," replied Max.

"I could let some air out of them, maybe."

"No, that wouldn't work, it happens with little ones too. Try to forget it, okay?"

"Yeah, okay."

So they returned again to the matter in hand. Soon their passion began to take control again. The gasping returned. He grunted, she squeaked. She squeaked, he grunted. She arched her back, he plunged his hands under her buttocks.

"Yes," she said. "Yes, yes, yes!"

"Oh!" he said. "Mh! Ah! Ooooh!"

Krystal's body was dissolving, making ready to orgasm. As she got warmer and wetter, Max thrust with ever-greater passion. The inevitable happened. There was a squelch that made Krystal's cleavage sound positively polite.

"Damn! I hate it when my crotch makes that noise," said Krystal. "Sorry."

"It's me, too, I'm creating the vacuum," Max observed

reasonably and nuzzled up to Krystal's ear. "Try not to think about it. It's beautiful."

"Beautiful! My crotch is blowing reveille, and you're saying it's beautiful!"

"Well, it is."

Krystal liked Max's attitude. She held him tighter, and gasping and squelching away, they rushed toward climax, and astonishingly it looked as if they were going to reach the tape together. Almost. Almost. Gasp, squelch, squelch, gasp. Sadly, at the last moment, as Krystal began to come and Max drew back for a last glorious plunge . . . it came out, and he banged it into her thigh, bending it double and making him screech in pain.

"Yes!" said Krystal.

"Ouch," said Max.

And so the brief marriage ended, amicably, painfully, and messily. Afterward they had a cup of coffee and discussed the upcoming divorce.

"Who shall we sell the story to?" Krystal asked.

"Well, I'm having lunch with my agent at the studio. I'll have a talk with her about it, she'll get us a good price."

So Max headed into Hollywood for lunch at the DigiMac Studio commissary. Which was, as it happens, where Rosalie and her team of ecoterrorists were heading in their helicopter.

Meanwhile, far away in Europe, where the morning was early evening, the man often celebrated as the last sane person on Earth was addressing the European parliament on the subject of environmental destruction. To emphasize his arguments, live footage of the Alaskan oil tanker disaster was playing on screens hung about the Grand Chamber. The same disaster that Plastic Tolstoy was watching in his kitchen and above which Judy Schwartz was hanging on a winch, still puzzling over the surprising nature and extent of the ruptures in the tanker's sides.

7

A gunpowder plot

The house that Jacques built.

JURGEN THOR STOOD, MASSIVE AND IMPOSING, BEHIND THE MARble podium inside the magnificent European Federation Parliament building in Brussels.

The place had only been open a week. It had been scheduled to open fifteen years ago, but, having been designed by a committee of architects from all thirty-six Federal States, it had overrun somewhat. Also, and for the same reason, there were no lavatories. No country was prepared to take responsibility for so mundane an area. No proud Euro Head of State was going to be the one who had to stand before that great, imposing repulsive marble palace and say, "Our man did the toilets."

There were no cloakrooms either, no kitchens, no committee rooms, and no offices, just thirty-six Grand Chambers. Everybody had wanted to design the Grand Chamber, and in the end everybody did. The Palace of Peace and Profit (for such was the Euro building's name) was almost two square miles of Grand Chamber. Thirty-six Grand Chambers contained within an edifice of such striking horror that children ran crying in fear to their mothers' arms after a single glance at it. If an infinite number of monkeys were given an infinite amount of graphic design equipment, never, in an infinite number of years, could they have designed such a stupid and repulsive building. But then that could have been said about most of the new buildings in the thrusting modern Europe.

The Palace stood in the center of what had been beautiful Brussels, mile upon mile of marble and precious hardwoods almost entirely obscured from view by the ring of Portosans that surrounded it. As it happened, the Portosans were not really necessary because there were so many statues, fountains, and frescoes symbolizing the Euro ideals of peace, liberty, and ruining the rest of the world's trade, that it was a simple matter, even for female delegates, to find some large symbolic lump behind which to relieve themselves.

Jurgen points the finger.

The European Federation had invited Jurgen Thor to address the opening session at the Palace because it wanted to demonstrate to the world Europe's continued commitment to defending the environment. It was, after all, a lot cheaper to give a platform to a green politico than to legislate against polluters.

Jurgen was, as always, pulling no punches.

"When you buy a private Claustrosphere!" he thundered. "When your taxes help build a municipal Claustrosphere! By that very action you accept as fact the dreadful possibility that we are about to destroy the Earth! In essence you yourself destroy the Earth! You commit planetary treason!"

The various delegates, lobbyists, and Euro Members of Parliament listened in uncomfortable silence. They were uncomfortable partly because the seats of the particular

Grand Chamber in which they were sitting had been designed for purely aesthetic purposes. They *looked* all right.
The architect (a Latvian) had attempted to create a pris-
matic effect, making all the seats out of Plexiglas pyramids,
and when the room was empty, light bounced from seat
to seat, creating a dazzling effect. However, when the room
was full of delegates (which was, after all, what it was
there for), the effect was merely one of lots of people winc-
ing because they had hard plastic points up their behinds.
The Euro delegates were also uncomfortable, however, because of what Jurgen Thor was saying. It was horrid to be
accused of planetary treason, particularly if secretly you
felt the accusation to be a fair one. There was not a person
in that huge chamber, with the probable exception of Jurgen Thor, who did not own a Claustrosphere. Everybody
had of course agonized over buying one, but what could
you do? Everybody knew that the Earth was half dead and
that there was every possibility of it going whole hog at
any moment. A person would feel something of a fool
standing outside some pal's Claustrosphere, explaining
with his or her last gasp that the pal had hastened the
situation that was about to kill the person. It was, when
everything was said and done, all very well having principles, but no principle was worth sacrificing your children
for, was it?

"You tell me you have to protect your children!" Jurgen
Thor beat his mighty fist down upon the lectern. "Will
your children thank you for bequeathing them a rathole in
exchange for a paradise?"

Jurgen Thor was demanding, as he had a thousand times
in the previous twenty years, immediate legislation against
Claustrospheres. He might as well have gone to Texas and
demanded immediate legislation against a man's right to
buy a machine gun in a service station.

Jurgen was not stupid. He knew his argument was un-
winnable; it was riddled with inherent contradictions. You
could not, on the one hand, say, as Jurgen often did, that

world ecodegradation was at the point of going critical, that we were all about to die horribly with bubbling flesh and phlegm-choked lungs, then on the other hand seek to deny people a small, sealed, self-sustainable environment in which they might survive this unpleasant prospect. All the same, he kept plugging away. Endlessly pointing out that, by purchasing an alternative to Earth health, you gave up on tackling pollution.

"Not so," the Euro delegates said. "If you buy a burglar alarm, does it mean you've given up on crime?"

"Yes," cried Jurgen Thor, "yes, yes, yes! You stupid Euro delegates! Crime is a very pleasant and perfect metaphor! The world is staggering toward violence and anarchy, and what do we do? We lock our doors! Employ guards! Buy guns and hide! We *have* given up on crime, and we've given up on the environment also! What is air, yes, if you can't breathe it, huh? What is food, I don't think, if you can't eat it?"

Jurgen was a Viking. His first language was Norwegian, and when much moved his English lapsed into the Euro-American MTV-speak of his youth, that strange language that seems to be a constant series of questions.

"I'm going to save the world, yes?" he had said in one of his first interviews, decades previously, before Natura, the world political party of which he was principal spokesperson, had even been formed. "I am the champion for all living things, okay? You dig it?" he had said, and hopeless though his battle sometimes seemed, the world could not have had a more convincing champion.

Green God.

Jurgen Thor was almost too good to be true. From his great mane of shaggy golden hair to his enormous sixteen-hole, tan leather Timberland work boots he was more god than man. His gimlet-sharp clear gray eyes could puncture a

61

politician across a hundred-yard conference room. They were more than just piercing, they were armor-piercing, and a thousand women had felt the prick.

Jurgen was huge. It was as if when the Almighty was making him He (or She) had always intended to make two, perhaps even three, environmental activists, but had decided to save time by making one big one. Muscles coiled like serpents about his colossal frame. His chest was a giant's chest, the nipples were in different time zones; this was a chest that exerted its own gravitational pull.

Legends of Jurgen's strength and physical powers rang around the world. Stories abounded of his days with the Mother Earth Direct Action Group, before he had renounced terrorism. It was said that he had once plugged a shallow water toxic outfall with his own body, withstanding the immense pressure for many desperate hours while a team of activists had made good the sabotage with steel and cement. People whispered in awe about how the great man had once personally dragged a stranded pilot whale from a polluted beach and swum it out to sea. His body was pockmarked with scars from numerous bullet wounds he had received during attacks on Claustrosphere factories in the early years. It was said that, on the occasional times when his vast consumption of chilled peach schnapps got the better of him, Jurgen's party trick was to crack walnuts with his foreskin.

Concerned constituents.

"Mr. Thor, what can you tell us about the activities of the terrorist group Mother Earth?" Colin Carper, the Member of Euro Parliament for Essex, England, and a paid Claustrosphere lobbyist inquired.

"As I have said many times, although I support their intentions, I do not support their methods," Jurgen answered.

"But surely you were yourself once a terrorist, Mr. Thor?"

"I do not accept the term terrorist, sir. Yes, I have committed acts against local laws, you know? In pursuit of a wider justice, yes? However, in my capacity as principal spokesperson for Natura, I, of course, acknowledge that it is not acceptable to take the law into one's own hands."

"Oh, come now, Mr. Thor. Enough of this pious bunkum," Carper sneered.

"Bunk up? What is the bunk up, please?" Jurgen replied.

"Bunkum, Mr. Thor! Bunkum! It is common knowledge that you are still a Mother Earth activist, and that Mother Earth itself is nothing less than the armed wing of Natura."

"Sir! If the European parliament is to be reduced to a forum for the perpetration of gossip, suspicion, and innuendo, okay? Then let me say that you, matey boy, are internationally recognized as a paid lackey of the Claustrophere conglomerate . . ."

The odious Carper reddened visibly at this outrageous slur.

"If I seek to make the case for Claustrosphere, Mr. Thor, that is because ninety percent of my constituents own them, and the others are protected by municipal arrangements!"

"The majority of your constituents also have vermin and rat infestations. Do you see it as your duty to endlessly represent those interests too?"

People occasionally noted, with some surprise, that Jurgen Thor's English could be as articulate and perfectly formed as the proverbial King's, when he wanted. Those in the know knew that he put the Norwegian inflections and stumbling, half-Americanized word formations into his speech for effect. He felt that it gave him a vulnerable air, which was useful in debate and also made women want to sleep with him. This latter was a goal that Jurgen Thor was rumored to treasure even more highly than an ecofriendly world.

"Mr. Thor, who is funding Mother Earth?" Carper demanded.

"What has this question to do with me, Mr. Carper?"

"Oh, for God's sake, Mr. Thor, your attitude insults this

house! The Mother Earth Direct Action Group has colossal resources. Its activities become ever grander and more daring. It has an air force, a small navy; it has been able to operate effectively in space, destroying countless commercial launches. Antisatellite ballistics cost billions of dollars, Mr. Thor. Who the hell is providing that sort of cash! I say that it is you, Mr. Thor! I contend that it is the saintly Natura party that funds this murderous terrorism!"

"Natura, Mr. Carper?" Jurgen laughed. "We are a political party, not Fort Knox Incorporated, okay, yes, you foolish dude. We exist by private donations and membership fees. We have less money worldwide than either of the two main parties in the U.S. alone. . . ."

Colin Carper's exasperation was getting the better of him.

"Claustrosphere factories have been attacked countless times, Mr. Thor! Causing billions of dollars in lost revenue! My constituents have a right to know who is funding these outrages. . . ."

It is a particularly gruesome characteristic of parliamentarians worldwide that, in order to legitimize their own prejudices and self-interests, they place them in the mouth of some shadowy collective constituent. Thus they lobby the cause of those who pay them in the guise of voicing the fears of those who vote for them. Jurgen was in fact about to point this out, but at that moment an enormous bomb went off.

European disunity.

The marble cracked, and the chandeliers shattered. The blast was truly terrible. Repulsive sculptures and meaningless murals were found hundreds of yards away. Metal shapes representing the Euro ideals of peace, diversity, and a strong currency were still landing in the suburbs of Brussels minutes after the initial explosion. A vast silk collage entitled "Vive la Différence," which had been commissioned to represent the twin Euro goals of cultural diversity and keeping out penniless refugees from the East, could be seen flapping in the wind, skewered on the spire of the secular chapel. Great blobby sculptures, which looked like huge, fat, multicheeked bottoms, but were in fact symbolic of the smaller European states, were sent rolling across the Euro Piazza and off down the busy shopping streets of the capital. All was chaos and confusion, a nightmare of smashed modern art mixed up with dead and dying delegates.

There were dismembered corpses everywhere. It was a harsh irony that only in death could those earnest European representatives find the unity of body and soul that had eluded them in life. The arms of staunch Flemish fundamentalists were to be found embracing the torsos of die-hard Norman separatists. The brains of Sicilian secessionists could be seen spread across the faces of Ulster unionists. Bits of socialists from Schleswig embedded themselves in bits of their sworn enemy, the socialists of Holstein. Christians were plastered over Muslims. Communists blended with Fascists. Jews, or at least parts of them, mingled freely and unchallenged throughout the chamber. For one shining moment, all creeds and nationalities— both real and dreamed of—became one nation. Croats, Serbs, Basques, Cornish separatists, Slovak nationalists, all pureed together in one grand multilimbed, multibrained, amorphous delegate. In the short period after the dust settled and before the finger pointing began, Europe was, in a strange way, and for the first time, unified.

When the finger pointing did begin, the directions in which it pointed were as many and varied as the special interest groups that were doing the pointing. All were convinced that the dreadful carnage had been caused by the secret agents of those whom they most despised. But as it happened, the bomb was not in fact planted by a secret agent at all. It was planted by an advertising agent. The bomb was a marketing ploy.

8

Dangerous investigations, a broken heart, and a terrorist attack

Getting your head around the news.

PLASTIC COULD ALMOST FEEL THE GREAT BLACK GLUTINOUS MOVEment of the sea as it beat against the ruined shore. He had forsaken conventional screen-fed communication for Virtual Reality television. From inside the helmet he was able to accompany the news teams as the full horrors were revealed. It was not a type of broadcasting that appealed to everybody. The three-dimensional images that surrounded the viewer tended to induce a certain degree of motion sickness. However, it suited Plastic's purposes. He wanted to get a feel for the disaster.

The rupture was complete; the oil was out. The booms were already being breached, the detergents washed about pathetically on top of the impenetrable slick. There could not have been a worse mess if it had been created by a giant two-year-old with bad hand and eye coordination, instead of responsible adults. Adults with awesome technical skills and a wealth of bitter experience to guide them.

They just don't learn, do they? thought Plastic, as he watched the last two people being winched off the fast-disintegrating tanker.

On the horizon he could see the Natura ship approaching at speed.

"Wow, those Natura protest people got on the case fast," the news reporter said, and inside the VR helmet it seemed as if he were addressing Plastic personally.

"They sure did," Plastic murmured in reply, ruefully comparing their performance with that of his own sales team, who had let a donut ad get between them and their target.

Further investigation.

Judy Schwartz was also marveling at the rapid appearance of a Natura protest vehicle.

"How the hell did those guys get here so quick?" he remarked to Jackson as they swung together on the line hanging from the coast guard helicopter.

"They've been trailing us for days," Jackson replied.

"Interesting, isn't it?"

"What?" snapped Jackson. She was getting a bit tired of Judy's interest in everything.

"That they've been trailing you. There are literally thousands of supertankers at sea at the moment, and Natura just happens to be hanging around the one that goes down."

"Tankers sink all the time," Jackson replied. "There's so much oil in the Atlantic, you could use it to make french fries."

At that point, further conversation was cut short because they had to clamber into the helicopter and be disconnected from the wire that had winched them up.

"Well, Agent Schwartz," the pilot said sarcastically, "if you've seen everything you wanted to see, perhaps we might go home now."

Judy did not answer. He was watching the Natura ship through the open door of the helicopter. He turned back to Jackson.

"How well did you know your crew?" he asked.

"Not well. It was a short trip. Why?" Jackson replied.

"So they were all new to you?"

"Not all, there were some faces from previous trips. What are you getting at? You think one of us deliberately ran the ship aground?"

Judy looked around the interior of the helicopter and wished Jackson would keep her voice down. There were some very tough types lining the walls of the craft, and he didn't want them to think he was accusing them of being saboteurs.

"Give me a break, will you?" he said. "I have to write something down in my report, don't I? Who recruits the crew?"

"The oil company, of course."

"Not the captain?"

"Well, obviously not. He doesn't pay the wages, does he? If the captain isn't happy with a sailor, then he can ask the company to change him. That's all."

"And the captain was happy? I mean, apart from killing himself, obviously."

"It was a good ship and a good crew, okay?" Jackson was getting angry.

"Until you ran aground."

"Okay, mister, that's it. I don't know what you're getting at, and I don't care. Maybe you think we sank our own ship, I don't know, but I'm fed up with your questions, and if you know what's good for you, you'll shut up. Because you're looking at one lady who's getting ready to throw you out of this helicopter, and there're twenty-five witnesses here who'll swear an oath you tripped."

Dressed to kill.

Meanwhile, Nathan was still negotiating with the private cops at the gates of the Beverly Hills Fortified Village. "So you're meeting with Plastic Tolstoy, huh?" they said, not really wanting to believe it. "Okay, writer, let's just check this one out."

They strutted back to their little hut, positively sparkling in their gleaming black BioTech flak suits. Their shiny boots crunched on the ground in a tough, aggressive manner. Not for the first time, Nathan reflected on the dubious value of allowing policemen to dress up like Nazis.

They wouldn't look so tough if they took off all their guns and stuff, he thought. Which was true, but since they were not likely to, rather irrelevant.

Cops had not always looked like this. Once upon a time, when policemen were first invented, they had looked rather stupid in a cozy sort of way. In Britain they wore top hats and frock coats and often sported enormous side whiskers, in which it was possible for small criminals to hide. On the continent of Europe their brother officers strutted about the place in shiny breastplates, big hats, and any amount of plumes and feathers. Streets had to be widened in the Paris of Napolean III, simply to make room for the epaulettes.

It was a wonderful system whereby those in authority were brought face-to-face with their own human frailty by being made to look very silly. It's rather difficult to act like an arrogant bully when you're dressed like a complete twerp. Sadly, things changed. First, a leather jacket appeared. Next, a visored cap, then a pair of shades. Slowly but surely, over the years it became commonplace to see those in whom the community was expected to place its trust decked out like a cross between a Hell's Angel and Heinrich Himmler.

Nathan resented it deeply. Before leaving Britain he had actually recorded a whinge about it for the Boring Channel.

Whinge was an open access program, where members of the public (preferably university professors) were invited to whinge for fifteen minutes on a subject of their choice. Nathan had chosen to pontificate on police uniforms.

"Those entrusted with power and authority should not be encouraged to strut around the place getting a great big stiffy about it," he had argued earnestly. "I mean, why do people become police officers?" he asked. "There are basically only two reasons. It is either because they want to serve the community or because they like being paid to look tough and push people around. The latter should not be encouraged with fascistic paraphernalia."

Nathan demanded that police uniforms be changed. That all officers, male or female, should be required to carry out their duties in stripy Lycra tights, pink dresses, and enormous leprechaun hats with shiny silver buckles on them. According to Nathan, the effect would be immediate. Cops would feel too self-conscious to intimidate people; crooks would not be able to bring themselves to shoot such jolly looking officers; victims of crimes would suddenly feel relaxed about approaching the police; witnesses would come forward. The whole community would rise up in support of such brave men and women, who were prepared to uphold the law no matter how stupid they looked.

Nathan extended his idea to include the military.

"While I accept the need for some form of collective security," he said, "I object strongly to the constant glamorization of something that is, when all's said and done, an unpleasant necessity. I mean, calling ships things like HMS *Indomitable* is just silly."

Nathan argued that there was something dangerously seductive about giving weapons tough macho names. Nothing made a politician happier than being able to announce, "HMS *Indomitable* was deployed today in the Gulf, carrying officers and men of the Second Armored Division." Would it not be better to rename these things? A politician pandering to jingoistic public opinion would find it much less tempting to deploy "HMS *Dubious Use of the World's Resources,* carrying officers and men of the Very Small Penis Division."

The program format of *Whinge* allowed for a right of reply by anyone taking issue with the speaker. Strangely, nobody from the police or armed forces took up the offer. The entertainment industry, however, sent along a spokesperson to object in the strongest possible terms to these pernicious efforts to undermine their livelihood. Geared, as it is, to providing entertainment exclusively for mentally challenged teenage boys, film and television producers found the idea of policemen dressed as clowns and battleships called the USS *Stupid* entirely unacceptable. There was simply nothing exciting about a Terminator in a dress.

Fool in Paradise.

The guards checked their list. The clipboard and ballpoint pen seemed curiously anachronistic in the hands of these distinctly high-tech cops. The reason for such archaic communications technology was, of course, that, unlike computers, Bics are very difficult to hack into. If you want to change a name that's been written on a piece of paper in ink, you have to scribble it out and write another one on the top. A subterfuge that even the stupidest goon could recognize.

Finding that his name was indeed on their list, the guards waved Nathan through the huge electric gates. As he put his window down and let in the clean, filtered air of the Fortified Village, Nathan's mood lightened.

Beverly Hills! he thought. He was driving through Beverly Hills on his way to play tennis and make a pitch to the most powerful communications mogul in the world. It didn't get any bigger than this. He was inside the oyster, inside the *pearl*. What would Flossie make of it?

Damn! He'd done it. He'd let his mind wander, and of course it had wandered straight back to Flossie, as it always did. Nathan had to be constantly vigilant because the moment he let his guard drop, the little devils that lived inside him would put that big heavy piece of lead in his stomach again.

"Screwed it up, didn't you?" the little devils would whisper in his ear. "You had a beautiful, perfect girl and you screwed it up . . . and why did you screw it up?" they asked, although they already knew the answer. "Because you're a complete git, that's why. What are you?"

"I'm a complete git," Nathan whispered to himself. Then louder, "I'm a complete git. A complete and utter git!" His voice rose to a shout and he banged his head on the steering wheel as he drove.

Suddenly his car was surrounded by Beverly Hills private cops. They leapt in droves from out of the lush plastic vegetation that enclosed the quiet road. Shouting at yourself and banging your head on a steering wheel was crazy behavior in anybody's books. The Beverly Hills private cops were certain that they'd caught themselves a live one.

Some say love is blind, but in fact it doesn't see half that well.

"Why were you shouting to yourself and banging your head against the steering wheel?" the first leather-clad gunman demanded of Nathan.

Nathan faced a positive sea of ballistics. One wrong move and he'd be vaporized. He decided honesty was the best policy.

"Because I spent two years trying to leave my wife, under the impression that I didn't love her and also because I wanted to screw other women. Then one day *she left me,* and I realized that I did love her madly, and ever since then my life has been a pointless joke."

The cops considered this for a moment. Weighing their response. Eventually their leader spoke.

"You have to fly to her," said the tough, hard-bitten cop. "You have to fly to your beautiful lady and smother her with wild, burning kisses. You have to put a cartload of flowers on her bed and say, 'Hey, sexy pants, I made you a meadow, get in it so I can bang you till your ears rattle.' That's what you have to do. Otherwise, you ain't even a man."

Nathan thanked the officer for his advice, adding that this course of action had not occurred to him before, but now that it had been pointed out, it was certainly what he would do. Secretly, however, he suspected that these were not tactics that would work on his beautiful Flossie.

His beautiful Flossie! Ha! Nathan had not called her that twelve short months before. No, then Flossie's charms had been lost to him. They had been together for eight years, and for the final two Nathan had wanted out. He had wanted to sleep with other women. He had wanted to sleep with just about every woman he passed in the street. What's more, he had wanted to sleep with women who put the top back on the toothpaste after they had used it. He had wanted to sleep with a woman who always left her keys and money in the same place, and hence was able to find them again when they were next needed. Flossie never knew where her keys were, and Nathan had hated it. Most of all, he had hated it when she stole his and lost those too. Nathan always, *always* put his own keys back in the same place, so he always knew where they were. Unfortunately, so did Flossie, and it was a source of constant irritation. She never put the milk or the butter back in the fridge after using them, either.

Nathan often reflected that the God of Love was at best a fickle, indecisive type and at worst a total raving schizo and bastard. When Nathan had first known Flossie he had been obsessed with her sexuality. Later he grew indifferent to her charms, and now here he was again, desperate to take her to bed. How could such conflicting passions exist within the same person? Every aspect of his attitude to Flossie had swung like a pendulum. It was absurd that a woman's personal habits could appear cute one day, utterly irritating the next, and back to cute again the day after. Nathan, who only a year before had thought Flossie's lifestyle bordered on the disgusting, now longed to see her underpants flung anyhow on the bathroom floor and to discover his special bedroom nail clippers in the pantry. Flossie never finished a cup of coffee; she always left it half full to be knocked over at a later date. There was a time when this habit had wrenched Nathan's guts with frustration. Now he looked back upon it as the most endearing of characteristics.

Yes, the God of Love was fickle, and he had turned Nathan upside down. A year ago Nathan had almost hated Flossie. He was sick of her and their relationship. He had moped through his life, cold and distant, wondering how he could get away from this woman whom he no longer loved.

"Do you love me?" Flossie would ask.

"Of course I love you," Nathan would reply.

"It doesn't seem like you love me," Flossie would insist, and although Nathan denied it, he knew she was right. A combination of sexual frustration and domestic irritation had convinced him that he wanted out.

Every day he had tried to think of a way to leave. He didn't want to hurt her, and he didn't want to have a row about who owned the house, but he had to get out. The months went by, while he continued to assure her that he loved her . . . and continued to try to figure out a way of escape. He was a coward, and he could not face the unpleasantness, but he knew that he would do it soon.

Then, one day, Flossie had announced that she was leaving him for another man, and from that second onward he had loved no one but her.

Terror hit.

As Max drove into the DigiMac Studio for lunch with his agent, having left his beautiful, nearly ex-wife Krystal (who will play no further part in this story) slumbering on their satin bed, he too was reflecting on affairs of the heart. Although he did not feel quite as desperate as Nathan, he could certainly take no satisfaction from his position.

Being asked for a divorce by a wife whom he did not even recognize had really brought it home to Max just how aimless his life had become. It was all very well being a great big star, but if you were also a sad drunk whose idea of a long relationship was making it to the second screw, then surely something was wrong. There was a hollow feeling inside him that he could not place. Was he hungry? Starting a cold, perhaps? No, it did not feel like either of those things. It was sort of empty and melancholic. Max arrived at the studio gates and drove through onto the main boulevard. There he saw two young lovers strolling arm in arm inside the sidewalk BioTube. The scene touched a nerve. That was it! He had it now. Max recognized the hollow sensation. He was feeling lonely.

Inside the commissary, Max's agent, Geraldine Koch, was waiting to have lunch. She had great news, news that instantly returned Max to his customary good humor.

"You have a meeting with Plastic Tolstoy at three forty-five today."

Max's eyes widened with excitement, and Geraldine could not restrain a grin of triumph from spreading across her face. A face that was usually so sour, people's jaw muscles prickled just looking at it.

"He wants to put you together with a British writer called Nathan Hoddy. I believe he has a feature in mind."

"You mean a full-length commercial?" Max asked, trying not to get overexcited.

"No, I mean a feature, Max. He's planning a huge advertainment around the theme of the battles between

Claustrosphere and the Green Movement. I've convinced his people that you're mature enough now for major adult leads."

This was just the kind of break Max needed. He and Geraldine had been discussing for months how he was going to make the difficult transition from idol to icon. There were some stars who were merely of the moment, and some, a few, who became stars for life. Despite his huge celebrity, in many ways Max was still the Levi's guy. That all-important leap from being a fashion to being an institution had so far eluded him, and the sands were running out. Working for Tolstoy would change all that. It would confirm Max as a true, grown-up megastar and place him on an exalted level from which he could never be knocked.

As Geraldine was giving Max the details of the meeting, Rosalie and the terrorists arrived. Not at the table; they landed on the translucent BioDome roof of the commissary with a loud thudding. Everybody looked up at the shadowy figures moving about on the dark-blue-tinted filter shield. Most people, including Geraldine, were rather scared, but Max loved any kind of excitement and found the scene exhilarating.

"Look at those guys," he said. "They certainly know their stuff."

"The security people should shoot them," Geraldine replied.

Max watched, fascinated, as above him the five masked figures in green fatigues mined the BioShield with well-rehearsed efficiency. They laid the charges at fifteen-foot intervals across the great domed canopy while their helicopter clattered above them.

"What are they doing!" asked Geraldine.

"I think they're going to blow a lot of holes in the roof."

And before Geraldine could respond to Max's calm observation, there was a series of bangs as Rosalie detonated the charges, and fragments of BioShield rained down on the screaming diners below.

"What are they doing?"

"I guess we'll find out in a minute," said Max excitedly.

And of course they did. Rosalie attached a grappling iron to the largest hole in the roof, and then she and the rest of the team climbed back into the helicopter.

"I think they're going to try and pull the roof off," observed Max. They could see the shadowy blue shape of the terrorist craft pulling slowly away from the canopy. Thirty feet above the roof, however, the helicopter stopped, hovering in midair, tethered firmly by the grappling rope stretched taut below. The mighty engines roared and tugged, but the roof was tougher than the terrorists had allowed for in their otherwise flawless planning.

Downstairs Geraldine laughed. They all laughed. They could see that what was clearly a plot to expose their pristine epidermises to killer ultraviolet sunshine had gone wrong.

"Roof's too strong, huh?" they shouted upward. "Fuck you, green assholes."

Up in the Mother Earth craft there was consternation.

"We'll have to cut her free," the pilot shouted above the scream of the laboring engines. "I give the cops another two minutes."

But Rosalie was having no such defeatest nonsense. This was the DigiMac Studio, a world-famous location in the middle of the most public town on the planet. Mother Earth could not be exposed as incompetent fools in such a dazzlingly high-profile arena. Grabbing her bag of detonators, Rosalie launched herself down the straining grappling rope and back onto the commissary roof. Quickly she laid a second line of charges close to the gaping holes. Down below, people did not know whether to scatter or stay put; most opted for cowering under their tables. Only Max remained calmly seated, although his heart was pumping.

He was trying to make out the face of the woman crouching high above him.

Rosalie finished laying the new charges and ran back over the blue-gray dome to the straining rope that attached the roof to the helicopter. Grabbing it, she activated the detonator. Her idea was that as the terrorist chopper rose into the air, taking with it that detested symbol of ecocomplacency, the BioShield, she would be hanging on to the tow rope. She would then be whisked away to the comparative safety of a life of international terrorism. Unfortunately, the roof came away with such a jerk, and the helicopter lurched upward with such violence, that Rosalie lost her grip on the rope, and she was thrown through the great jagged hole in the BioShield, of which she was the principal creator. She fell fifty feet into the dining room below, landing with great good fortune in Rupert's cake.

9

The dream factory and the dead sea

Rupert's cake.

FORTUNATELY FOR ROSALIE, EVEN IN SUCH ELEVATED SURROUND-
ings as the commissary of DigiMac Studio, the dreaded
birthday interruption could occur. As hazards of dining
out go, the birthday interruption is not the worst. It is not
as bad as being poisoned by the seafood or getting a table
next to fifteen guys on a stag night, but it's still a pain.
You're in the middle of your meal, in the middle of a
conversation, maybe even in the middle of suggesting that
coffee be skipped in favor of screwing all night like crazed
rabbits. What's more, rabbits who have grown tired of life
and lettuce and decided to fuck each other to death instead. Then suddenly the lights dim, "Happy Birthday"
(or one of the groovier pop options) is cranked up on the
sound system, and a mound of whipped cream and spark-
lers is brought in and plonked in front of whoever's birthday it is. This is always a pretty gruesome affair. The self-

conscious smiles of the recipient and pals; the scarcely veiled hostility of the other diners; the show-off waiter letting it all go on a bit too long. The occasion at the Digi-Mac commissary was rendered even more horrid by the fact that the birthday person was a child star. Hence everybody had to profess themselves absolutely delighted that this youngster, who had everything, had got just a little bit more.

Rupert, who was only eleven, accepted the ten-foot-tall cake with the practiced grace of a true professional. He was a wonderful actor, one of the studio's hottest properties, and he had been a huge hit in the *Child Star* Virtual Reality games. In these incredibly popular entertainments, the player is faced with a fictitious juvenile Hollywood supercelebrity, played by Rupert. The player is then allowed to punch, throttle, and, if he or she can, run over the Child Star with a truck.

The game was already in its twelfth mutation: *Child Star 12: The Premiere.* In this version, the player inside the VR helmet encounters the Child Star at the opening of *Smirk,* the Star's latest kiddy picture. The Star does an interview, in which he goes on about how his mom only gives him ordinary pocket money like the other kids and how neat it is to get to meet all those big stars, etc. At the point at which the Child Star says, "I'm just a regular kid. I guess I like to do what all kids do," the player has fifteen seconds to throttle him before the handlers arrive. The player must kill the Child Star immediately, because with each throttling the Child Star survives, the more obnoxious the interview gets: "I'm just a regular kid, I eat pizza, go to movies, and hang out with the guys in the mall. Girls are cool, but I don't have a regular date." Eventually, if the player has failed, the Child Star, still grinning his endearing grin, gets awarded a special juvenile Oscar by Mickey Mouse.

Surprisingly, Rupert himself was popular in actual reality as well as Virtual Reality because he was, in fact, a nice child. While the trend for many decades had been for pint-sized little shits to play witty, decent, inventive boys and girls, Rupert, who was actually a fairly well-adjusted young person, had made a hit playing a pint-sized little shit.

Cross-dressing.

As she fell, Rosalie caught a momentary glimpse of the terrible pandemonium she had created. Sunlight was pouring in! Pure, unscreened, naked sunlight! Not one square inch of flawless white skin in the room had felt such a harsh glare in years. It was a beautiful bit of terrorism. The sort of witty, brutal protest for which Mother Earth was justly notorious. To pour sunlight on the beautiful people of the Golden State and watch them run screaming for their BioShield parasols was to remind the world yet again just how far people had drifted into simply accepting ecodegradation.

Rosalie was in and out of the cake in a moment. It was as if she'd been falling into and leaping out of cakes all her life. However, one glance showed her that it was out of the frying pan and into the fire. Or in this case, out of the cake and into the arms of the studio security officers. Five of them were closing in on her, although they had heavy going among the upturned tables and panicking beautiful people. Rosalie scanned the room for a means of escape. The ladies' room was only yards away; she made for it. Rushing in, she surprised a beautiful young starlet at the basin. The starlet had no idea what had been happening, having been restapling a chin tuck while all the excitement was going on.

"Get your dress off!" shouted Rosalie, already stepping out of her cake-covered green dungarees.

The starlet wondered. This could be her big break. True, the casting couch was a coin to be spent sparingly. If you dropped your drawers every time anyone with a two-picture development deal on the outer edges of the lot suggested it, you might as well leave them off altogether. On the other hand, this woman in dungarees had a pretty commanding presence. A lot of gay girls made pictures these days; a couple were even production heads. The starlet thought that perhaps now was the time to swallow her pride.

"Hey, listen, you're real nice, I like you," she said, trying to hedge her bets. "But, you know, I don't want you to think I get it on with just anyone, you know?"

"Get your dress off now, you repulsive little bitch, or I'll kill you." The wire-strippers Rosalie found in her belt gleamed inches from the girl's face.

The starlet was thrilled. This woman had power attitude. In Hollywood, the more powerful you are, the ruder you can afford to be, and this lady was rude enough to be a production head, maybe even a studio chief. The wire-strippers were a bit of a worry, but nobody ever said a career in movies would be easy.

"Okay, but you can't hurt me, all right? Like, I don't do that at all, okay?" the girl said, slipping out of her dress. "No pain, just fun stuff, right? Are we going in a cubicle?"

"Gimme the shoes," said Rosalie, kicking off her own boots.

"My name's Tori Doherty. I'm an actress," the starlet said, feeling that she really ought to get the business side of the transaction sorted out, but not really knowing what the procedure was. "Um, maybe you can help me, I don't know, some advice perhaps or . . . ."

"My advice is separate all your garbage, avoid plastic containers, and insulate your attic."

Rosalie pulled off her woolen hat, letting her hair fall to her shoulders. Then, wearing Tori's dress and high heels, she ran out of the toilet screaming. The security people had only just arrived at the ladies' lavatory, and Rosalie pushed past them, shouting, "There's a weirdo in the rest room."

As the guards ran into the room, Rosalie dived into the panicking crowd. Within moments she was out of the commissary and trying to find a way off the studio lot.

Lost in Development.

Rosalie was running along the little sun-drenched lanes looking for an exit. The UV was ferocious, and the skimpy dress she had taken from the starlet was specifically designed to let just about anything through. Rosalie could feel her skin burning, but she could not afford to get trapped in a sidewalk BioTube. She blessed the fact that she had only recently had her pores reblocked. They'd hold for an hour at least, and if she wasn't out in an hour, she wasn't going to get out. On she ran through the blinding sun, between rows and rows of little pale bungalows. She turned one way . . . there were little pale bungalows. She turned another . . . there were little pale bungalows. She was in a maze of little pale bungalows.

"Where's the exit?" she said to a strange, distracted-looking fellow in glasses who was loitering beneath a curbside shelter.

"Why?" he replied, a weird tinge of panic in his high voice. "Is something happening at the exit? Do you have a *deal* at the exit?"

Rosalie had no time to confer with weirdos. She ran on. Two people, a man and a woman, were emerging from a little pale bungalow. Rosalie accosted them before they could get into the BioTube.

"I need the exit," Rosalie demanded.

"We can give you that," said the woman with a desperately ingratiating smile. "In fact, we have a whole bunch of ideas around the theme of exiting. Death, departure, decay. We have a treatment right here."

"But funny," the man chipped in. "Death meets funny. It's about what's happening now, today."

The two dazed people wandered off into the sunlight together. Rosalie feared that she had stumbled into an insane asylum, but she was actually somewhere far more confused and paranoid. She burst into the bungalow that the two people had just left.

"Where's the exit?" she blurted to the lady behind the desk, a forceful-looking woman of about fifty, cut up to a fairly convincing thirty-five. Her name was Shannon.

"If your treatment is on micro, leave the chip in the bucket. We accept no other format," Shannon said.

Rosalie had had enough. The studio security staff would not take long to work out that she was wearing somebody else's dress. She had to get out.

"Okay, love, I don't know what kind of loony bin I've wandered into here, but you listen to me and you listen hard." Rosalie was employing the kind of look and tone that had cowed whale murderers on the bridges of their own ships and unmanned SWAT teams in the bowels of nuclear power stations. "This is very important."

But Rosalie wasn't on the bridge of an illegal whaler, nor was she attempting to interfere with a nation's civil domestic nuclear capacity. She was in a little pale bungalow on a back lot in Hollywood, facing the most formidable attack beast ever developed. The producer's secretary.

"Everybody's treatment is important, dear." Shannon's smile never left her lips, but the voice was honeyed steel. "Everybody's idea is an idea whose time is now. Just place your microchip in the bucket provided, dear, and I'll see that—"

Rosalie lunged forward, intending to grab Shannon's lapels and shake the information out of her. Instead, she found herself staring down the barrel of a stun-thrower. She had not even seen Shannon move.

"You know, dear, I can't tell you how much I miss the

days when writers went off and killed themselves instead of trying to kill me."

"I'm not a bloody writer," Rosalie shouted. "I'm a terrorist."

"I never met anyone on this lot who didn't think there was something special about themselves, dear. Take a hike."

Rosalie stumbled out of the little pale bungalow.

Where ideas go to die.

In the midst of Hollywood, the dream town, Rosalie had stumbled upon the place where there were only nightmares. For in those quiet little buildings the desperate met the scared. Desperate writers and scared producers. Writers, desperate to be used; producers, scared of making the wrong decision.

The place where ideas went to die.

There are two ways for an idea to die in that sunny bungalow world, fast and slow. Fast is easier. Fast is when it gets rejected outright. Of course, even then the idea only dies for the studio; for the writer it will never die, but since the writer is one of the living dead anyway, that's irrelevant. The slow way for an idea to die is in development. This happens when a person inside a bungalow takes an interest in an idea. This special privilege is reserved for very few ideas indeed. These are special ideas, and for them a very special form of torture has been devised: They will be discussed to death. Considered from every possible angle by as many people as the producer can afford to employ until nobody can remember what was good about the idea in the first place. Then somebody will say: "I think we've gotten real complex here. We need to get back to what we had in the beginning," and slowly the idea will fade and die.

There is a haze that hangs over Los Angeles. Many people say it's pollution, others say it's something to do with what happens when cold water meets warm air out over the ocean. The truth is that it is the haze of a million ideas slowly fading away.

A way out appears.

Rosalie knew she had to get out, not merely because she had just perpetrated a violent act of terrorism, and the forces of the law were closing in on her, but also because she could sense something strange and terrible about the place in which she had found herself. Rosalie was born and brought up in Dublin; she was fourth-generation hippy and had listened to poetry and song all her life. She knew when a place had bad karma, and this one had it. She was not a writer nor an actor. She had nothing to do with the entertainment industry, but quite suddenly she knew she was surrounded by lost souls and unhappy spirits. The ghosts of a hundred years of unrequited artists, all of whom had died in development.

She began to run, sensing that if she stayed much longer she would never leave. A strange sensation was beginning to overtake her. She felt a desire to buy the daily trade papers, to attend improv classes, to talk to kindred spirits about which heads had rolled at the majors, to drop a mention or two of a potential meeting over at Fox. . . . She ran, up one avenue, down another, past sound stages, more bungalows . . .

A car pulled up beside her.

"Jump in," said Max.

Max had followed Rosalie out of the commissary. Her disguise had not fooled him for a moment. He was a good actor, and he knew a performance when he saw one. Also, the girl who had originally owned the dress had only a few moments previously approached Max at his table and mentioned that she admired his work. Max remembered the dress, and he remembered the girl. Now there was the dress again, but on a very different girl. A much more interesting-looking one. Max had watched, fascinated, as the strange woman in the stolen dress made her escape. He was hugely impressed. Here was somebody who clearly had a purpose. Somebody who had worked out what it was she wanted to do and was doing it. What's more, that thing had nothing to do with show business. To Max, this was quite incredible. He wanted to know more about this woman. That was why he had followed her out and was now offering her a lift.

For a moment, Rosalie thought about punching Max out and taking the car. However, reflecting that she still had absolutely no idea how to get off the lot, this did not seem like a very clever move. Besides, Rosalie may have been a green terrorist, but she read magazines and went to the pictures. This was Max Maximus. If she ever got back to Dublin, this would make for great gossip down at Flannagan's. "So there I was, driving about in Hollywood with your man Maximus himself. Would I lie to you?"

She got into the car, and Max headed for the studio gates.

Horn of a dilemma.

Once they were out on the public highway, Rosalie asked Max something she had wanted to know for months.

"Why did you have the horn done?"

"I'm getting rid of the horn."

Max hated that horn. Why the hell had he done it? Drunk, that's why, drunk enough to get a stupid, dumb, simulated-bone spike grafted to the front of his head. Dr. Rock said he could take it off again in about a month, and it wouldn't scar, but then Dr. Rock was a BioQuack and a casualty. Dr. Rock's principal source of income was doing dick extensions for porno stars, which fell apart if you so much as gave them a slap.

At first, having a horn had felt great. Nobody had had a horn before. Krystal had liked it, and Geraldine, his agent, thought it was a terrific idea.

"Sure, a horn, why not? It goes with the whole wildman thing, and it kind of resonates solidarity with endangered species. Like rhinos. Do they still have rhinos, by the way, or did they get dodoed?"

Rhinos had definitely got dodoed some fifteen years earlier. What's more, a drunk movie star with an imitation horn surgically grafted onto his forehead was not going to bring them back. Still, it did look pretty wild. Geraldine had immediately organized a major stills photo shoot, which had gone over big. Max had looked great. Torn jeans, slashed open at the fly to reveal a flat, hard stomach rising to a lean, wiry torso. Arms spread wide like Christ. The expression on his sweetly handsome face that of a wounded beast, sad, tortured, noble, and come-fuck-me all at once. And atop it all, that majestic spike, twelve inches of smooth, clean imitation bone. What a pose. Eight pages in *Vanity Fair* plus the cover. The teens had gone crazy for it. Within a week the shops had been full of plastic stick-on horns, and Max got twelve percent of all the marketing. Of course, as always, some kids went too far, and Max had to go on the TV and try to look responsible; not an easy thing to do with a horn grafted onto your head.

"Mr. Maximus," the talk show guys had said, "how do you feel about reports of kids whose parents can't afford decent subcellular surgery getting cheap horn jobs from backstreet BioQuacks and ending up scarred and maimed and totally socially dysfunctional for life?"

Max had been very firm on this one. "Don't do it, kids," he had said. "The easily removable, glue-on 'Horno Maximus' is available at any K mart, so you can look keen and stay safe."

But all that was weeks ago. Now Max was sick to death of the thing. He couldn't wear a hat, toughs had started throwing doughnuts at it in bars, and it banged against the faucet when he was in the shower.

"I'm having it removed next month," Max said to Rosalie and changed the subject. "So what do you do, then?"

"I kill people who murder planets."

"That sounds pretty radical. Did you ever think about trying to talk to them first? You know, put love out to them and keep it there?"

Coincidence considered.

The stricken tanker was a stricken tanker no more; it was a wreck. Only the port side of the forward section could now be seen above the water. It stood out like the tombstone that it was. A tombstone for a dead sea.

The water surrounding the wreck was a mass of activity. The coast defenses had been scrambled, and the "cleanup" was underway. "Cleanup" was of course a strange description for a process that really consisted of nothing more than spreading the mess about a bit. Worse, the detergents and chemicals used in the pointless operation were in themselves dangerous pollutants. Basically, the whole effort was entirely cosmetic, and a cynical world knew it. The reason that they knew it was largely because of the constant efforts of Natura to put the facts before the public. For more decades than anybody cared to remember, Natura had battled against terrible and dangerous odds to get to the heart of environmental disaster. Its aim was always to expose the cover-up efforts of those who profited most from those disasters, or at least from the industrial and economic activities that made such disasters inevitable.

The Natura scientists were hard at work as the little coastguard launch, upon which Judy Schwartz had hitched a lift, approached their ship. Once aboard, Judy and the other authority figures were met with the cold hostility they had come to expect from any encounter with green activists. As far as Natura was concerned, the FBI, the coast guard, and all other law enforcement agencies were there to protect the interests of the polluters.

"You see this!" an irate biology professor from Princeton said, addressing the news cameras that had also arrived at the ship. "Now, the coast guard turn up! Coast guard! That's got to be the sickest joke on record. Did they guard this coast? I don't think so, because this coast is now dead. So what do they do now? Subpoena the people that created this hell? No, they come and hassle us!"

"Your ship is impeding the cleanup operation," the chief coastguardsman said, employing that stiff "only doing my job" manner that cops of any description adopt when they find themselves in front of a camera. "You have no authority to sail in these waters."

"The cleanup operation is a crock of shit and these waters are not waters, they are a stew of oil, heavy metals, and dead fish," the Princeton professor stated, addressing both coast guard and cameras. "As regards who has authority to be here, Natura is a world party and claims the moral authority to be wherever ecodeath is being covered up and sanitized."

One thing was for sure, Judy noted. He might be losing the environmental war, but Natura certainly won all the propaganda battles. The little confrontation that he was witnessing would play heavily on all the news broadcasts. Judy drifted away from the group. As usual, he was able to do this because of his appearance. He looked so harmless, the casual observer would certainly have picked him for a greenie rather than a Fed. Judy reasoned that although the activists on the ship would know each other, extra personnel would now be arriving on board to help cope with the disaster. He decided to see how far he could get before he was challenged.

"Looks pretty bad, doesn't it?" he observed to a couple

of scientists who were drawing up buckets of polluted sea-water for analysis.

"Worse than I've seen for a while," said one of the scientists, clearly very upset. "It'll dilute a little, farther out to sea, but what's it going to dilute into? It's shit out there too."

"Still," said Judy. "Kind of fortunate in a way, though, isn't it? I mean, not fortunate, but sort of, well . . . you know."

"What the hell are you talking about? Fortunate? What do you mean 'fortunate'?"

"Just that the Natura ship was here and everything when it happened. You know, to exploit the propaganda value of it and all. It's a lucky coincidence."

"That's a damn strange way to look at things. Who the hell are you, anyway? I don't know you." The scientist turned to his companion. "Do you know this guy?"

"I do."

There was a voice behind Judy that he thought he recognized. Turning around, he found himself facing an old adversary, a man whom he had first encountered during a Mother Earth blockade of a leaking nuclear facility.

"Hello, Pierre," Judy said. "How are you? Any tumors yet?"

The man called Pierre was in no mood for comradely reminiscences.

"You have no jurisdiction here, Schwartz," he said, making no attempt to conceal his hostility.

"We're in U.S. coastal waters, Pierre. Sorry," Judy reminded him.

Pierre changed his tack, although not his manner.

"Well, you'll get no cooperation from us. . . . This man is an FBI agent!" Pierre loudly informed the scientists working on the deck. "Offer him no assistance, answer no questions, show him nothing unless he produces a warrant."

Judy glanced around. Suddenly he was the focus of attention. Angry, hostile faces glared at him wherever he looked.

"I have no warrant," he said. "This is a peaceful Natura protest ship, why would I need one?"

"Exactly," said Pierre.

"So what are Mother Earth terrorists doing here?" Judy asked.

Pierre did not reply. Instead, with calm deliberation he spat on the deck at Judy's feet.

The scientist whom Judy had first approached spoke up.

"A whole sea is dying, so what do they do? They send the FBI. Brilliant." The man's voice shook with anger and contempt.

Judy turned and walked away. He knew that he would learn nothing more, now that he had been unmasked as an agent. Nonetheless, his trip had not been wasted. He had made an important discovery: Mother Earth terrorists were present at the scene of the disaster. Judy felt they would have done better to keep themselves hidden.

10

Holistic bullets, robotic needles, and Cupid's arrow

Script conference with God.

NATHAN PEERED OVER THE TOP OF HIS KNEES. HE WAS IN PLASTIC Tolstoy's study, seated on quite the softest, lowest couch he had ever encountered. It was like sitting in a luxuriously cushioned hole. On the table in front of him stood a glass of carbonated water, but he could not reach it, not without a rope to haul him out of the couch. His shoulders were at a lower level than his knees, and his head was sunk deep into his chest. Where his neck had gone, Nathan did not know. He presumed it would reappear when he emerged from the couch, should he ever find himself in a position to do so. He did not need his neck at the moment, anyway. At the moment he cared for neither neck nor water. All Nathan cared about was how Plastic was reacting to his treatment.

This was the biggest break it was possible to have. Nathan was past every hurdle, every script reader, every consultant, every vice president in charge of development. He was pitching direct to the man. It was unheard of. To pitch direct to Plastic Tolstoy was a writer's Holy Grail. This man owned the largest communications empire on Earth. He commissioned more copy than everybody else in advertainment put together. He took a direct personal interest in probably no more than one in a thousand of the projects his companies developed for production. Writers would plead to be allowed to compromise every artistic principle they ever had just to eat in the same commissary as the lowliest of Plastic's people. A few years previously, before it was made illegal, some Harvard undergraduates had isolated Shakespeare's DNA and fast-grown another Bard of Avon. Plastic's office had not even bothered to return the guy's call.

Nathan watched nervously as the great man paced about. Plastic spoke without looking up from the synopsis that Nathan had procrastinated over for so many lonely nights in his hotel room.

"So the rat's going to go eat the kid?" he said.

"Yes," said Nathan, "I thought that might make us care . . . in a warm way."

"You want me to put a rodent carnivore about to orally defile a cute little girl on prime time?"

Nathan sensed some criticism in Plastic's tone.

"Well, I don't know about orally defile . . . I mean . . . eat, yes."

"Did your mother reject you?" Plastic inquired with bitter sarcasm. "Were you denied the breast? Is that where the sicko stuff started? You think a *rat* eating a sweet little girl is not a defiling thing? You think that it is somehow *nice!*"

The combination of power and indignation was terrifying. Nathan sank so far into his seat that he was in danger of disappearing altogether. Plastic towered over him, shaking the few pathetic pages.

"Here's an idea—why doesn't the rat *screw* the kid first?

Yeah, that's right, he could screw her, *then* eat her. Would that be sick enough for you? Huh? What is it with you English guys? Is Digusting Pervert on the syllabus at Eton? Can't you even pitch a script treatment without flaunting your sadomasochistic pedophile obsessions?"

Plastic had been in California for about a thousand years, but he still spoke New York Media Jewish. Rhetorical questions and heavy-handed sarcasm were his conversational armory, and he was always at war. He did not really mean to hurt. In fact, what he really liked to do was amuse. Plastic loved to get a laugh, and if none was forthcoming from his audience of cowering employees, he was always happy to provide his own. He certainly had to do his own laughing in this case, for Nathan could not laugh. He was too horrified, terrified, and bent double inside a couch.

"We don't actually see the rat eat the girl," Nathan murmured. "It's implied."

"Oh, it's *implied!!* I'm *so sorry,* Jeeves, old boy! I missed the subtext, don't you know, what ho and pip-fucking-pip!" Plastic's English accent was no less biting for the fact that it sounded about as English as the Statue of Liberty.

"Implied! Don't give me your fucking English fucking subtlety." He seemed almost in despair. "What are you? T. S. Eliot? You think a prime-time vision bite gives you time to indulge your obscure pretensions? You think people who clean cars and wait tables want to spend their precious leisure dollar trying to work out some up-its-ass limey bullshit?"

Nathan gulped in fear and confusion, something to be avoided when folded in half with your ears resting on your shoulders and your knees forced against your chin. It was an action almost certain to bring on the hiccups, and it did.

"Why stop there with your pretentious fucking subtlety? How about this, how about we don't even *have* a little girl?" said Plastic, who, as always, liked to milk any comic theme he found himself developing till its tits squeaked. "Maybe we should have a packet of Pop-Tarts that *represents* a little girl, so ten years from now, when we're all on welfare because our product stank, some fag English professor from UCLA can tell the world that the whole thing was actually a masterpiece, if only we coulda worked out what was *implied!*"

"Hic."

"What, are you going to puke on my couch now?" asked Plastic.

"No, I have hiccups," said Nathan, and with a monumental effort he rocked himself forward far enough to grab the bottle of water on the table before plunging back into the bottomless couch.

"Like, I want to hear about your hiccups. Like that *really* interests me. You know what the Claustrosphere advertainment budget is each year, Nathan?" Plastic asked. "Twenty billion minimum, in the U.S. alone. Work out how many dollars just got spent so you could tell me about your damn digestive problems. We brought you here . . . we sent a *limo* to the damn airport! So you could pitch. So pitch!"

"Um . . . hic . . . do you think perhaps, hic, we might show something of the little girl's fate, but tastefully, you know, avoiding the more graphic details."

" 'Do I think perhaps hic'!" Plastic quoted Nathan with such withering sarcasm that all the pot plants died. "Do *I* think! *I'm* not the damn writer! *You're* the damn writer. I'm just the moron who *pays* the damn writer." Plastic punched his intercom. "Sarah! You know that outrageously inflated sum Nathan Hoddy's agent demanded for her client's pathetic services? Get her on the line and tell her since Mr. Hoddy seems to desire me to do half his work, would she object to me taking half his fee."

Nathan hiccuped miserably.

"You think I'm being hard on you, don't you? You think I'm being unnecessarily negative," said Plastic.

Nathan did not reply. He had nothing to say but hic.

"You want to see negative!" barked Plastic. "This is negative."

Suddenly Plastic pulled open a drawer of his mighty desk and took out a gun. Nathan could not have moved had he wanted to, being stuck in a couch as he was, but there was no time anyway. It was over in a second. Plastic took two steps toward him, pointed the gun into Nathan's astonished face, and fired. Three shots, point-blank range. The gun flashed, the noise in the confined space was deafening, the glass rattled as acrid smoke filled the room.

"Have they gone?" Plastic inquired mildly.

Nathan could not reply; you cannot talk when your heart is in your mouth.

"The hiccups, have they gone?" Plastic asked again. "All that eerk-eerk-eerk was making me nauseous. Thought I'd try this out on you."

The gun disappeared, and in its place Plastic held a small tube with a switch on it.

"It's a holographic projector," Plastic explained. "We're going to give them away at gas stations. Look." He held the tube as if it were the butt of a pistol, flicked the switch, and the three-dimensional image of the pistol reappeared in his hand. "Did it cure your hiccups?"

"Yes, they've gone," whispered Nathan.

"Okay, let's play some tennis."

"All right," said Nathan, struggling out of the couch.

"We'll play in the Claustrosphere."

Play? In the Claustrosphere? Play *tennis* in a Claustrosphere? Nathan thought Plastic must mean table tennis, but he didn't. Set in the grounds of Plastic's house in Beverly Hills was quite the biggest Claustrosphere Nathan had ever seen. In fact, it wasn't really set in the grounds, it was the grounds.

"Hey, who wants a damn garden?" Nathan said. "At least in a Claustrosphere your grass don't die."

Nobody likes it, but what can you do?

They walked down the connecting BioTube and through the EcoLock into the central dome.

Nathan was stunned; he had never in his life encountered such opulence. The thing must have covered well over four acres and contained everything: living quarters, gardens, a little stream. The air was fresh and sweet, birds chattered in the upper reaches, butterflies fluttered over a small field of wheat, fish went "glop" in the pond.

"Of course, it's all BioMechanically generated," Plastic explained. "A genuine ecocyle is impossible on such a small scale. This whole cycle is kept functioning with subcellular protein concentrates and fast-grow organic engineering. It'll work for at least a hundred years though, so who's complaining? This is the kind of development that Mother Earth has been trying to knock out for years. Stupid hippy schmucks, always bombing the wrong labs."

Nathan had of course been aware, as everyone who read a Sunday color supplement was aware, that BioSphere technology had improved; but he had not quite realized how good it had got. Plastic's dome made his and Flossie's ancient old backyard job look like exactly what it was: a crappy little ecoshelter. A basic Eden Three, no frills. It had water rotation and a basic food cycle. It could break down and reconstitute human waste, and it could maintain a breathable atmosphere. It had come with a free gift miniaturized bonsai rain forest, but that was about its only luxury. Even the video library was manual . . . you actually had to eject the microtapes yourself. Flossie and Nathan had debated whether to purchase the optional day and night cycle, but had decided that they couldn't really afford it. Those eye guards you get for sleeping on airplanes would be just as good anyway.

The truth of the matter was that they had both been rather reluctant to buy a Claustrosphere at all. They had not been the first of their friends to do it, but they were not the last, either. They had, in fact, wrestled with their consciences for about the average amount of time taken by most middle-class liberal couples before buying one. Nathan often reflected that his generation seemed to have spent its entire adult life sitting around dinner tables drinking red wine, eating Tuscan bean soup, and trying to justify the morality of buying a Claustrosphere.

"I mean you don't *want* to do it, for God's sake. Do you?" they all said.

"Nobody *wants* to do it."

Of course, as students they had all been deeply opposed to Claustrospheres. Natura was big on campus, and when their parents had slowly begun to think about buying an Eden One they had all reacted with horror. Referred to their dear old folks as "Pollution Fascists" and "Planet Traitors." However, when they themselves reached maturity, the situation looked a bit different.

Dying of consumption.

The Earth just wasn't getting any healthier. How could it? The one single and abiding criterion by which the success of countries is judged is in terms of their "growth." Each year the great nations agonize over how much they have "grown." How much more they have made, how much more they have consumed.

Consumer confidence is actually considered a measure of a country's relative economic strength. When a load of poor, deluded losers are down at the stores running up debts on their credit cards, economists claim that the economy is "growing" and start celebrating. Recessions are deemed to be over the moment people start spending money that they don't have on things that they don't need. Consumption is synonymous with "growth," and growth is good. It is always good, whenever and wherever. Hence, clearly consumption is good, all consumption, anywhere, anytime. Judged by the logic of world economics, the death of the planet will be the zenith of human achievement, because if consumption is always good, then to consume a whole planet must be the best thing of all.

Acting sensibly.

And so, faced with the fact that the world was growing to death, slowly but surely people began to buy their Edens. Just as their grandparents and great-grandparents had moved out of the dirty inner cities into the suburbs. Nobody wanted to do it, but on the other hand, things were as they were and privately martyring yourself was not going to change things.

Every night Jurgen Thor and all the other self-righteous greenies were on the TV, ranting on about planet death. What were you supposed to do? It was obvious: Send Greenpeace a donation, and start digging the foundations for your Claustrosphere.

It was, of course, self-perpetuating. The more people bought them, the more difficult they were to resist. Those who had taken the plunge became Claustrosphere's most passionate advocates. Every time another tanker sank or a nuclear power station went pop, they would silently congratulate themselves on having made the right decision. They scarcely liked to admit it even to themselves, but there was almost a grim satisfaction to be had out of the daily worsening ecostatistics.

"I see that two-fifths of Russia is no longer habitable," they would say to each other over breakfast. "I knew getting a Claustrosphere was a sensible decision. I mean nobody *wants* the Earth to die, but you only have to look at the papers. . . . I wonder what Mr. Holier-Than-Fucking-Thou next-door will say when it's two-fifths of the fucking United States you can't live in? I know what he'll fucking say. He'll say, 'Any room in your Eden for me and the wife?' "

The question of what non-Claustrosphere owners would do in the event of planet death added considerable piquancy to the delicate social politics of the whole issue. In the early days those who owned a Sphere were in the minority, and they had looked rather selfish and antisocial, but as Claustrospheres became more and more common, the moral balance switched. So that it was those without a shelter who began to appear selfish. Once it came about that there were only a few houses left in any street without a Claustrosphere, the majority became obsessed with what those people would do if the Rat Run were announced. More and more, those who held out (be it for moral or financial reasons) began to look like the irresponsible, anti-social ones. In many communities, those who were neglecting to take due precautions to ensure a future for themselves and their families in the event of ecodeath, came to be held in contempt.

"It's all very well being green, we're *all fucking green*," people would say. "But they'll be banging on my door trying to get in when the Rat Run starts. I know they will."

These debates were even more heated when it came to apartment dwellers. Many people in communal living situations had begun to band together to purchase land out of town and commission larger, group Claustrospheres. The question of who was in and who was out divided previously friendly neighborhoods.

Finally the whole community became involved in the issue as politicians began to plan for mass, public Claustrospheres, for the use of the broader population. They claimed that they were concerned for the well-being of all citizens in the event of eco-Armageddon, but the real reason was, of course, fear of the mob. If you have a nice backyard Claustrosphere, just right for you and your family, and up the road there is a housing project containing thousands of people with no ecocover whatsoever, then you're going to get a little nervous about what all those people are going to do on the day of the Rat Run. Therefore, in order that the rich might feel confident about using their Claustrospheres unmolested, some arrangement had to be made for the poor. Right across the industrialized world, borders began to be reinforced and legislation passed to make it a local government responsibility to provide basic ecocover. The Community Claustrosphere became as much the responsibility of City Hall as the roads and the police.

Everyone could see which way this type of thinking was leading. It didn't need a Jurgen Thor to spot it. The more effort that went into what would happen *after* planet death, the less effort people were putting into preventing that death. Coupled with which, the Claustrospheres themselves consumed colossal Earth resources in their actual production. The extraordinary irony was clear to all but the stupidest. The world was actually hastening its own destruction in order to survive it.

Some people like Nathan and Flossie agonized over this paradox; other people said, "Shit happens." Everybody made sure they had access to a Claustrosphere.

Discussing death.

As Plastic Tolstoy led an astonished Nathan into his palatial Claustrosphere, Plastic's most public and bitter enemy, Jurgen Thor, was being sewn back together after the explosion of the European parliament.

Jurgen allowed only local anesthetics to be used. This was partly because he wanted to keep his mind clear to consider the implications of the outrage, and partly because the press were outside the room and he wanted to look tough. It never does a politician any harm to be seen showing physical courage, and also it helps when trying to get laid.

"I tell you, this was a company job, and we go public with the story."

Jurgen was addressing a small group of senior Natura officials, announcing his theory that the bomb blast had been aimed at him as part of a seasonal Claustrosphere marketing push. He spoke through gritted teeth as the laser surgeons worked to sew his massive limbs back on. "Hey, take it easy with that," he shouted as his colossal Nordic penis was unpacked from the ice and prepared for surgery. "It's the basis of my legend."

"You're lucky we saved it at all," the surgeon said. "It landed in the smorgasbord at a reception given by the Norwegian fisheries people. It was a chilled plate, and the herring kept it cool."

"You mean my prick's been saved by the whaling lobby!" Jurgen roared with laughter. "Imagine what all the earnest little hippies who vote for us would think? Jurgen Thor had his dick in a whaler's smorgasbord. Ha, ha! Maybe I won't get so lucky with all the 'right on' girls! What will they say?" Jurgen affected a high squeaky tone. "No, Jurgen, you cannot rumpy-pumpy me! Your wang has the blood of innocent whales upon it!"

Jurgen's great frame shuddered with amusement at his own jollities. The chief surgeon looked up from her delicate work.

"Mr. Thor, I am trying to sew your penis back on, here. Could you kindly lie still?"

"Ha! Doctors! You pretend you are such special people!" Jurgen laughed. "We all know the Robosurgeon does the difficult bits."

"Even Robosurgeons have to be programmed, Mr. Thor. I would hate for you to walk out of here with your penis disappearing up your backside."

Jurgen felt this was a good point and decided to stop making jokes for a minute, much to the relief of all concerned. The brief respite gave a chance for Natura's Chief of Press Liaison to observe that Jurgen's theories regarding the source of the bomb were unsubstantiated slander.

"The police say the blast could have been planted by one of any number of nationalist groups. What on earth makes you so sure that the company tried to hit you, Jurgen?"

"Hey, groover, two things for a start. First, as a rule of your thumb, right? Whatever the Belgian police say, you take the opposite. Right? Okay? Ciao, baby, wake up and smell the flowers. Second, the bomb was indiscriminate, no? Too big by far to have been targeted at any one group. In fact every group suffered casualties, right? You think people plant bombs to kill themselves? I don't think. No, the bomb was designed to breach the security screen that protects the speaker. The speaker was me, okay, babe? But I was lucky, the screen was strong, and so am I. All that happens is my love pump got a little damaged."

"It certainly did," said the surgeon, again looking up from her work. "Look, there are burn marks on it."

"Hey, baby." Jurgen smiled. "Those burn marks didn't come from no bomb, okay? Right? You know what I'm saying here!"

Jurgen rarely failed to make a strong impression on women, and this occasion was no exception. The micro-surgeon would have liked to have taken that big, long, fat dick of which Jurgen was so clearly proud and throttle him with it; but she was professional, and so she returned quietly to her work, making a mental note to spread around that she had actually seen the great Jurgen Thor's legendary appendage, and it was tiny.

"I'm telling you," Jurgen continued, "that bomb was meant for me."

"Well, maybe," conceded the Chief of Press Liaison. "If it was, you sure are lucky they installed such a tough screen."

"Oh, yes, that's for sure and certain, okay? They designed it for when the British hold the rotating presidency of the Euro parliament . . . everyone in Europe wants to kill them, right?"

"But the company?" the press officer protested. "It would be pretty audacious, I mean, it could easily backfire. Killing you could provoke a green backlash."

"Not if I got killed by someone else's bomb! Look, it's simple, man. Claustrosphere wants me dead, right? They always have, but they know that if I die, bang! Immediately I'm a martyr. The Guevara syndrome, right? Okay? Unless, of course, I die stupidly, like getting blown up by someone else's bomb. Then it's kind of a stupid, embarrassing way to die, like those people who get sucked into airline toilets. So what do they do? Wait till I'm addressing the European

Federation, bomb capital of the damn Universe, goddamn and damnit, and hit me with a bomb so big that every nationalistic zealot will be crying foul. They want me dead! I am more than a mere man, I am an idol, an inspiration, a prophet! In many people's eyes I am just too wonderful to be allowed to live."

The surgeon raised her head from her work again.

"I can certainly understand people wanting to kill you," she said.

"Exactly. Of course the Claustrosphere Company will kill me if they can do it safely. Believe me, babe, I am lying here today in fourteen separate pieces because the boys at Claustrosphere *have added murder to their marketing strategy*. I want you to knock up a press release explaining our opinion. They won't sue, I'm telling you."

"But it seems so wild, I mean . . ."

"Listen, man, ask yourself this: If one of our people got the chance to knock off Plastic Tolstoy. Wouldn't they take it?"

A meeting to kill for.

"Hey, how would you like to meet Plastic Tolstoy?" Max asked Rosalie. It was a last-ditch attempt to interest her.

Max was already halfway smitten by Rosalie. She was exciting. She had purpose. He wondered whether her sweet face and pale, slightly freckled skin could possibly be real. It wasn't that she was perfectly constructed like Krystal or anything, far from it; but Max was aware that some girls deliberately had slightly flawed, kooky face jobs done, so that people would think it was natural. Having lived in Hollywood all his life, Max was only vaguely aware that there was a big world outside where people did not have themselves routinely reconstructed to suit their clothes.

He had asked her to lunch. He had suggested a drink, a

swim in his pool, a trip to the BioDome-enclosed beach at Venice; but all this Rosalie had politely declined. She reminded him that she was an international terrorist who had just tried to give a whole crowd of media stars a dose of cancer and was now on the run from the forces of justice. So could he kindly drop her at the airport so that she could make her escape before her description got circulated.

That was when Max suggested introducing her to Plastic Tolstoy. Max occasionally caught the news, and he had a vague idea that Mother Earth and Natura people considered Tolstoy a figure of some significance.

There was a pause. Rosalie was wondering if this was a joke, or perhaps a trap of some kind. "You can get me in to see Plastic Tolstoy?" she asked warily.

"Sure, I have a three-forty-five at his place in the Hills . . . You green guys are kind of down on him, aren't you?"

"Oh, well, you know," said Rosalie, "these things get blown out of proportion."

"He's actually a pretty cool person. I think you'd like him. You know, you're both kind of energetic, 'in your face' type of people. You get things done. He's a legend in the industry. . . ." Max put on his most impressive tone of voice. "He wants me for a picture."

They were maneuvering through the traffic that was, as usual, gruesome. But for once Rosalie did not go into her traffic-jam rant. For once she was appreciative of the delay. She needed time to think. Despite her tough talk, Rosalie was not a killer. She *had* killed, in an indirect sense. During Mother Earth actions she had often been fired upon and had occasionally returned fire. She might have hit someone, she didn't know. She had never hung around long enough to find out. Also, she had blown up a lot of things around and about the world, polluters, dodo-makers (as the traders in near-extinct species were called), Claustrosphere showrooms. There must have been casualties then, she supposed. Her own side had certainly suffered many losses, so she presumed that the enemy must have had them too. She had, however, never specifically or deliberately killed anyone.

Could she do it now? Should she do it now? Rosalie's mind was racing. Plastic Tolstoy was not, after all, directly responsible for the dead seas and extinct species. Except in a small way he was. He was, after all, the prophet of the alternative to saving the planet. . . . But that was stupid. If there were no Plastic Tolstoy there would still be Claustrospheres. He had not invented them; what's more somebody would still be selling them. It was people who were destroying the Earth, not any single person. . . . But then again, Tolstoy did encourage them. Every day, he cynically tempted people to neglect their true responsibilities. . . . History was full of leaders, and Plastic Tolstoy was definitely a leader and an incredibly powerful one at that. More so than any politician. It wasn't politicians who shaped the world anymore, it was the marketing people, the people who perpetrated and justified the myth of consumption. Plastic Tolstoy was the biggest marketer of all.

"I don't think you heard me." Max interrupted Rosalie's reverie. He was very disappointed that his news had not gone over bigger. "Plastic Tolstoy wants me for a picture! Have you any idea what kind of huge shit that is?"

Rosalie was anxious not to arouse Max's suspicions. She pretended to take an interest.

"Why is it so special? You're a big star, everyone knows that. I've read that you could work with anyone you wanted to."

"Anyone but Tolstoy. He's so far ahead of everybody else he's an industry in himself, he *is* the industry. No matter how big you are, you're still small compared to him, and if I play my cards right, he's going to make a picture with me!"

Not if Rosalie could help it he wasn't.

11
Career opportunities

The games people play.

PLASTIC AND NATHAN WERE NOT PLAYING TENNIS IN THE conventional sense. Big though Plastic's Sphere was, it did not actually contain a court. It did not need to. It was equipped with state-of-the-art game-suits that offered a tennis court, a baseball diamond, in fact, any playing field one desired. The suits were Virtual Reality body stockings that the player wore while suspended, weightless, inside a vacuum tank. You could run, kick, and jump in them without going anywhere. You could play any sport, either against a great player of your choice, via computer, or against a real person whose suit was linked to yours. Thus, Plastic and Nathan played two hard sets of tennis involving some pretty impressive serving and net play, and yet all an outside observer would have seen was something akin to two frogmen squirming and writhing in a big fish tank.

"That's the kind of leisure accessory that is going to make New Generation Eden absolutely irresistible," Plastic remarked over a glass of fruit punch as they sat relaxing under the great geodesic dome on the edge of the desert, next to the rain forest. "Inside one of those suits you can join any team you ever dreamed of playing for and play against any team you ever wanted to beat. Some great match you think your team should never have lost? Join the side, play it again, and see if you can make the difference. Many times I've come down here on my own, got in that tank, and shot hoops with the 1980s L.A. Lakers when Magic was playing. Of course, your average guy couldn't afford one of these suits if he saved for a thousand years, but the price will come down, it always does."

Nathan was quite interested, but only quite. He didn't want a game, he wanted a job. He guessed that, despite Plastic's rough treatment of his synopsis, he must still be in some kind of contention or he would not still be in the great man's company. All he could do was sit and wait. Eventually Plastic returned to the point.

Marketing lesson.

"Your treatment is good," said Plastic. "The rat is going to eat the kid, that moves me. It's a little down, a little somber, maybe, but it's good."

Obviously, Nathan, not being privy to Plastic's sense of humor, was a little surprised, considering what had been said in the office, but he was happy to take his luck where he found it.

"But, with respect, I would contend that it *has* to be down," he said, launching into his pitch. "You market a product that will protect people from the death of the Earth, surely the best way to do that is to push the total planetary screwup we're in. Environmental degradation is the best sales tool you've got. You can't talk it up enough."

Plastic smiled at Nathan's naive enthusiasm.

"Oh, like, and that never occurred to us, right?" he said, returning to his favorite tone of aggressive sarcasm.

"Well, I just thought—"

"Like, there's all us dummies sitting around here in Hollywood without an idea in our heads, just waiting for some genius Englishman to come and reveal the dazzlingly obvious to us. Thank you, Mr. Einstein, thank you for striking the scales from my eyes. I feel so stupid my dick has shrunk."

Nathan was at a loss.

"The reason that we have avoided the scare commercial for nearly thirty years, you feebleminded jerk," Plastic shouted, "is because we market a product that shames us all, that's why! Jurgen Thor and the Natura guys are right. It's absolutely disgusting that people are investing in post-Armageddon life insurance. Jesus! We should all be putting every penny we have into saving what we've got."

"Well, yes, of course, but—"

"But nothing! Shut up and listen. Claustrospheres are the thing everybody says they wish they didn't have to have. It's like private education! People would like to support the state system; on the other hand, they don't want their kid getting shot for his eraser. Now if we'd been playing the doom card all these years we'd have looked like we were exploiting a terrible situation. Like we were *happy* the Earth is screwed—which of course we are—but if we say that, we look tacky, right? We've had to be positive and upbeat! We've had to say *'Because we hope you'll never need it.'* If we had said, 'your kids will die unless you buy our product,' people would have smelled a rat, and the rat would have been them. Nobody likes getting the mote in their eye shoved in their face."

"So you don't like my treatment, then?"

"I just said I liked it!"

"But then you said—"

"Listen, Nathan, just let me do the talking here, okay? You shut up, and maybe we'll get somewhere. The situation has changed. Just about everybody in the developed world has a Claustrosphere. You have one, right?"

"Well, actually it's part of a property dispute with my ex-wi—"

"Like I should care? Nathan, please. We will be here all day. Everyone has a damn Claustrosphere, the market is drying up, right? We've been so damned successful we have consumed our consumers. Now this ain't a new thing, right? Producers have faced the problem before, like everybody has a freezer, a car, a semiautomatic weapon. The point is that with other products you get around the problem with built-in obsolescence. You just make a damn freezer that falls apart after two years, it's easy. Unfortunately, built-in obsolescence would kind of defeat the object of a Claustrosphere. By definition, it's got to last at least a couple of generations. So what's the solution?"

Nathan decided not to risk attempting an answer. He knew that whatever he said, Plastic would twist it so that he was wrong.

"We gotta get people to upgrade, that's what. People have to realize that their present units, Eden Ones, Twos, and Threes, are crap. What are you and your wife fighting over?"

"A Mark Three with a bottled rain forest."

"Exactly. Crap. An escape hatch, nothing more. Sure, it'll keep you alive, but who wants to live like that? I'll bet the video library doesn't even have Virtual Reality."

Nathan could only nod at this casual exposure of the woeful inadequacy of his arrangements.

"The point is that all the time people have been sort of presuming that in the end they won't actually have to use the thing. You know, it's been like insurance. Nice to have it there, but you hope you'll never have to claim it. What we need to do now is change the emphasis. We have to make people believe that *they're actually going to have to use their Claustrosphere,* which, let's face it, they probably are. People have got to realize it's a pretty good bet that they're going to spend the rest of their lives inside a geodesic dome, existing off a Biosphere technology. We've got to have them asking, 'Hey, do we lay new carpets in the house? Or do we stick a rain water simulator in the Sphere?' They've got to say, 'Well, hell, where are we likely to be five years from now?' That's what we've got to do, Nathan, we've got to get people to upgrade their Claustrospheres before they change their cars. It is finally time to play the doom card—the one that you seem to be under the impression you're the only person to have thought of!"

Consumer control.

"So you're going to make my ad, then?"

"Yes, I'm going to make your stupid little dumb ad," Plastic replied irritably. "But that wasn't why I asked you up here. You think I ask every pen-pushing little scribbler I commission into my private Sphere to play tennis? Let me tell you, under normal circumstances I *shit* you kind of people. I actually shit little guys like you and then use another little guy like you to clean my ass. Understand?"

Nathan nodded.

"I brought you here because I think you can write, and I want to make a movie. A real movie, a centerpiece to the new campaign. I want a real old-fashioned advertainment and I want you to work on the words, okay?"

Nathan was stunned. A proper movie! So few were made these days. To be asked to be involved in one was to join an echelon so upper it gave Nathan vertigo.

Only a few years previously it had seemed as if nobody would ever make a real movie ever again. Not one with actors and a real fixed plot, that people had to go to a cinema to see. A series of technical innovations seemed to have made the genre obsolete. The feeling was that technology was more interesting than art and that if you didn't need a million-dollar helmet to watch a show, then it wasn't worth seeing.

Interactive entertainment became the miracle ingredient that was going to revitalize a depressed industry. The consumer was going to be put in control.

"Like the consumer knows anything!" Plastic and a few like-minded visionaries had complained at the time. "Remind me because I forget, did the consumer write *Oliver Twist?* Or Beethoven's Fifth? No, I don't think so. As I recall it was *artists* who did those things, people with special talents. And what did the consumer do? The consumer *consumed* it, didn't he? Sucked it right up and went away with his life enriched."

But for a while the revolution was unstoppable. It was presumed that since the technology existed by which an audience could be presented with an infinite number of possible solutions to a drama, then that must be what they would want. Likewise, since it was now possible for viewers to don helmets and suits that would enable them to enter the action along with their favorite heroes, then it was presumed that the public would jump at the chance.

Plastic still felt bitterly about the way art had been hijacked by technology. He ranted at Nathan as if it had been Nathan who was responsible for the development of interactive entertainment.

"The public *always* had the technology to get involved with the action if it wanted to. Right back to the Greeks. All they had to do was get up on stage and join in. But they didn't do it, did they? Weird, huh? Maybe, just maybe, they kind of guessed that it would completely screw up the show. The public could *always* choose their own endings when they read books. All they had to do was get a damn pen and write in that Scrooge never got nice and Moby Dick was a chipmunk. But they didn't, and why? Because the public doesn't pay for entertainment in order to have to provide it themselves. The whole damn nightmare was a conspiracy by scientists and computer brains to make everyone in the world as boring as them."

But now the tide was turning. The public was returning

to more traditional forms of entertainment; movies, in particular, and it seemed that Nathan was being commissioned to write one. What's more, Max Maximus, who was just driving up to the house with Rosalie fidgeting nervously at his side, was going to star in it.

Stormy meeting.

"Here's what I want," said Plastic. "I was a straight megabuck advertainment to sell new-generation Claustrospheres. It's got to be the biggest hit of the year. I want everybody to go and see it, and I want it to star Max Maximus, okay?"

The BioLock entry screen leapt into life. An electronic voice announced that Max and a friend were outside. Max and Rosalie appeared on the screen.

"Come on up, Max. We're in the Claustrosphere," Plastic said. The screen went dark, and he turned to Nathan. "Can you believe this guy, brings a chick to a meeting? I've got a good mind not to put him in the picture. Chicks always distract things. Am I right?"

Plastic was about to find out how right he was.

Max and Rosalie emerged through the BioLock.

"Hi, Plastic. Great Sphere, cool," said Max, like an overeager schoolboy visiting a much-respected master at his home. "Wow, you have a minimountain," he said, referring to a hundred-yard-high rock structure complete with snow on its upper reaches. "I've been thinking of putting one of those into mine, but I'd have to extend. I don't have the height for a split-level climate."

If Rosalie had been having trouble making her decision, that was behind her now. The sheer obscenity of what she was looking at confirmed her resolve. She did not consider herself Plastic's judge and jury. That task lay with all the dead animals and sick, dying people she had encountered in her years of struggle. The devastated area where peasant populations skulked in the shade, nursing their tumors, waiting for night to fall so they could harvest their mutated crops. *They* had tried and convicted Plastic Tolstoy. It was merely Rosalie's job to carry out the sentence. Of course, she knew it wasn't all his fault, but there he was, inside a private paradise that he had built for himself in a doomed world, and Rosalie was in no mood to make excuses for him.

"So, who's your little pal?" Plastic said, turning to Rosalie only to find himself staring down the barrel of a gun.

"Plastic Tolstoy!" Rosalie announced, her hand trembling on the trigger. "I am a Mother Earth activist. Dedicated to the principle that the ultimate human responsibility is to the planet that supports us. The idea that we can exist separate from the planet is treason. You are the principal perpetrator of this fiction, and therefore, on behalf of the planet Earth and all the people, animals, and plants that live on it, I am now going to execute you. . . ."

Rosalie had never been so lucid in her life. Conviction lent her eloquence. Plastic Tolstoy was dead. She knew it, and he knew it. Rosalie's finger tightened on the trigger.

It was pure ambition and naked careerism that saved Plastic.

For a moment, both Max and Nathan had simply watched in horror while Rosalie announced her sentence of execution. Then, separately and simultaneously, it dawned on them that this mad bitch was about to murder the biggest break either of them had ever had. For Nathan in particular it would be an unbearable fate . . . to be commissioned to write a screenplay by the top producer in the world, only to have that producer murdered, minutes later. People spent their whole lives looking for a break like this. Nathan couldn't let it go now. The planet was all very well, but this was a *movie,* for God's sake!

Max was in a similar position. He needed Tolstoy badly. Yes, he already had a huge career, but as his agent, Geraldine, never tired of pointing out, it was trend-based. He was the current big thing, a teen idol. He had to move on from that; he had to mature and become a genuine star. A Tolstoy project was his chance at real longevity.

For both Nathan and Max, saving Plastic Tolstoy was a career move, pure and simple. Hence, just as Rosalie's finger began to tighten on the trigger, the two of them launched themselves at her, and as the gun fired, all three collapsed together on to the ground. As she fired, the gun flew out of Rosalie's hand. The bullet went wild, missed Plastic, bounced off the geodesic wall and rebounded, killing a rare breed of domestic pig that was feeding on supagrass concentrate by the pond. The noise of the shot rang around the dome, causing a cloud of airborne wildlife to rise in fear above the canopy of the rain forest and an androgynous self-breeding bull/cow to emerge from its stable and tread on all the chickens.

Around the world in eight minutes.

Rosalie was up in a moment, but Plastic, who had had to defend himself before, already had the gun.

"Okay, stay where you are, young lady," he said as two armed servants appeared at the mouth of the BioLock.

But Rosalie had no intention of staying where she was. Instead, she dived into the dense vegetation of the rain forest. In a moment she had disappeared within its generous foliage. The two muscular servants plunged in after her, trampling down millions of dollars worth of Tuf-Plant. Tuf-Plant was greenery genetically engineered to withstand pretty much anything, although not, as it happened, a couple of two-hundred-pound armed thugs jumping all over it.

"Watch out for the fucking rain forest!" Plastic shouted. "And don't kill her. Dead babes look bad!"

Rosalie plunged on through the jungle that covered about a third of the whole Claustrosphere. Plastic tried to

116

run around it to cut her off on the other side, but was prevented from doing so by the babbling stream.

"Nathan," Plastic yelled over his shoulder. "You're a writer, make a note. I have to have a bridge built."

Rosalie emerged from under the dark canopy of the rain forest and jumped into a small field containing various giant Hi-Yield cereal crops. Pushing through that, she leapt over a small mangrove swamp and started to skirt around the rocky outcrops at the bottom of the mountain.

"Where is she?" shouted Plastic, as the two servants thrashed their way out of the forest.

"I think she headed for the hills," one of them replied.

Rosalie continued skirting the mountain, the foothills of which lay at the very edge of the Claustrosphere, right up against the walls of the geodesic dome. As she crouched behind a large rock, she could hear her pursuers circumnavigating the foot of the mountain from both sides. Her only option was to head upward. As she broke cover to scramble up the scree that lay all about on the lower slopes, one of the servants spotted her. He fired a couple of warning shots, hitting a small herd of geep.

"Mind my geep! You asshole!" Plastic shouted.

Geep were one of the most successful products of a genetic engineering revolution that had been going on in deadly secrecy for years. The original genetic project had been started by a group of very rich men who had been hoping to breed a camel that would fit through the eye of a needle. They spent years on it, until one day it occurred to them that it would be easier and cheaper simply to build an enormous needle. They got out of genetics immediately, selling their research to the Claustrosphere company.

Geep were a cross between a sheep and a goat. They were incredibly hardy, living for over a hundred years, and all the while provided wool, milk, and, quite astonishingly, meat. So resilient were these creatures that you could cut glamb chops out of the hindquarters for supper, and the animal would have healed up by the next morning.

This Kwik-Heal flesh was developed out of DNA isolated from those insects that grow another leg if you pull one off. Therefore Plastic Tolstoy need not have worried about his geep. The bullets scarcely made them flinch. They had resulted from such brutal grafting and cloning experiments that being shot at was just like the old days in the lab to them.

Rosalie reached the snow line and looked back. Seventy-five yards below, in near tropical conditions, she could see one of her pursuers beginning to climb up after her, while Plastic and the other guard doubled back around the base of the mountain, clearly planning to cut off her descent. She had no choice but to press on. She breasted the summit and began to run back down the opposite slope, hoping to arrive at the bottom before Plastic came around through the foot-hills. It was a tough descent, with alpine conditions for the first twenty feet. Almost inevitably, she slipped on a glacier and fell into a minigully. Fortunately, nothing was broken, but she was pretty winded, and it slowed her down. So much so that by the time she had completed her descent, the first of her muscular pursuers was emerging around the mountain with Plastic Tolstoy puffing behind.

"Okay," said the pursuer, by way of a warning, "I don't want to hurt you."

"Whereas I do want to hurt you," replied Rosalie.

She had taken the precaution of picking up a fist-sized boulder on the lower slopes of the scree, and she smashed this into the face of her assailant, causing him to offer no further opinions. Plastic arrived next, just in time for Rosalie to deal him a mighty kick in the balls before running for the BioLock.

Career decision.

Unfortunately for Rosalie, by now the second of the muscular types had descended the mountain. He charged after her, covering the entire desert in four strides before bringing her down with a flying tackle. The man was an aikido master, and despite Rosalie's formidable fighting skills, he was easily able to fix her in a body lock. Crushed as she was by a large martial arts expert, Rosalie knew that the game was up.

Max had to make a career decision. This woman had just tried to murder the most powerful producer in the world, a producer for whom Max very much wanted to work. On the other hand, this same woman was very attractive indeed, and her announcement of execution had contained some extremely valid points. What to do? Max usually left difficult decisions to his agent, but he knew that she would have been in no doubt. There was no point even calling her to ask. Max knew what her answer would be. "Stand back and let the girl be taken," Geraldine would have said, "and just pray Tolstoy forgets you were the one who brought her here."

Yes, that is certainly what Geraldine would have said. Then, again, Geraldine was not in full possession of the facts. For one thing, she did not fancy the girl. In fact, to the best of Max's knowledge, Geraldine had not even met her, and if she had Max doubted that she would have found something wild and compelling about the girl's behavior. Max certainly did. Everything about Rosalie spoke to Max's very soul. She seemed to throw his own pointless and dissolute existence into shameful contrast. Max was by nature both romantic and a bit mad. It was these two factors that led him to decide to lay professional considerations aside and be romantic and a bit mad now. Except that he did not really decide; he just did it, because, as has already been pointed out, he was a bit mad. Running over, he took a huge kick at the aikido master's head. Rosalie rolled her unconscious man off her and leapt to her feet.

"Here," said Max and threw her his car keys.

"Thanks," said Rosalie.

Max would love to have believed that there was a poignant glance, a meeting of eyes, an unmistakable moment of understanding, and perhaps even affection, between them. But there wasn't. She just grabbed the keys and took off.

"See you sometime," he murmured as Rosalie flipped the switch on the BioLock and disappeared into the tube that led to the carport.

Max turned to face Plastic, who was staggering to his feet in some considerable pain. Plastic had, of course, witnessed Max's craven disloyalty. What is more, that disloyalty was not over yet. As the BioLock closed behind Rosalie, Max marched over to Plastic.

"I don't want you to call your security people, Plastic. I want you to let the girl go."

Max gulped, Nathan gulped, even Tolstoy gurgled slightly. None of them could quite believe that Max was aiding and abetting the escape of someone who had just kicked the most powerful person in Hollywood in the balls. Everyone knew that Max was a bit mad, but this was insane.

"You want me to let her go?" Plastic inquired.

"Yes," said Max.

Plastic could see that Max was clearly determined. He also knew that Max was young, fit, and very strong. He shrugged.

"Looks like she's going to get away then."

There was a pause in which nobody made a sound except the numerous mutant animals that were still voicing their protest at the sudden disturbance.

"Um . . . listen, Plastic, . . . Mr. Tolstoy," Max mumbled, reason returning to its throne, "I hope this incident won't affect our working relationship."

"You hope it won't affect our working relationship?"

"Yes."

"You take sides with a woman who tries to execute me, and you hope it won't affect our working relationship?"

"If that's okay by you."

"All right then," said Plastic, ever the pragmatist. "I don't know what we would have done with her if we'd caught her anyway. The last thing I need is to be seen dragging some cute little greenie through the courts. You can bet your bottom dollar she'd get all the sympathy. Just as a matter of interest, though, may I inquire why you brought this homicidal lunatic along to a creative meeting?"

"I just met her at DigiMac. . . . I thought you might be interested. I didn't know she was going to try and execute you."

"Thank you. That's nice to know. Are you porking her?"

"Well, I . . ."

"Good, because it's a connection we can use. Nathan here is going to write me a movie for you to star in. A movie about the battle between Mother Earth and Claustrosphere. He's going to write about how those decent but misguided souls in the Green Movement learn that, far from threatening the survival of the human race, Claustrosphere is in fact ensuring it. Isn't that right, Nathan?"

"That's exactly the type of plot I had in mind," Nathan said hastily.

"Good."

Broadening the campaign.

After Max and Nathan had left, Plastic returned to his communications room in the house. A marketing strategy has to be many-leveled. You can't just make a decent ad. A well-designed package alone is not enough. A marketing strategy has to set the agenda for consumption. A perfect marketing strategy not only provides the product, it also identifies and promotes the need. All his life Plastic Tolstoy had known that the easiest market to exploit is the one that you create yourself.

12

The paranoid conspiracy theorist

Trapped nerd.

JUDY WAS CORNERED, AND HE KNEW IT. THERE WERE TWO OF THEM outside the cubicle. What's more, they were armed, and Judy was not. Normally, in these circumstances, when an agent is trapped in a toilet cubicle, there is a convenient back window through which to make an escape. This time, however, there was no window and probably a good thing too, considering that the lavatory was on the 190th floor.

"Come on out, man." The tone was violent, with the hint of a sneer. "Unless you want them to find you with your pants down."

It was a point, thought the terrified Judy. If one has to fight, best not to have to do it with your trousers around your ankles. He pulled them up and readied himself for the inevitable. Outside they were laughing; they had their man, and they knew it. Judy desperately tried to recall his training. It was a while since he had found himself in a combat situation and in truth, he had never been very good at it anyway.

"Make a plan," he said to himself. That was what he had been taught. If your opponent is confident, then he is at his most vulnerable. The idea being that an assailant who thinks he has the attack in the bag will move sloppily, he will make mistakes. This is the point where clear thinking and properly planned actions can turn the tables.

Okay, thought Judy, there are two men outside the door, which is my only exit. They are bigger and tougher than I am; they are also armed. Clearly they are going to be feeling confident. Hence, according to combat training, they are at their most vulnerable.

Judy's plan was simple. He knew from the voices that one of his assailants was standing directly outside the cubicle door and that the other was slightly off to one side. What Judy would do was kick the door open with all his might, slamming it into the face of the first of his enemies. He must then follow through instantly. He must be out of the cubicle before the first man's nose had even started to bleed. Having emerged from the cubicle, he must immediately stick his fingers in the eyes of the second man, the one who was off to the side. He would have to move fast enough to give the second man no time to raise his guard. Then, with both assailants briefly disabled, he would run out of the men's room. He would not pause, he would make no witty cracks, he would simply run, for his foes would surely not take long to revive. So that then was the plan. One: kick the door open. Two: emerge and stab eyes with fingers. Three: run away. In this manner, Judy, a weedy man of five-foot-five with one leg slightly longer than the other, would get the better of two enormous, armed thugs.

Very gently he edged open the lock of the door, a necessary prerequisite for kicking it open. It was a tense moment. If they heard the bolt slip, he was dead. They didn't, and Judy had the door unlocked. Holding on to the toilet paper dispenser, he drew his foot back against the toilet bowl, getting ready for the mighty kick.

"Are you still out there?" he inquired, attempting a casual tone.

"That's right, and now we're coming in to get you," the thug replied, thus establishing to Judy's satisfaction that the first assailant was still in the same position.

"Good," said Judy, and with all the force that fear and loathing could summon up in his small body, he drove his boot against the cubicle door.

Sadly, the door was an inward opener. The whole cubicle shook with the impact, and pain shot up all the way from the tip of Judy's toes to deep within his testicles. From there, the pain proceeded upward through his agonized body, finally coming to rest at the back of his head and making his eyeballs rattle. Judy sank back onto the toilet seat as the two thugs burst in and started to beat him with rolled-up magazines.

"Please, please, guys!" Judy screamed as the blows fell about his head and shoulders.

"Repeat after me," said Cruise, beating Judy all the while, "I am a stupid little queer and a disgrace to the Bureau."

Agent Cruise had been nursing a deep resentment for Judy ever since Rosalie had cut his arm open in the desert. The humiliation of being cut up by some freaky little green chick had weighed heavily on him in the weeks since his return, and he had come, irrationally, to blame Judy for the failure of his mission. Somehow he felt there must have been something in the environmental briefing he had been given that had been inadequate. Cruise concluded that Schwartz had set him up. Therefore when Judy returned from his adventure on the stricken oil tanker, he found Cruise waiting for him and looking for trouble.

"I am a stupid little queer and a disgrace to the Bureau," Judy shouted.

"And don't you forget it," said Cruise, administering a final swipe with the magazine.

"Hey," said Cruise's companion. "It's nearly noon, we'd better get into the meeting, you know what Klaw's like if you're late."

The man was referring to the monthly meeting of the FBI's Environmental Department, which all three of them had been on their way to when the ambush had occurred.

"Okay," said Cruise. "Looks like you're off the hook for now, Schwartz, but you'll be back next month, and I'm going to get you all over again."

But by now Judy had had a moment's breathing space to size up his opponent and prepare a counterattack.

"No, you aren't," Judy replied, "because in the meantime I'm going to devote my life to hacking my way into your file and compiling a comprehensive list of every single bar tab, taxi ride, and hotel room you have ever claimed on expenses. Then if you hit me with a rolled-up magazine again, I will send that list to one of the numerous congressmen who got elected by promising to cut waste in government, so they can use your name in their personal crusade to haul in big-spending federal agencies like the FBI."

It was a complicated plan, but Cruise for one could see how effective it might be.

"Yes, well . . . ," he said after a moment's thought. "Just watch it, that's all," he added rather weakly, and with that they all went into the meeting.

Dark suspicions.

The departmental meeting was not going very much better for Judy than the meeting in the men's room.

"You're saying you don't think the captain of the stricken tanker killed himself." The voice of Judy's boss, Bill Klaw, was heavy with sarcasm.

"That is correct, sir," said Judy, trying to sound firm.

"You find the guy, a known drunk, I might add, dead in his sinking ship, a bottle in one hand, a smoking gun in the other, his brains in the trash basket, and you don't think he killed himself?"

"I've looked into his background, sir. I've found nothing that suggests a suicidal personality."

"Oh, I see. In that case, of course, there's *no way* he could have killed himself," Klaw said, showing his exasperation to the whole room, in which thirty or so equally exasperated field officers were assembled. It was nearly lunchtime, and nobody was interested in Schwartz's paranoid investigations. "Brilliant deduction work, Schwartz." Klaw continued in this withering vein. "The captain never tried to kill himself *before,* so why should he now? Did you by any chance discover whether the guy had ever *lost a billion-dollar tanker and destroyed three hundred miles of coastline* before!! And if not, did it not occur to you that this might have been a factor in dampening his normally sunny disposition!"

"I don't think he killed himself, sir. I believe his ship was sabotaged and that the captain was murdered to prevent the discovery of that sabotage. I inspected the hold of the tanker, sir, accompanied by the ship's number two, a woman named Jackson. I have her testimony here. . . ." Judy could see that Klaw was losing patience. He pressed on quickly. "The condition of the rupture in the walls of the ship were not conducive to the reasons given by the coast guard for the wreck, sir. I noted that the lip of the tears were predominately curling outward, sir, which, you will agree, is very strange. A ship holed externally by treacherous rocks would have shown damage caving inward, which it did to a certain extent, but not entirely. Some of the damage distinctly suggested pressure from within. The kind of pressure that could only have been caused by an internal explosion."

"What is this, Schwartz? The coast guard is satisfied that

the ship got caught in a rocky channel. Are you moon-lighting for the insurance company or something?"

"Insurance is not an issue, sir. There is no claim because the captain is presumed to have been drunk."

"In that case, there's no possible motive for anybody wanting to sink the damn thing now. . . ."

"What about the close proximity of the Natura ship, sir?"

"What about it? They're always there, aren't they? The little cockroaches."

"Exactly, sir. In every case we've heard today, the Natura people were on the spot before even the emergency services. I've been studying the files, sir. It's happened numerous times; nuclear meltdowns, toxic leaks, dodo syndromes, conveniently placed disasters occurring where no one could have predicted them, and with no one left to say what happened—"

"Schwartz, that's what happens with disasters, they pop up, and they kill the people who are around."

"And every time, Natura is there to extract the maximum propa—"

"Are you saying these people are being tipped off? That these well-meaning and highly respected greenies are somehow being *used* by nastier, more sinister, less principled people?"

"I think it's possible, sir."

"Who?"

"Mother Earth, sir," said Judy firmly. "They were definitely present on the Natura ship that approached the stricken tanker. I know, I encountered an activist on board. We've heard today from other agents who have detected a covert presence at similar disaster scenes. Agent Thompson," Judy addressed a colleague sitting behind him, "is it not true that Mother Earth people were present at the scene of the most recent Five Mile Island meltdown?"

"Of course they were, it's in my report," said Thompson

testily. "It was they who first alerted us to the leakage. They discovered it."

"Oh, they 'discovered' it, did they? Isn't that rather convenient?" said Judy. "Sir, I believe we may be facing the nastiest piece of black propaganda in history."

"Okay, that's lunch," said Klaw, closing his file.

As people began to leave the room, Judy approached his boss.

"Something strange is happening, I swear it. If I could just infiltrate them, get inside the organization. Please. I've made numerous requests."

"I know that, Schwartz, it's me that keeps knocking them down. . . . Listen, Judy," said Klaw, for a moment trying to be nice. "You're keen, I like that, but you're not a cool, glamorous spy, and you never will be. You're a shitty little assessment officer whose job is to compile shitty little assessments. That's it, no more. Now in words of one syllable, get the fuck out of my face."

Despite his best intentions, Klaw just simply was not very good at being nice.

LFS.

The next day, Judy's luck changed. He was summoned to Klaw's office and shown a series of photos of the recent Mother Earth raid on the roof of the DigiMac Studio.

"Yes, I read about that," Judy admitted. "Pretty audacious stuff, eh? The leader escaped via a birthday cake, didn't she?"

"Yes, she did," Klaw replied. "And we're getting a lot of heat to make an arrest. The studio wants blood. It's getting sued by just about everybody who was at the damn restaurant. There's a full LFS developing."

"That bad, huh?" Judy was impressed.

LFS, or Litigation Frenzy Syndrome, could leave families and communities divided, it could destroy vast corporations, it could leave grand and respected institutions broken in the dust. Studies had suggested that, left unchecked, LFS could eventually develop into civil war. LFS was, however, always checked eventually, due to the first law of legal dynamics. The first law of legal dynamics states that litigation will expand to absorb the amount of money available; a corollary of this law clearly being that all litigation will cease when the money runs out.

The LFS that was consuming the DigiMac Studio, and hence causing so much concern to Klaw, was a textbook example. A potentially dangerous situation of some kind had occurred, in this case, exposure to sunlight. Medically a very simple problem, legally a potential minefield. The moment the first rays of light had fallen on the beautiful people in the DigiMac commissary, the anguished cry had gone up, "For God's sake, somebody phone a lawyer."

Within minutes, the streets approaching the studio had been jammed with Rapid Response Litigation Teams. Over the years this type of development had become a major headache for the emergency services. It was not uncommon in the aftermath of an accident for the fire and ambulance people to find themselves unable to get to the scene because the roads were blocked with lawyers. As it happened, the DigiMac disaster required no medical assistance because the UV exposure had been so brief. This was great news for the law firms, it being recognized that the absence of specific injury was a classic catalyst in the development of LFS. With no actual physical problem to get in the way of vague speculation, the leap to the fantastical was much more easily made.

The first claims were obvious. Compensation would be required for the emotional stress caused by the *potential* damage via exposure to sunlight. The studio instantly recognized the danger it was in and mobilized its own damage control teams to counterclaim, their assertion being that their reputation as a responsible and caring employer was being irrevocably damaged by such wild accusations.

Also, that the mere fact of being beautiful and famous meant that the litigants had set themselves up as terrorist targets, so in real terms, the attack had been their fault, and they should pay for the roof.

All this had happened within minutes of the attack. A legal meltdown was occurring even before Rosalie had escaped from the building. Faced with the studio's counterattack, the original litigants hit back furiously. The second phase began, as claims were made on behalf of the children of the litigants. Children whose home life would be rendered dysfunctional by the suffering caused through fear of their parents' getting cancer. The logical consequence of this, of course, was phase three: representations made on behalf of the as yet unborn and indeed unconceived offspring of the litigants, notional children whose future existence would be adversely affected by the case, should they ever materialize.

It was the acceptance in the courts of the principle of cross-generational suffering that made LFS such a terrifying phenomenon, because once it was accepted that a hypothetical future child could be affected, then clearly so could future grandchildren and indeed great-grandchildren. Presuming a reproductive rate of two children per adult, a lawyer who extrapolated a mere ten generations into the future could find him or herself representing over a thousand hypothetically injured hypothetical parties, all of whose costs would be awarded against the plaintiff should their case prevail. This was, of course, presuming that the original litigant had only one family, something extremely rare in Hollywood. Then, inevitably, there were all the claims from friends and relatives (plus *their* future offspring) whose lives had also been adversely affected due to stress caused by knowing somebody who might have been exposed to dangerous sunlight.

All in all, it was a classic case of Litigation Frenzy, which, within a year or two, would certainly destroy a mighty studio unless it could be contained. Obviously the money would run out in the end, and the first law of legal dynamics would apply, but that was scarcely a contingency to be desired. This was why an arrest was required. If a conviction could be secured against a person or group directly responsible for the outrage, then all other actions would go on hold for fear of prejudicing the case. The trial, with all its appeals and counterappeals, would hopefully carry on long enough to dampen the worst excesses of LFS, possibly extinguishing them altogether.

Target.

"So we need to make an arrest," said Klaw.

"How can we arrest anyone? They got away. I mean, we're the FBI. Investigation's not really our strong point, is it?"

"Don't get smart with me, Schwartz. We know who one of them is." Judy was shown a series of photos of a woman falling through a BioDome roof into a cake and then running into the ladies' lavatory.

"We took these stills from the security videotape."

"She's a bit blurred," said Judy, stating the obvious.

"I know that, jerk, but not when she comes out of the john." He held out another series of pictures of a small, pale woman in a saucy little dress rushing out of the ladies.

"That's her, she took the dress off a bimbo in the bathroom."

"Very clever."

"Sloppy security work. In these situations the only way to avoid suspects escaping is to shoot everybody. I tell these people till I'm blue in the puss, but do they listen? Like hell they do."

Judy studied the photos.

"She's a unit leader," Klaw continued. "Agent Cruise was on to her, but his cover was blown."

"Yes, I heard about that," confessed Judy. "You know, I think he kind of blamed me."

"Of course he blamed you, you were the briefing officer."

"Yes, and I also sabotaged his parents' gene pool, so that they'd give birth to a complete dickhead."

"Shut up, Schwartz, and stick to the point. The girl's Irish. She works out of the Dublin Natura office. We've had her marked for a year or so, always hoped if we tailed her we might get something on Jurgen Thor. But now we've got to bust her. DigiMac and the city want an arrest, so the chick gets thrown to the scheisters."

"You do know that we're not allowed to bust people in Ireland, don't you, sir?" Judy had often noticed a tendency in certain Federal agencies to presume that since America was the world's policeman, then the planet was their precinct and U.S. law applied.

"Yes, I know that we can't bust people in Ireland, you little fuck!" Klaw replied. "But we have an extradition treaty with Europe on terrorism. The Garda will arrest her and hand her over to you for escort back to the U.S."

"Why me?" asked Judy.

"Because she's a cute little girl, concerned for the planet, and we are the FBI, which is slang for Satan to the liberal press. If she gets off a plane in cuffs with some big, hairy thug bearing down on her, *we* look like the bullies even though *she's* the terrorist. I was going to send a woman, but then I thought, no, Judy's the one. Christ, you're such a nerdy little shit, people will feel sorry for you."

"Thank you, sir. That's a lovely thing to say."

Judy decided on this occasion to let what was clearly a palpable bit of nerdism go unchallenged. For he could see that, if he played his cards right, he would get what he wanted: a chance to infiltrate Mother Earth.

13

Astonishing vegetables and other surprising developments

City of the night.

DUBLIN WAS A NIGHTTIME CITY. NOT IN THE TRADITIONAL, PARI-
sian sense of an exotic world that occupies the town after
dark, but in a literal sense. Dublin had become a nighttime
city. Most cities had. It was all a question of money. If a
municipality could afford orbital filters like Beverly Hills,
or if they had the money to enclose their pavements in
BioTubes, then some semblance of traditional daytime activity could be maintained. But Dublin had never been
rich, and so most activities now took place at night. It had
begun gradually. For years people had simply put up with
the inconvenience of ozone depletion. As the sun's rays
became ever more deadly, they had dodged from doorway
to doorway and borrowed each other's BioBrellas, perhaps
having their pores blocked as a special treat at Christmas.

Slowly, however, all over the world, it began to dawn on people that there were a good eight to ten hours in every day when the sun wasn't around at all. When it was possible to walk down a street or kick a fluorescent ball around a park without fear (from the sun, that is—you still had to breathe, of course). At first, in many western cities there was a strong objection to switching to nighttime. It was thought of as something that only mutated peasants did in faraway places.

"We'd look like a piss-poor little fourth-world country," people said to each other, flattering themselves that they did not look that way already.

However, good sense eventually prevailed, and stores and offices began to open after sunset. The whole structure of the day changed. Twilight became morning, and people started to go to work at around six in the afternoon. Their evening's leisure time began at about four A.M. and the bars closed sometime toward noon.

Of course, the European Federation had been promising to locate orbital shields for years, but they never did. Not over the cities, anyway. As always in Europe, agriculture came first. Hundreds of billions of European Currency Units had been spent sunscreening large patches of the countryside. This was so that quaint old ladies dressed in black could continue to bend their backs in tiny, chemically saturated fields while their husbands pissed it up in the local bar. In this manner, traditional country life was maintained. Also, vast quantities of semipoisonous crops were produced that were then piled up into enormous food mountains, whose only use was that they provided some shade.

"What about us?" the city dwellers' representatives would occasionally ask. They would have liked to have asked more frequently, but they could not normally get past the near-constant demonstrations organized by the farmers. It was an accepted feature of European government that it existed under a state of siege, and that mad farmers in huge combine harvesters would spend their lives blockading the various buildings designated for democratic debate and terrorist attack.

The representatives of the Euro city dwellers knew that their requests for BioShields were useless. Euro administration was entirely crisis-led. Every time the coffers in Brussels were deemed to be sufficiently full to start thinking about sunscreening cities, another civil war would break out. These wars smoldered endlessly across the vast continent from Lisbon to the Urals and could break out at any time, meaning, of course, that all the cash had to be spent sending soldiers to observe the genocide and say very firmly how horrid it was.

The European Federation's budget priorities were quite clear and had been for over half a century: first, the bureaucratic apparatus itself; second, the agricultural subsidy; third, observing genocide whenever it occurred and making a point of saying what a bad thing it was; fourth, everything else. Sadly, there was very rarely any money left for fourth, so any city that wanted an ecodefense was forced to pay for it from its own local taxes.

Hence, some of the countryside was on daytime, but not all, and some of the cities were on nighttime, but again not all of them. The situation was much the same in America and Southeast Asia. It was of course far more confused in Russia, where the whole thing changed on a twenty-four-hour basis and, indeed, from street to street. It was quite possible for a Russian to get out of bed, ready for a full eight hours' work, walk five minutes up the road, and arrive in time to clock out at the end of the working day. By this means it was possible for people to rack up vast amounts of overtime and still spend upward of twenty-three hours out of twenty-four in bed.

An actor does his research.

Max and Nathan were sitting in the bar of the Dublin Shelbourne Hotel at about three-thirty in the morning, watching the office workers drift in for an after-work refresher. They were waiting for their drinks. It had already been half an hour, but that is nothing at all if you have ordered Guinness. It is an article of faith for bartenders in Dublin that a pint is not worth drinking unless it has taken about an hour to pour and another hour to settle. Those with any experience in these things call the pub and put in an order before leaving home, but Max and Nathan hadn't worked that out yet.

They had been in Dublin for three days, searching for Rosalie, and had so far drawn a blank. The reason for trying to locate Rosalie, apart from the fact that Max had developed a crush on her, was in order to use her to research the movie that Plastic Tolstoy had commissioned. They wanted to get inside a Mother Earth unit. Actually, it was Max who wanted to get inside a Mother Earth unit. He was thrilled with excitement at the idea. Nathan would quite happily have made the whole thing up. He was not big on research.

"Shakespeare had no experience of the Roman Empire, but he still wrote *Julius Caesar,*" he was fond of saying. In Nathan's opinion, if you took the experience and reality theory to its proper conclusion, he could only ever write about emotionally shattered middle-class Englishmen who had screwed up their lives and lost the only person they had ever loved.

"Exactly," said Max. "And that's just about all most English writers do ever write about. I admire that, it has integrity . . . it's dull, but it has integrity."

Max believed that artists had to inhabit the thing that they wished to portray.

"You have to live the experience. *Be* the experience. If you're lying to yourself, then you'll be lying to the audience, and believe me, they'll know."

"Oh, for God's sake, Max," said Nathan. "The last thing I wrote, a bloke cut off his own leg because a rat was eating it."

"Then you should have cut your leg off," said Max piously. "My last role was about this guy who is indulgence-obsessed, right? It was a harrowing drama about a man addicted to having a great time. All he does is eat, drink, and screw beautiful women. The guy's a hollow shell, right? His existence is empty and pointless. Do you think that scared me off? Do you think I shirked confronting the debilitating properties of excess? No way, man. I did my research! I went out and ate and drank and screwed around like some jerk trying to party himself to death. That's the point, man. I have commitment. Without commitment you're Jack Shit."

"Okay, so what about *Yellow Ribbon,* when you played that POW who got tortured and put in solitary for twenty years?"

"I researched that."

"You did?" Max was surprised.

"Sure. The thing I figured was that the horror of the guy's situation had to lie in his *back history,* right? Back history is the whole thing for an actor. I thought, the guy gets tortured, right? So what? A lot of guys get tortured. How can I make this torture different? How can I make it *special?* Then it hits me. I think, if this man has lived a life of unadulterated luxury, that would make his suffering more acute and more ironic. You see what I'm saying. To give the characterization depth, in my own mind I needed to juxtapose his present torture and loneliness with a previous life of—"

"Eating, drinking, and screwing beautiful women?" Nathan inquired.

"Exactly. I felt if I could get that side of things right, the suffering would develop naturally from there."

Picked up by the greenies.

A sweet-looking little old lady approached Max and Nathan at their table.

"Mr. Maximus?" the sweet old lady inquired.

"Sure, it would be a pleasure," said Max, producing a pen and paper. "Whom shall I dedicate it to?"

Although Max was disguised, he was still being recognized and always gave autographs when asked. This was partly because he was a nice person who did not like to disappoint people and partly because he was normally followed around by ten or fifteen journalists, waiting for him to refuse to sign an autograph, so that they could write stories about how rude and arrogant he was and how he had forgotten the people who made him what he was. On this occasion, however, Max need not have worried.

"I don't want a fucking autograph," the sweet-looking little old lady said. "You've been making inquiries at the Natura shop about a friend of mine. Follow me."

They walked outside into the darkened, bustling street. In the park opposite the hotel, some kids were playing a game of fluoro-soccer. The bright, glowing shoulder sashes danced about in pursuit of the moonlike ball. Max and Nathan stood on the pavement while the sweet old lady made a signal. Up the street a large car pulled into the traffic and across toward the hotel entrance. It was a big new Japanese limo, a real ecocar, greener than green, as befitted a Natura vehicle. So copious were its filters that it emitted not one single poisonous gas of any sort. You could have put a flatulent elephant on the backseat, and nobody would have been any the wiser.

Not for the first time, Nathan wondered where the hell these people got their funding. Natura always had the best transport. Mother Earth always had the best assault choppers. While the IRA and the Basque separatists were making bombs out of fertilizer in their garages, Mother Earth bought the best, direct from British and German businessmen, paying top dollar.

"Nice car," Nathan observed. "How many tin rattling volunteers does it take to buy one of those?"

"Get in," said the woman, as the hotel doorman opened the back door for them.

They got in the car, Nathan experiencing his never-ending hotel dilemma of whether to tip the doorman or not. Max, of course, had no such problem. He was so rich and famous it would not have occurred to him to do something so mundane as tip a person. Max had people to do that for him. In fact, he was so big and special that even his people were too important to tip, they too had people to do things like that. It is a strange fact of power, fame, riches, and general celebrity that the more you have, the more you get. Real celebrities never pay for a ticket to a show. They endlessly eat for free, it being generally assumed that, by simply gracing an event with their presence, the mega-celeb is making contribution enough. It is, in fact, possible to be so rich that you have no need for money at all.

Nathan tipped the doorman the price of a pint for five seconds' labor that he would have preferred to have done himself, and they got in the car. Once inside, Nathan noticed that the rear windows were all blacked out. Max did not notice because, despite its being nighttime, he was wearing shades. The sweet-looking, foul-mouthed old lady did not join them, and they were left alone as the big limo pulled away. They could not see the driver because there was a screen between the front and the back of the car. Max lifted the screen. There were two men in the front.

"Hey, guys," he said. "Where are we going?"

The front passenger pointed an automatic handgun in Max's face.

"Put the blind back down. If you lift it up again, even once, I'll kill you."

Max put the blind down and looked at Nathan. Nathan was white with fear and shock. Max pulled the blind back up again. He and the gunman stared at each other for a few very tense moments as Nathan struggled to maintain control of his bowels.

"Ha! I knew you wouldn't do it," Max said and dropped the screen again. "You have to call guys like that," he said to Nathan. "It's a point of principle."

They drove for at least three hours. First along straightish roads, then on what they guessed were winding country lanes, and finally along what were clearly dirt tracks. Nathan passed the time by continuing to dwell on the cruel irony of his longing for Flossie.

"You see, I know now that I've always loved her. How could I not have known it then? I suppose, in a way, I made my biggest mistakes early on in the relationship, when I thought we were still happy. . . ."

Max wondered whether, if he lifted the blind again, he could persuade the gunman to shoot Nathan.

The little stone cottage.

Max and Nathan were led blindfolded into a room filled with a wonderful smell. They heard their captors retreat and the door close behind them. The two men stood for a moment, unseeing and, they thought, alone, breathing in the splendid aroma.

"Cool smell," ventured Max.

"Yes," Nathan replied.

Something about the smell struck a chord in Nathan's memory. It took him far back to his childhood. Back past years and years of tired, joyless, fantastically expensive media lunches in Soho, back to an almost forgotten time when he had still enjoyed food. A time when the only connection between the words *eating* and *meeting* was that they rhymed. A time before irradiation, before menus featured "lite alternatives" and butter carried a government health warning. Yes, that smell took him back. It also plonked him right down in the present. He was hungry, very hungry.

"Stew," he said out loud. "Stew with dumplings."

"That's right, it's nearly ready," they heard a soft, female voice say. It was an oldish voice with a strong Irish accent. "You can take your blindfolds off now, boys."

The two men removed their blindfolds and found themselves in the kitchen of a little stone cottage. An old lady was sitting at a wooden table. A very old lady. Max would have put her at a hundred and fifty plus. Her hair was gray and there was far too much skin on her face, enough skin, in fact, for two faces, Max thought, maybe three. This wasn't age, this was disease. Max felt a little ill just looking at her. What sort of horrible affliction could cause such deformity? Was the woman a leper? Whatever it was, Max sure didn't want to catch it. He moved a step back toward the door.

The woman was peeling a pile of strange brown lumpy things, stranger even than she was. They looked like tumors hacked from the body of a fourth-world nuclear power worker. Beside the tumors, spread out on a bit of newspaper, were some weird, bent, orangy long things with hairs growing out of them and knobbly bits sprouting out at various angles. Neither Nathan nor Max had ever seen anything like these ugly-looking lumps. Instantly, the hunger that they had been feeling so keenly vanished. They did not want tumors with their stew, no matter how nice the smell. Nor hairy lumps. Perhaps it was eating the tumors and lumps that had made the old lady look the way she did.

"Where are we?" Nathan asked, wishing he were somewhere else.

"Well now," the old lady replied, "we're hardly likely to be going to the trouble of bringing you here in darkened cars, blindfolded and all, just to tell you where you are the minute you arrive, are we?"

There was a brief silence, then Max asked the question that was actually foremost in both their minds.

"What the hell is that stuff on the table?"

"Potatoes and carrots," the lady replied.

"No way," said Max. "I've seen potatoes, and I've seen

carrots, and they aren't anything like that stuff. That stuff looks like dogs' balls. In fact, it looks like something you'd cut off a dog's balls."

"I don't wish to hear language like that in this house, young man," the old lady said.

The money.

Max was rather taken aback. He was so rarely ticked off by anyone that he did not know how to react. If you are a star, and you live in L.A., you will literally never be contradicted.

In movie language, a star is known as "the money." This is because it is very difficult to get a project financed without a star attached. In any industry, money is virtually all that matters. Hence in the entertainment industry, stars are virtually all that matter. Their power and influence are awesome and far outstrip any talent or ability they might have. This is not to say that stars have no talent; many are fine actors. It is just that it is not physically possible to be talented enough to justify the kind of money that really big stars earn. God simply does not make human beings that good. This is why stars are not measured by ability, but by what they earn.

"Hey, granted, the guy's screen presence was hewn from a block of solid teak, but have you any idea how much he *earns?*"

The star is not an actor. He or she is the money. Hollywood is an industry town. Everyone has a script to be read or a portfolio to be looked at. You do not get those sorts of breaks by badmouthing the money. Hence, no star is ever contradicted.

Back in the cottage.

The old lady (whose name was Ruth), however, did not have a script she wanted read, or a portfolio to be looked at. It was years since Max had met anyone like that.

"You don't walk into a person's kitchen and start being foul about her veggies," Ruth said. "What on earth would your mother think?"

Max considered a moment.

"My mother wouldn't mind," he said. "She likes foul. In her case, foul is a lifestyle choice. She just did a centerspread in *Penthouse,* split beaver, the lot."

Now it was Ruth's turn to be taken aback. She raised an eyebrow as if to say, "it takes all sorts" and returned to her peeling. The door opened, and an old man entered. He had clearly contracted the same disease as the old lady, for his face too was baggy and creased. If anything, he seemed to have the plague worse than her, for there were great sacks under his eyes, red veins all over his nose, and great tufts of pubic hair coming out of his ears. Max was nearly nauseous.

"This is my husband, Sean," the old lady said, putting the chopped potatoes and carrots into boiling water. "My name's Ruth. We're Rosalie's grandparents. She'll be along in a while. Meanwhile, will you have something to eat? It's nothing much, stew with dumplings, taters, and carrots."

Both men hesitated.

"Those potatoes?" Max inquired.

"These are what spuds actually look like, you know," Ruth said. "The knobbly bits and the eyes, that's a real potato."

"You're kidding me," said Max.

The great visual food joke.

But the old lady was right. Generations ago, before the great visual food joke had been perpetrated upon the public by supermarket owners, potatoes had eyes and carrots had hairs.

Unfortunately, real food is notoriously volatile. Filled as it is with endless bacteria and trace elements, it is delicate

143

to grow and goes rotten easily. This is a problem for accountants trying to use shelf space cost-effectively. What the food suppliers needed was to get the public to accept vegetables and meat that were entirely anesthetized and uniform. Anemic, tasteless crap of a constant shape and size that would be easy to grow and transport and would last a long time. The joke was that it turned out that the public actually preferred their food this way because it looked nice. People were attracted to small, hard, pale red tomatoes and small, hard, pale yellow potatoes; they looked clean and fresh, with no horrid bits to have to cut out.

Only two groups objected: the blind, obviously, and the makers of magazine-style, public-involvement TV programs. The producers' problem was that they had, of course, lost their best visual gag. With uniform-shaped vegetables there were no longer any to be found that were shaped like genitalia. The vegetable nob gag was a hardy annual that had kept generations of television viewers amused. People had vied with each other to send in the crudest-shaped carrots and the most suggestive zucchini. Sadly, the great visual food joke had put an end to the laughter.

Revelation stew.

Max and Nathan could not believe their tastebuds. The meal was a sensation. Never had they imagined such carrotyness or potatoeyness. The lamb in the stew tasted as though a thousand lambs had been blended into a single chop. The onions and herbs created an orgasmic richness that left their tongues lying at the bottom of their mouths, exhausted, satiated, and saying, "That was wonderful, darling."

"We still farm organically here," said Sean. "You can't do it entirely properly—the water table's as poisoned for us as for everybody else—and we have to use artificial sun. But we do all right."

"You do fantastically," said Nathan, mopping up the gravy with bread. For a moment he almost felt happy, then he remembered that Flossie didn't love him anymore and reminded himself that he would never feel happy again.

"And that's not all," said Ruth, having modestly received Max and Nathan's unstinting praise. "Look at this!" and from her apron pocket she produced a carrot that looked exactly like a big dick with two little balls. "I just couldn't bear to cut it up until I'd shown it to Sean," she said, her eyes damp with laughter. "Isn't it a scream?"

They all agreed that it was indeed a scream, and after they had stopped laughing, Max and Nathan had second helpings. When they had all finished eating, Max felt so kindly disposed to the two old people that he decided to bring up the subject of their illness.

"Listen, guys," he said nervously, "I don't know what's wrong with you, but I'm sure I could recommend someone who could help. You know with your . . . faces." Ruth and Sean were clearly not following Max's gist, so he attempted to explain. "You know, all the flaps of skin and the ear hair and . . . well, there are doctors who can— Ouch!"

He said "ouch" because Nathan had kicked him under the table. Nathan understood that there was nothing at all wrong with Ruth and Sean. They were just old. Although, even to Nathan, who lived in a far less cosmetically adjusted world than Max, the old couple did look weird. Just about everybody had *something* done when their faces began to sag. A little tuck, a touch of electrolysis, a hint of color, but these two had absolutely left nature to take its course.

"There's lots like us, you know," said Sean.

Max hoped not.

The meal over, they sat around with a glass of beer and

chatted. They could have talked about anything. Between them they had a world of experience. However, within thirty seconds Nathan had worked the subject around to him and Flossie.

"People say I'm just experiencing classic jealousy, but I don't agree. You see, Ruth, I love her, I truly do, I know that now. . . ."

Fortunately for Nathan, just as Max was about to strangle him, they heard a truck outside. Dawn had not yet broken, but when Ruth crossed nervously to the window, she could make out a familiar shape. Moments later, Rosalie had joined them in the cottage.

"Hello again," said Rosalie to Max as she entered, hanging up her beret and gun.

Max did not know what to say. What he felt like saying was, "Hubba! Hubba! Hubba!" which was the preferred method by which he and his friends at school had informed each other that they had met the girl of their dreams. If Rosalie had spoken to the depths of Max's soul before, now she was shouting through a megaphone. To see her in the wild country (anywhere out of town was wild for Max) with a beret and a machine gun, was to see a vision, a vision of strength and sauciness. Max thought about asking her to marry him, but he recognized that this might be considered a little presumptuous on only their second meeting. Anyway, he had only been divorced a few days, and did not wish to appear flighty. Particularly in front of his future granny-in-law.

"Hi," he said, feeling that he could have done better.

"Well now," said Rosalie. "Who's your friend?"

"His name's Nathan Hoddy."

"I'm a screenwriter," said Nathan, "and I thought I didn't love my wife, but then she left me and it turned out that I did love her after all. Actually, you and I met at Plastic Tolstoy's, when you tried to kill him and had to hide in the rain forest, but you probably don't remember."

146

The long arm of the law.

Outside, the Garda, as the Irish police are known, were surrounding the cottage. They were acting on a request from the FBI, who wanted, as Judy had learned from Klaw, to bring Rosalie back to the United States in order that she might face trial for the DigiMac hit. Had the FBI not wanted Rosalie, the Garda would have happily left her alone. Europe was full of terrorists. If a police officer really felt like busting one, they could be picked up in the local pub. There was certainly no need to schlep all the way across the country to do it. Particularly if it meant creeping about in the damp grass. "For Christ's sake, will you stop your complaining," the Garda sergeant said to his constables. "Some coppers have to work for a living, you know, and it's not as if this is going to tax your powers as police officers."

The sergeant was right. It certainly did not look as if it would be a difficult arrest. The truck that had brought Rosalie had left, as had the limo in which Max and Nathan had arrived. The cottage was entirely undefended, and the occupants were on their own.

We are talking about a movie here.

Inside the cottage, Nathan was making his pitch. Pitching in the only way he knew how, desperately. As if he were in that terrible land of pale bungalows where ideas went to die.

"We see this picture as committed, ideology-wise, it will be *very* committed. Bimbo pic, this is not. *No way* are we in the business of compromise. *Principle* is a big word to us, prin-see-pull, three *very* important syllables. But we want to be number one. Of course we want to be number one. We don't *know any other numbers*. We want to be number one, and *you* want to be number one because nobody remembers the guys who came sec—"

"Excuse me," said Rosalie, who had never been pitched at before and hence was unused to such copious quantities of bullshit. "Would you mind leaving aside the crap at all?"

"Of course not, no way! Let's leave the crap aside," Nathan agreed.

Nathan always agreed. He was a writer, and so during any pitch he simply agreed on instinct. The only way a writer can get his ideas across is through a process of aggressive agreement. The process is simple. The writer states his or her idea and then waits for the executive's objections. Having heard and considered them, the writer then fervently agrees with everything the executive has said, adding that he or she feels a complete fool for not having seen it himself. The writer then repeats his or her idea as if it were a summation of all the executive's points, thanking the executive for making it all so clear.

It sometimes works, but only if the writer is talking to an executive. Rosalie was not an executive, and she was deeply unimpressed.

"Will you let me get this straight?" she said. "You say that your man Plastic Tolstoy wants to do a movie about Mother Earth, and you want me to let you join my active service unit so that you can get all the details and the atmosphere down perfect. Am I right?" she asked.

"Exactly," Nathan agreed, "I *think* that's what I was trying to say, but I did not see it so clearly until you explained it."

"You do recall, I'm sure, that I'm the woman who just tried to shoot the very fellow you want me to work for?"

"Ah, but that's the point," Max chipped in. "Plastic thinks he's going to use you, but really you're going to use him. We're in the driving seat! I'm the star, I have veto on any director, Nathan here will write it. Don't you see? We're in control. We can do a movie that makes you people look great, that makes *you* look great. A real hero."

"I never heard such nonsense," said Rosalie, and how

148

Max loved the way she spoke. "I'm sure I don't know much about Hollywood, but I do know that the only person in the driving seat on a Plastic Tolstoy film would be the man himself."

"Fillum?" asked Max. "What's a fillum?"

"Film," Nathan translated. "Rosalie means a Tolstoy movie."

"Oh, right. . . . Well, sure, we'll have to put the case for Claustrosphere a little in the fillum too," Max conceded, "but balance is good."

"I like balance. Balance is sexy," Nathan agreed.

"Damn balance," Rosalie said, adding, "Sorry, Granny."

"I agree with the point Rosalie just made about balance," said Nathan, "I don't think we need it. I'm sure Granny agrees with me on this one."

"Of course we need balance," said Max.

"Exactly," Nathan agreed furiously. "We need balance, we don't need balance. It's a both ways thing, it *has* to be."

"That's right," said Max. "Balance shows what big people Mother Earth are. People who are not afraid to see the other guy's point of view. Vulnerability is very big right now."

"It's huge," Nathan agreed, "believe me, Rosalie. Vulnerability is huge. There was a new fillum premiered last month: No vulnerability, it *died*. Complete turkey. You could smell the gravy and the Brussels sprouts from outside the theater."

"You're both completely out of your little minds." Rosalie picked up her mobile phone. "I'll give the fellows who brought you here a call—they're only in the village. They'll take you back to Dublin."

"What? Now?" asked Max.

"Certainly, now. The sooner you complete idiots go away and stop wasting my precious time, the better. And I might add that I don't care if I never see or hear from either of you again."

"So it's a 'maybe' then?" said Nathan.

"Rosalie," pleaded Max, seeing his chance to get to know her better slipping away. "We are going to make you into a national hero!"

"We are talking about a *fillum* here," Nathan added.

Neither he nor Max could begin to comprehend Rosalie's attitude. They thought it must be a joke. In the world in which they lived, a green-lighted movie with the budget in place was *the* life goal. Nobody turned it down.

"Mr. Hoddy," Rosalie asked, "if this *movie* goes ahead, how long before it gets shown?"

"From now? Ideally eighteen months. Realistically two years tops."

"Yes, well, it's my belief that there may not be a world to show it to in two years' time. Perhaps everyone can take a little video of it into their Claustrospheres when the Rat Run happens! Good heavens, Mr. Maximus, when I heard you were looking for us, I thought perhaps you genuinely wanted to join us."

"I do! I do!" Max exclaimed.

"No, you don't! You just want to use us, that's all. It's a damn shame, that's what it is. A figure like you could have helped us with getting through to younger people and . . ."

Rosalie's voice trailed away. She scarcely liked to admit it even to herself, but she had been rather excited about seeing Max again. What is more, not for merely professional reasons. She had liked him the day they met at the DigiMac Studio. Liked him, even considering that he had had a horn grafted to his head at the time. He had also, of course, saved her from Plastic Tolstoy. Rosalie liked men who did that sort of thing. Yes, there was no doubt about it, Rosalie had been a bit taken with Max Maximus. Now it turned out he was just another shit who was working for Claustrosphere.

"I wouldn't let you near one of my operations if you were Jurgen Thor himself."

Max could see that he had a lot of ground to make up. He was just about to start the process when events overtook them.

14

A standing ovation

Under siege.

OUTSIDE, THE GARDA WERE IN POSITION. THE INSPECTOR OF PO-
lice in charge of the arresting party fired his revolver into
the air and informed the occupants of the cottage via megaphone that they were surrounded. The inspector added
that he and his men were there in order to arrest the
woman known as Rosalie Connolly. If she came out quietly, nobody would be hurt, and no other person would
be arrested.

Inside the cottage there was silence for a moment. Rosalie's eyes burned into Max. She was wondering why the
Garda had come now. Did this American and this Englishman have something to do with it? Rosalie did not
mind Yanks, but she was not big on the Brits at the best
of times, and it did seem strange that the Garda had followed so hot on the heels of the two movie men. Max
shrank under Rosalie's gaze. He was a fine actor, he had
made a career out of communicating a thought with just a
look. He could also read the thoughts on other people's
faces. He knew what Rosalie was thinking.

"Rosalie, I swear I—" he started to protest his innocence, but Rosalie's gran cut him short.

"This has nothing to do with you. So shut up, keep your head down, and you won't get hurt."

Her husband was sweeping china ornaments from the beautiful old chest that stood in the corner of the room. Having cleared the top, he opened it to reveal a stash of arms.

"If you fight," said Max, "I fight too."

"What!" Nathan gasped.

Ruth too was surprised, but she was not about to look a gift horse in the mouth.

"Can you use a gun?" she asked. Max gave her a pitying glance.

"Ruth, I come from L.A. Most times it's a question of trying to remember how *not* to use a gun."

Sean thrust an automatic rifle into Max's hands. He offered one to Nathan.

"We are here to pitch a *movie*," Nathan pleaded in horror.

"Not any more!" cried Max. "We're defending the homestead!"

Max was terribly excited. He loved to do mad things, and they did not come much madder than this. In fact, the only thing he loved more than doing mad things was doing mad things in front of beautiful girls. Particularly beautiful girls with whom he would dearly love to spend long romantic evenings, drinking wine, talking, and eventually screwing for an inordinately long time and in a variety of interesting positions and different domestic locations.

Nathan could see that trying to reason with Max would be useless, and dived under the kitchen table. He could think of nothing better to do.

Ruth and Sean were both armed now. Sean ran out of the kitchen to cover the back of the cottage, while Ruth knocked out one of the kitchen windows and prepared to fire. Max, taking his cue from the gun-toting granny, also knocked out a window and then inspected his weapon. He wanted to ensure that he fully understood its working and would not be fumbling to reload when the heat got hot. Rosalie too had got her weapon from the wall and for a moment she seemed ready to start shooting; then, however, she stopped and her face fell. She stood dejected in the middle of the kitchen.

"Gran," she said, "this is stupid. We're trapped, we can't shoot it out, they have us cornered. Besides, we don't want to kill a load of innocent coppers. I mean, that's no good, is it?"

"But, sweetie," said her gran. "The stuff they've got on you, they'll put you away forever. You'll do thirty years."

"There aren't thirty years left, Gran."

"Exactly, darling, which is why you have to be free to fight." The old lady's knuckles were white over the trigger. "No copper ever stopped your mother and father getting shot outside Sellafield nuclear plant, did they? The police may just be innocent boys, but their job is to defend the things that are killing us all."

Sean shouted from the other room. "Your gran's right, Rosalie! They mustn't take you. The trail bike's all ready in the sheep shed. If we cover you, you can get along the stream gully to the dry-stone wall and be away!"

"Sure, and have my own grandparents tried as cop killers."

"We don't have to hit them," Max interjected. "We just use our fire to pin them down."

But Rosalie was adamant. The place was surrounded by armed police, and as far as she was concerned, she was caught. Outside, the Inspector of Police reacted to the clear signs that the cottage was preparing to defend itself. He informed them in no uncertain terms that they were hugely outgunned and that any threat to his officers would be met with the full force at his disposal. The inspector's point was basically that Rosalie was cornered good and proper, so why should anybody have to get killed? Rosalie agreed with him and decided to give herself up.

Inside the cottage Max started to take his clothes off.

The actor prepares.

Max's plan was simple. He was, he reminded them, short and slim and also a brilliant actor. It was still only half light outside, and as far as anyone knew, none of the Garda had ever seen Rosalie personally. Yes, they had probably seen her arrive, but it would have been at a distance and in the dark. Even if they had used night-sights, they would really only have been able to make out her clothes. Max explained all this while stripping down to his underwear before the startled group.

"Come on, come on," he snapped. "Give me your clothes! They would have seen your clothes."

"Don't be bloody stupid. You don't look a bit like me."

"Hey, lady! This is my bag, okay? My space. I know what goes down. . . . It's dark, it's cold, the cops want to bust some ass and go home. So, let them bust my ass. Believe me, acting is about bluff. If you do it with chutzpah people will buy it, no matter how unconvincing you are." Max spoke with conviction, having recently attended an Arnold Schwarzenegger retrospective at the American Film Institute. "If I go out there with your beret pulled over my ears, a little bit of makeup, and a dress, they won't think Jack Shit about it. Get real, Rosalie, what are the chances of an American movie star walking out of this cottage dressed as a babe terrorist? Zilch. The cops wouldn't believe it even if I showed them my dick. They saw you go in, they'll see you come out. . . . Besides which, what have you got to lose . . . to be sure, my little darling?" This last, Max delivered in a good approximation of Rosalie's Irish accent. He also raised the pitch of his voice a little, not a great deal, just enough. Not all women have high voices by any means, and there is nothing less convincing than a man squeaking to sound like a woman.

Rosalie wavered no longer. She pulled off her jumper and dress.

"What do I have to lose? If they suss you, which they will, so what?"

"Exactly," said Max. "But they won't."

"They will if you say 'to be sure,' " said Ruth. "I don't think I've ever heard an Irish person say that in my life."

"I'll need the bra, I'm afraid," said Max, unable to stop himself glancing appreciatively at Rosalie's body. It seemed so, he didn't know, real . . . "And something to stuff it with."

"You won't need much, I'm not one of your Hollywood types."

She turned her back to him and took off her bra, replacing it with a T-shirt that her gran handed her from the clotheshorse by the fire.

Max began to construct his character. He had shaved only a few hours earlier at the hotel, and by adding a little powder that Ruth supplied, he managed to conjure up an acceptably smooth skin. Some lipstick and a tiny nod toward eyeliner changed him out of all recognition . . . although, of course, he still did not look a bit like Rosalie. Rosalie had been wearing big walking boots with her dress, long woolen socks, a coat over it all, and her chestnut hair tucked into a black beret. Max's hair was nearly shoulder length so he was able to get away with that, and having borrowed a pair of farmer's boots from Sean, his magic was beginning to work.

"You know something, Max," said Nathan, who had emerged from underneath the table, "you might just get away with it."

"I don't know any Max," replied Max in his gentle Irish accent. "Jesus, you know I'm still half tempted to shoot it out with these Garda bastards."

Nathan couldn't believe it. Max had only just popped the dress on and he was already doing the usual actor crap. Nothing in the world frustrates writers more than when actors claim to be getting "inside" a role, and refuse to drop it. This is because the writer, who has normally created the character, suddenly finds him or herself being told that they understand nothing about it, that only the actor can truly inhabit the soul of the part. Nathan had no such investment in Max's current characterization, but he still hated the way actors tried to imply that acting was "real" and not just pretending.

Max squatted down and did some deep breathing. He stood up and did some stretching. He stood on his head. He lay on his back and hummed, the hum growing into an articulated note . . . "mmmmmmaaaaAAAAHHHHH." He got up. He was ready. He walked to the window.

"If I come out," he shouted in his Rosalie voice, "will you be after leaving my Ma and Pa be?" Rosalie winced somewhat at his choice of language, which seemed to be rooted somewhere in the nineteenth century, but she could not deny that the accent and voice were good.

"We're not interested in the old couple," the Inspector of Police replied. "You're all we want, miss. We'll bring a truck up, you can walk out, we'll put you in it, and be gone."

"All right," Max shouted. "I'm coming out. If you break your word now, the sweet Holy Virgin Mother of God and Jesus will know about it."

Max turned away from the window. Rosalie decided to venture a bit of advice.

"Maybe a bit less of the Irish stuff," she whispered.

Nathan could have told her it was madness. You just did not criticize an actor midperformance. Max may have been falling in love with Rosalie, but an actor is always an actor first and a human being second. He turned on her with a look of such ferocity and contempt that she actually backed away.

"Look, *babe!*" he hissed, *"I'm* the poor bastard who's actually got to make some sense of this crappy little part! *I'm the dumb schmuck* who's actually got to get out there and *fucking do it!"*

"Sorry," Rosalie whispered. "Actually, I think it's brilliant. I really do."

She was catching on fast.

Max collected himself. They could hear a truck drawing up outside.

"Just go out there and *fucking enjoy it,"* Nathan murmured under his breath.

Max picked up his automatic rifle and, holding it above his head, kicked open the cottage door and stood, silhouetted in the dawn light. He paused for a moment and then cried, "Before God I surrender my worthless body to you, but my immortal soul you shall not have! That I keep for myself and the Earth which bore me. And I tell you now, you agents of immoral laws, better men and women shall follow me, and a new law will prevail! A law for life and for the planet! A law for children! A law for the future! You cannot stop us, for we are the Earth and all that lives upon it!"

With that, Max hurled his gun down and stepped forward toward the truck where the Inspector of Police was waiting, visibly moved.

"Miss," he said, "I have to take you in, but let me say it grieves me to do so."

"You must do your duty as you see it, Inspector," said Max and, walking past him coldly, he climbed into the back of the Garda truck, handling the dress like he'd been born in one.

From the cottage they watched as the Garda pulled away, police gunmen retreating from behind every bush and rock.

"All I hope," Rosalie said, "is that when I do go, I go one-half as well as that."

BEN ELTON

The sign of a good performance.

God he had been good.

As the Garda truck pulled away from the tiny stone cottage and began to bump slowly along the rutted dirt track, it flooded in upon Max just how good he had been. The performance of a lifetime! Had such a triumph ever been presented at the New York Met or by the Royal Shakespeare Company? Max thought not. He had successfully hoodwinked armed police into accepting that he was a wanted green terrorist, a *female* wanted green terrorist. And the show was not over yet, the fat lady was a long way from singing "The Star-Spangled Banner." Here he was in the back of a truck, with two constables and an inspector not three feet from him, and still his extraordinary characterization continued to utterly encapsulate his audience. He had them eating out of his hands.

God, he was good.

But theater is a bitch of a mistress, as they say. She always wants more, more! More! She won't let go until she's handcuffed you to the bed, spanked you hard, and made you plead for mercy. Max knew he must focus! Concentrate and focus! That was all great acting consisted of, concentration and focus, and good bones, of course. Good bones were terribly important, but fortunately Max had been amply blessed in that department. Concentrate! Mustn't lose it now, must *focus*. Max discreetly checked that his knees were right . . . not glued together, just gently side by side, an unaffected, girlish, athletic grace was what was required, not some tarty come-on pose. . . . Perfect, the legs were perfect. Now, hold the body firm, don't slouch, you're Joan of Arc, not some used-up bar girl. Proud bust. "If you've got it," Max thought, "flaunt it." Don't thrust, though! Make the bosom work for *you* not vice versa. Now the head. Chin turned slightly away, let it drop, sullen, but defiant. The tiniest gap between the lips, short, angry breaths. . . . And the eyes! The eyes are everything. "If you

158

get the eyes right," Max's old triple-M (movement, massage, meditation) tutor used to say, "you can play the part in a tutu and rubber boots, and people will believe in you." Let the eyes blaze. Fire and defiance. A cornered dog. A wild thing trapped.

Max's spirits soared. How long could he maintain the pretense? To trial, perhaps? Could he actually get himself imprisoned? The theatrical possibilities were mind-boggling . . . and when the story came out! He would be the toast of Hollywood. A play would be written. A movie made! There would be personally sponsored VR games . . . "Max Maximus asks 'Could you act well enough to kid the cops and save the world?' " Max had struck a blow for all actors! He had proved that their very special and delicate talents could be used to protect the environment. That they were not just a bunch of neurotics who liked dressing up, but crack assault troops in the battle of life. Max was positively tingling with his triumph.

Not physically, of course. As far as the policeman and woman sitting opposite him were concerned, he was not triumphant but defeated. His whole body suggested a wild woman chained and captive. Except for one part. One part of his body suggested neither a woman nor captivity. For unbeknownst to Max, his private excitement was beginning to show. Just as it had done on his last morning with Krystal. Max had often teased a reluctant appendage into action by dwelling upon his enormous talent, and on this occasion the process was underway without even being prompted. The inspector and the woman constable watched in astonishment as a bulge appeared in their captive's lap. While inwardly discreetly congratulating himself on his brilliance, outwardly Max was taking a standing ovation. The Garda could not believe their eyes as the bulge strained at the cloth of the dress and thrust itself ever upward. Growing right there in front of them, reaching up to the feminine chin that rested in the delicate cupped hands above it. *"J'accuse,"* that straining bulge seemed to be saying, *"j'accuse*. This woman is not a woman, and I, a proud, full-blooded erection, am here to prove it."

Busted.

Back at Ruth and Sean's cottage, Rosalie was just getting ready to leave when the Garda returned.

It was a cruel blow. Moments before, they had been celebrating Max's extraordinary success. Rosalie knew that she owed him a favor, and she promised Nathan that if he remained in Dublin she would reestablish contact the moment Max reappeared.

"They won't keep him long." Rosalie was sure of that. "The last thing the Garda want is the papers telling the world that a famous American Virtual Reality star tricked them into believing that he was a wanted Irish girl. There're enough jokes about the Irish as it is."

She had just finished pulling on a change of clothes when they heard the roar of trucks hurtling back up the dirt track. There was no time to voice the disappointment they all felt. Rosalie moved as if she had to escape from armed police every day. She grabbed her automatic rifle, and pecking her granny and her grandad on the cheek, she ran out of the cottage and made for the outhouse, where the trail bike was hidden. She was just kicking the machine into life as the Garda arrived. In the cottage, Ruth and Sean made ready to fire at the police vehicles. Nathan returned to his position under the table. There was the high-pitched rev of an overtuned engine, and Rosalie roared out of the shed and headed for the gully of the little stream by the dry-stone wall.

It was over in moments; the Garda did not even leave their armored trucks. A single stun-shell from the riot cannon mounted on the front of the lead vehicle blew the bike out from under Rosalie, and she landed heavily in the stream. Nothing was broken, and she was on her feet in an instant. Peering out of the gully, she considered running, but what was the point? They'd got her and she knew it.

"Granny! Grandpa! Don't shoot," she called as she emerged from the stream, her hands held above her head. "No sense us all going to prison."

Poor Ruth and Sean had to watch helplessly through the broken window as their granddaughter was caught. Nathan tried to look elsewhere, furiously studying a magazine he found on the shelf. It is never a socially relaxing situation, being a guest in the house of people you do not know, as they watch a beloved relative get charged with numerous acts of terrorism and start what will almost certainly be decades in captivity.

"Don't you bastards understand!" they could hear Rosalie shout as she was handcuffed. "The Earth's being fucked rigid. We've got to do something."

"I have to tell you, miss," the Inspector of Police said, "this poof here in the dress made a much prettier job of getting arrested than you're doing."

Angry eyes.

They sat opposite each other in the back of the Garda truck, retracing the journey that Max had made so triumphantly a few minutes before. How different were things now! His costume, which previously had been his armor, his triumphal robe, was now just a stupid dress. Max had been hauled in by the law on many occasions, but this was the first time he had done it wearing women's clothes. He hated it. Still, in a way he was lucky. At least you don't get thirty years in the slammer for wearing lipstick and wasting police time. You did, however, for a five-year career as a terrorist, and both he and Rosalie knew it. She was going to watch the world die, helpless to stop it, from behind prison bars.

"How did they suss you?" she asked.

Max was ready for this one.

"Oh, you know, performance is a myriad of subtleties," he said earnestly. "You get one gesture or expression out of place, even a thought, one tiny nuance, and the edifice crumbles. A single tiny moment misjudged, and the whole house of cards collapses."

"Your man here got an erection," the policewoman said cheerfully.

"An erection!" Rosalie gasped in astonishment.

Max was mortified. With every moment he was becoming more and more attracted to Rosalie. And now this! Shame covered him as if it had been mixed with custard and poured on his head. He loved this girl, he knew that. He had felt it from the first moment they had met. He loved her soft Irish voice. He loved the tough things she did. He'd seen her in her underwear, and he loved that too. What he wanted most in the world was to impress her, and he had a sneaking suspicion that the manner of his exposure was unlikely to do so.

"I couldn't believe it," the policewoman continued happily. "A big whopper, right there in his lap. I nearly hung my cap on it!" She was having a lovely day, this Woman Police Constable. You didn't often get a chance to arrest movie stars in drag on the west coast of Ireland.

"That's enough of that, Constable," the inspector admonished sternly, and silence fell for a moment.

Rosalie looked around. Searching for the source of the hard-on. There were two policemen and a policewoman. Rosalie knew that Max was not gay, not only from his reputation, but also from the way she had noticed him looking at her. That left the Woman Police Constable. Rosalie was not one to judge a person by their appearance, but this girl did not look the sort to provoke uncontrollable trouser-based excitement. Particularly in a man who had recently been married to one of Hollywood's sexiest stars. The policewoman was large and rather dumpy . . . very attractive in many ways, no doubt, lovely hair, but scarcely an instant erection trigger.

"How come you got a hard-on then?" Rosalie asked Max finally, fixing him with her steady, unblinking green eyes. Eyes that Max usually found drop-dead gorgeous, but at the present time found intrusive and frankly intimidating.

"Um, well . . . I just couldn't help it," he replied.

"I presumed you couldn't help it," Rosalie snapped. "I didn't think you'd sat there and induced the damn thing. Why couldn't you help it?"

Somebody had once told Max that honesty was the best policy.

"Look, Rosalie . . . It was amazing, you know? My performance. To pull it off like that, to trick all those cops. It was like a career triumph, like winning an Oscar or something. . . ."

Rosalie's eyes said it all. Whoever had told Max that honesty was the best policy was wrong.

Parting of the ways.

By the time the police convoy arrived back in Dublin, Max was almost tired of those gorgeous green eyes that he had found so fascinating since the first day he had seen them. They had glared at him in silent fury for the entire journey. They were so fierce and strong that Max was actually beginning to fear that their impact might by now have left permanent marks on his face.

The reason for Rosalie's fury was not just that Max's vanity had been the cause of her being about to spend the rest of her life in a cell. She was a reasonable woman and aware that the Garda were clearly on to her, and that she would have got caught whether Max was there or not. No, her fury went much deeper than that, for it was fueled by a wounded heart.

She liked Max. He had already saved her life once, in

Plastic Tolstoy's Claustrosphere, and she had liked him then. Even tough, no-nonsense terrorist fighters have a romantic side, and Rosalie's was very well developed indeed. She was a wild country girl raised on fairy tales and ancient myths. If gorgeous handsome men wanted to risk their lives on her behalf, than she didn't mind a bit. Rosalie had wondered from the start whether Max might not be a little sweet on her, from the way she had caught him looking at her. However, she was not a vain woman, and thought it unlikely that such a colossal and rich star could be showing anything other than a passing interest. Therefore, when for a second time he had offered to save her bacon, she had been deeply moved. Rosalie had been brought up to believe that when you love someone you'll do anything to look after them and protect them. That certainly seemed to be what Max was doing. After all, aiding the escape of serious criminals was a pretty big crime in itself, and Max had walked into it without a murmur. Now it turned out the whole episode had just been about an actor's vanity, a vanity so great that it had eventually ended in Rosalie's getting arrested anyway. He didn't like her at all, he had just used her as an opportunity to show off. She hated him. She hated him because she had started to fall in love with him, and now she would never see him again.

The little Garda convoy eventually pulled up in the courtyard of Dublin's Central Police Station. Max was removed first.

"Rosalie, I'll—" he started to say.

"I wish I'd never met you at all," she said, her eyes no longer fierce and strong, but liquid with sadness. "And I never want to see you again."

"You won't, love," the inspector assured her. "They don't put men in women's prisons, not even transvestites."

15

Unlikely savior

Exit pursued by love.

MAX WAS DEPORTED THE NEXT DAY. NATHAN MET HIM AT THE airport and was with him when the Garda escorted him to the plane. Except, of course, they did not get as far as the plane, not for quite a while anyway. Dublin Airport Authority, like all airport authorities, seemed to see it as their principal duty to herd passengers as far down the departure process as possible, before informing them that there will be a two-hour delay. They do not inform you that you are passing the last lavatory or the last bar or the last newspaper shop. That is something you discover for yourself once ensconced in a place called a departure "lounge," which is defined as a room in which the sole facility is an inadequate number of plastic seats.

They stood, leaning against the wall. Nathan, Max, and the two cops. For once it was Max's mind that was utterly preoccupied with affairs of the heart. All Max could think about was those green eyes staring at him and then filling with tears. Astonishingly, Nathan was not, for the moment, thinking of his beloved and unattainable Flossie. When you are talking about a movie, even love sometimes has to take a backseat.

"I have this great idea for the plot of our film," he had said to Max when they met.

"If it's anything to do with cross-dressing, forget it. I'll kill you if you ever breathe a word of what happened," Max snapped, "and believe me, I know how to kill."

"No, no, it's a bigger thing, a thematic curve." Nathan was very, *very* excited. "I am very, *very* excited," he said.

"I don't care, I'm not interested. The world is a hollow and empty place, and I am the hollowest and emptiest thing in it." Max turned to the officers who were escorting him. "Listen, guys. I have let down a woman I think I am in love with. I have to make it up to her, please unlock the cuffs."

The officers did not move. Max pressed on.

"Please, guys. Try to forget for a minute that you're tough, hard, ball-breaking peace officers and get in touch with the child inside you. Ask that child what he would do."

"We're doing you a favor putting you on a plane, son," the first officer replied. "If you start a relationship by apologizing to a bird, you'll be under her thumb all your life. Jesus, you'll be after asking permission to go and get pissed in the pub."

"That's right, pal. You have to be tough, forceful," the second officer added. "If you love this little lady, then ring her from the States and say, 'All right, so I fucked up. So what? Do you have a problem with that, darling?' Tell her that, and if she does have a problem with it, then tell her that she can fuck right off. There's plenty of birds in the world that aren't so fucking choosy."

"That's right," said the fist officer. "Besides which, you're better off sitting in the pub anyway. At least your money's your own."

"Thanks, guys. You've been real," Max said, and the group lapsed into silence. The Irish cops' attitude reminded Nathan of the cops he had met at the Beverly Hills Fortified Village. He wondered whether this relaxed attitude to romance was common to all policemen. Maybe if he joined the police he would get over Flossie. Damn! He had let his mind wander on to Flossie again. Now he was as sad as Max.

Protective custody.

After Max had parted from Rosalie, she had been taken to an interrogation room and asked a lot of questions about Mother Earth. She, of course, had told the police nothing. Partly because she would rather have died than sing, and partly because, like all members of even vaguely efficient secret organizations, she actually knew very little.

She did not, for instance, know where Mother Earth's detailed knowledge of the next environmental hot spots came from. And she could not have told the police, even had she wanted to, how her unit and others like it were always able to be at the heart of the action so quickly.

"The intelligence people look after that stuff," she told her interrogators. "We just go where we're told."

"So who pays?" they had asked, as they always did in such circumstances, Mother Earth finances being so notoriously shadowy.

"Rich green fellas, I guess," Rosalie replied, and she knew no more than that. She had, of course, heard the rumors, as everyone had, that some megabillionaires were finally beginning to see sense. That they were turning the funds they had acquired destroying the Earth to the job of saving it. Rosalie did not, however, have any better idea than the police as to who these dubious philanthropists might be.

"Oh, come on!" barked the policeman. "The kind of equipment you people carry doesn't materialize out of thin air! That automatic rifle you were caught with is a state-of-the-art weapon. Our men don't have anything as good as that. Who the hell is supplying all that stuff?"

"I don't know, gentlemen, and if I did I certainly would not be after telling you, now, would I? Now, if you're going to torture me, will you please do me the courtesy of getting it over with?"

The chief officer adopted a slightly offended but still censorial tone.

"Sorry to disappoint you, miss, but contrary to hysterical rumor we do not torture people. Not unless you count the food. Take her down, Constable."

"When do I get to see a lawyer?" Rosalie asked as she was hauled to her feet by a tough Woman Police Constable.

"You can see a lawyer in America. Good day, miss."

And to Rosalie's surprise, she discovered that she was not to be tried in Ireland at all, but handed over to the FBI for extradition to America. There she would face trial for the DigiMac Studio raid. Her departure was set for the following day. A magistrate had already issued the appropriate authorization and there were no avenues of appeal. In vain did Rosalie protest that this was completely illegal, that they could not just hand over a European citizen to the American authorities. The truth was, of course, that they could do what they liked and were going to. The European Federation was so utterly plagued with terrorists (terrorism having taken over from car theft as the number one crime) that they were absolutely delighted when another country offered to take one off their hands. The head of the Irish Special Branch of EuroPol had actually phoned the U.S. ambassador to tell him that they had hundreds more suspected terrorists awaiting trial, and the FBI were welcome to as many of them as they wanted. On behalf of the Bureau, the ambassador had politely declined the offer.

What kind of G-man are you?

The following evening, the Garda handed Rosalie over to the custody of the American authorities, embodied in this case by Special Agent Judy Schwartz.

"Hi, I'm Special Agent Judy Schwartz," said Judy, offering Rosalie his hand. She kept hers, which were handcuffed together, firmly in her lap.

"You're a G-man?" she said. "You don't look like one."

"Oh, well, I can explain that. What happens is, when there's any rough stuff, what I do is I rush into a telephone box and put on two hundred pounds of pure muscle, and I get so handsome and cool it's terrifying."

Judy didn't know why he bothered really, it never changed. No matter how many times he tackled nerdism head on, it never got any better. Ever since he had arrived in Dublin and met his opposite numbers in the Garda Special Branch, he had been aware of the sniggering that followed him about. Judy sort of understood. The media had decreed many decades before what a secret agent should look like, and it just wasn't like Judy. Judy realized that it was not really the fault of the people who laughed at him. It was society in general. After all, if you're a policeman, and you're told that the FBI is sending an agent to pick up a terrorist, you do not expect somebody with one leg shorter than the other, thick glasses, and crooked teeth. Judy *sort* of understood, but it still hurt, even after all these years.

Judy would have been pleased to know that on this occasion his little antinerdism joke did at least hit home. Rosalie nearly apologized, but then stopped herself. This man was, after all, going to haul her off for trial in the States. On reflection, she didn't care if she had offended him or not.

"I'll take charge of the prisoner now," Judy said to the officers who were flanking Rosalie, but they did not move away. Instead, one of them snapped open one of the cuffs on Rosalie's wrist and locked it on his own.

"You're still on European soil, Agent Schwartz. We have to escort you and the prisoner to the airport and put you both on the plane."

"Yes, of course," Judy said. "Well, I'm afraid I'm going to have to insist that, in the interests of security, the suspect is handcuffed to me."

Judy met the surprised look of the big policeman steadily.

"This case is extremely important to the Bureau," he explained. "Ms. Connolly is an experienced criminal, known to be shrewd, resourceful, and tough. I cannot take any chances on our losing her."

It took some guts to say it. There were four Garda officers in the room, and any one of them, including the woman constable, could have just about put Judy in their pocket. They laughed at him, of course. Even Rosalie could not help sniggering at the man's nerve.

"So what you're saying, Agent Schwartz," the inspector asked, "is that, in the event of the suspect playing silly buggers, you feel that you will be better placed to prevent her escape than my officers? Is that it?"

"I have been very highly trained, sir. No offense is intended."

The inspector just laughed again and instructed his man to handcuff the suspect to the American, if that was what he wanted. Judy asked for the key, but was told perfunctorily that it was not Garda policy to leave the key with the man wearing the handcuffs. Judy could have it when they were on the plane.

And in this manner they left for the airport, Judy, Rosalie, and two Garda officers. It was pretty much at the same time that Max and Nathan were heading out the same way. Rosalie, however, was destined to miss her plane.

Riveting viewing.

Judy and Rosalie stood apart from the line as one of the officers checked them in for their flight. There were, as in all airports, numerous television sets hanging from the ceiling and attached to the walls. Some offered flight information, others offered what could loosely be called "entertainment": cable music video channels, local morning TV, and interactive games.

Many years previously, it had been decreed by the moguls of media and marketing that the human race was so utterly devoid of originality and creative powers that it was incapable of getting through even the simplest activity without some electronically delivered stimulus. Hence, shopping malls were suddenly suffused with tinny renditions of classic pop songs, wafting hither and thither among the discarded litter, dried-up fountains, and utterly repulsive sculptures. It was possible for old people to stand forever on escalators that had never worked and die to the sound of "Wonderful World." Elevators, stores, even buses, all began to sing. When people called for minicabs, they were forced to sit through fifteen minutes of commercial radio before being told that there was a three-day wait for cars at the present time. Noise joined the dazzling potpourri of pollutants that the industrialized world was devising in order to make the fact of being alive ever more unpleasant.

Nor was it just aural "entertainment" that was forced upon people who had previously been capable of doing their shopping without having to listen to orchestral arrangements of Beatles' hits. Televisions began to appear everywhere. The logic was that because people liked to watch the television in their living rooms, then they would surely like to watch it in all other circumstances. Buses, stores, and particularly pubs and bars were invaded. The appearance of TVs in pubs was surely the cruelest blow of all, for a pub is above all a place of social intercourse.

It evolved out of a natural human desire to go out, meet other people, and talk to them. A TV has no place in a pub. People do not have beer taps in their living rooms. A TV utterly destroys all possibility of conversation, for it is a physical property of all televisions that *the eye is inevitably drawn to them.* Its hypnotic powers know no bounds. If a TV is on in a public place, people cannot avoid staring at it. The sound does not even have to be on. No matter how boring the program, and no matter how interesting the conversation one is having at the time, the eye will slowly drift over to the television and have to be constantly dragged back. TVs can now be found in post offices, banks, and police stations. Surely it is only a matter of time before they appear in operating rooms, which will mean a lot of wrong pieces get cut off.

Handling the handlers.

Socially disastrous though these electronic intrusions usually are, they were good news for Rosalie, although she did not yet know it.

Judy had been waiting for his chance, and now he saw it. One police person was checking them in, the other was momentarily transfixed by the silent broadcast of a morning shopping show being presented on a wall-mounted television nearby.

"Hope the flight's on time," Judy ventured.

"Mmm," the policeman replied, his attention elsewhere.

"I'll bet the VR helmets on the plane don't work," Judy mused.

"Mmm," replied the distracted policeman.

"Would it be okay if Rosalie and I were to jump across that empty check-in station and disappear through the rubber curtains onto the luggage belt?" Judy asked in a bored voice.

"Mmm," the policeman replied.

Fortunately Judy had squeezed Rosalie's hand to get her attention, for she too had been staring at a TV set.

"Thanks," said Judy. "Let's go, Rosalie."

And, handcuffed together though they were, they jumped across the check-in bay and pushed themselves through the rubber curtains.

"What in the name of goodness is going on?" Rosalie cried as they began to glide along the conveyor belt with all the luggage.

"I don't think now is the time to explain," Judy answered.

Up ahead of them, the baggage handlers were performing their duties as laid down by the airport authority. These consisted of flipping one catch open on every fourth bag, sprinkling red wine and bits of broken glass on everything, and loosening one wheel on each baby stroller.

"Airport cops behind us," Judy shouted at the baggage handlers.

He was pretty sure what their reaction would be, and he was right. The idea that the airport police had been set upon them yet again was a red flag to a bull for airport baggage handlers. They are notoriously easy to offend. Baggage handlers know that everybody hates them. They know that every individual passenger feels personally victimized by them, believing that their own particular bag has been deliberately held back. They know that everybody firmly believes the lengthy time it takes to get the bags to the carousels is caused by the handlers trying to decide what to steal. They know that the tatty, forlorn little unclaimed suitcase that seems to have been bolted to every carousel by the manufacturers is taken by the public as evidence that the handlers remove only one bag at a time from the airplanes and refuse to get another until that one has been claimed. All this the baggage handlers know, and they do not like it. They believe it is the public who are the unreasonable and indeed immoral ones. They believe that the public deliberately fill any excess spaces left over after they have packed with lead ballast, in order to ensure that an adequate level of spinal injury is inflicted upon the handlers. They believe that it is the public who neglect to fasten their luggage properly, so that the bags explode in a flurry of dirty underwear on the conveyor belt. The handler is then expected to restuff them while an inadequately wrapped granite boulder is bearing down upon him.

The public hates handlers, and handlers hate the public. It is a universal truth and cannot be altered. If there is life elsewhere in space, then it may be safely presumed that there are little green men and women exchanging horror stories about how their cases ended up in the wrong solar system.

"What aliens must think of our planet when they visit I just don't know," the little green creatures will declaim loudly to each other as they mill aimlessly around the baggage collection transporter rooms. "When we can't even beam down a few damn cases from the mother ship."

All this antagonism has led to a sullen touchiness on the part of baggage handlers worldwide. It was these feelings of persecution that Judy was attempting to exploit when he announced that the two figures emerging through the rubber curtains behind them were airport police. He had judged the situation well.

"Right, that's it," the handlers said to each other and turned off the conveyor belt. "Yet again, we're being harassed by the company. Yet again, we're being categorized as a bunch of thieving bums who have to be constantly spied upon in case we try to pinch a plane."

And so a strike was called, which left the two Garda escorts stuck on the stationary belt, struggling to follow Judy and Rosalie, while angry handlers expressed their antagonism to authority by heaping luggage in their way.

A not very alert security alert.

Outside in the arrivals area alarm bells were ringing, and police and soldiers had started to run around all over the place. This was all to the good, as far as Judy was concerned. For the airport, like all European airports, was on hair-trigger alert for terrorist attack. Every day, the authorities planned in meticulous detail where every soldier and every police person should run to the moment the alarms went off. They held a full dress-rehearsal once a week, with smoke and blank bullets and everything. There were also regular false alarms that occurred when old ladies forgot to inform the authorities that they had packed a small bazooka in their hand bags for their personal protection. All this training meant that when the alarms went off, the soldiers and police at the airport operated with machine-like efficiency . . . only, however, if there was a terrorist attack underway. If, for instance, two handcuffed people were trying to slip quietly out of the airport together, the activities of the security forces were not merely irrelevant but actively counterproductive.

"This way," Judy instructed Rosalie, and jumping off the conveyor belt, he pulled her toward the next set of rubber curtains along the line.

"But that's back into the check-in area," Rosalie protested.

"I know," said Judy, trying not to resent her for acting as if he were an idiot. "Do what I tell you, and we may get out of this . . . okay?"

Rosalie had nothing to lose.

"Okay," she said.

"Good. Now when we go through the curtains, hold up your arm so that everybody can see the cuffs, right? And shout out that it's all right, you've got me, and everybody should be calm. All right?"

"But . . . ," Rosalie attempted to interject.

"Look! You're a tough, beautiful Irish girl, right? I'm an American nerd. In terms of bluffing our way out of Dublin Airport, who do you think should play the good guy?"

Rosalie could see the logic. She dragged him through the rubber curtains, emerging behind an Aer Lingus check-

in girl who was in the process of telling everybody to be
calm. The whole hall was a mass of confusion.

"Garda Special Branch," Rosalie shouted, holding their
arms aloft. "It's fine. I have him." And with that she thrust
herself forward past the Aer Lingus desk and into the astonished line of travelers. For a moment the crowd did not
part, and Rosalie experienced a split second of panic as
she thought the bluff had failed.

"Make way now! Clear a path," she shouted, pushing
on, dragging Judy with her. Rosalie need not have worried.
The momentary hesitation on the part of the crowd in front
of her was merely due to the fact that, even during a terrorist attack, the first instinct of people in an airport line is
to protect their place. The nagging suspicion that everything that happens is a ploy by some other traveler to push
in dies hard. Fortunately, Rosalie's natural ability to command and the inherent dignity of her bearing won through.

"Get out of the fucking way, all of you! I've got a killer
here," she screeched, flailing her free arm about, and the
people parted. They did more than part, they cheered and
clapped. Judy had again judged the psychology of the situation to perfection. The sight of a pretty little local girl
with flashing green eyes capturing such a nasty-looking
foreign weasel of a man filled the crowd with a sense of
romance and pride.

"Death to all papists!" Judy shouted in his broadest
Southern U.S. accent. "The Elitest Church of Christ the
Crew-Cut is the one true faith."

Judy knew that Ireland is a country that has suffered
more than most from religious bigotry over the years, and
he reasoned that people would be pretty happy to see a
bigot busted, particularly a Protestant one. He reasoned
correctly. How they cheered as their brave girl cop escorted the evil zealot across the arrivals area. People from
other lines heard the commotion and walked across to see
what the fuss was about. In a few moments, a large crowd

was celebrating the victory of law and order over bigotry and violence.

"Okay, let me through, this isn't a freak show," Rosalie shouted as the crowd pressed in. Judy began to regret inflaming the crowd, but help was on its way.

"Get back there, sharp now!"

The voice was that of an army sergeant who, seeing that a capture had been made, was following statutory instructions to facilitate an orderly arrest. Before they knew it, Rosalie was escorting Judy up an avenue of soldiers who, while grinning broadly, were holding back the cheering and rapidly growing crowd. People usually felt so helpless in the face of terrorism, that to see it temporarily vanquished was a massive thrill for everybody at the airport, soldiers and public alike.

"Good for you, you little darling," they shouted. "Hang the bastard."

As Rosalie and Judy arrived at the exit, the sergeant marched up to them. He stamped and saluted in his proudest manner.

"Well done, Sergeant," Rosalie said. "You moved very quickly."

"Thank you, ma'am," the proud sergeant replied, "and on behalf of the lads, may I congratulate you on nabbing the little shit."

"That's very kind, Sergeant. Thank you. Now if you'd just hold this door for a moment while I get my man here into the Special Branch car, I'd be grateful."

And while the army held back the crowd, Rosalie and Judy went out and caught a taxi.

16

The loneliest girl in the world

Bitchin' pitchin'.

"OKAY, IT'S LIKE THIS," SAID NATHAN, ATTEMPTING TO SOUND dynamic.

He was back in Plastic Tolstoy's office, perched on the very edge of the bottomless pit that Plastic called a couch, nervously gripping his empty soda glass and making his pitch. Nathan was at the crunch point. The point that must be faced in every pitch. The point when the pitcher knows that he or she can procrastinate no longer and that the actual idea must be stated. It is always a nerve-racking moment, because so often it is the last moment before igno- minious failure. Nathan, therefore, like all pitchers, had put it off for as long as possible, spending a full ten min- utes lucidly repeating the principles of his original brief.

"You don't want a story that runs down the greenies," he had said in about six different ways. "The greenies hold the high ground, we have to accept that. What you want your story to do is acknowledge the moral position of the Environmentalists, while showing the Claustrosphere company in a great light. Right?"

Plastic Tolstoy was losing patience.

"Nathan. I know this. *I* told *you*," he replied testily. "You think I'm renting you a house off Sunset to be told back what I told you already? Is that how things get done in England, huh? Jesus, excuse me! No wonder you guys lost an empire."

"Yes, yes, no, fine. Just restating our position," Nathan agreed hastily. "You know, checking we're both coming from the same place."

"Well, don't, because we ain't. You're coming from being poor, and I'm coming from being rich, which means *you* have to impress *me,* which, I would like to tell you, so far is not happening. No impact is being made. I am looking around my office here, and it is an impact-free zone. There is no zing in the air, no pow! No ideas bouncing off the walls. All there is, in fact, is nothing; and nothing, as the dead white guy said, comes of nothing. Certainly not enough to justify the exorbitant amounts of money—"

For just one moment, Nathan saw red.

"Oh, for God's sake, you smug bastard, will you shut your stupid face for a minute so I can explain my idea!!"

It was out before he could even believe he'd said it. Nathan went white with fear. He had shouted at Plastic Tolstoy. He had called Plastic Tolstoy an arrogant bastard. He had told Plastic Tolstoy to shut his stupid face. It is sometimes said that when a person is dying, their whole life passes before their eyes. When you die in Hollywood your whole future passes before your eyes. The beach house you won't own, the waiters who will not be crawling to you, the twenty-seven-page profiles that will not be commissioned about you for *Vanity Fair*. All this and more passed before Nathan's eyes as the realization of what he had done sank in on him, and the dark shadow of Shepherds Bush fell upon his soul. (Shepherds Bush being that place in West London where what was left of the once mighty BBC still lived.) A dark, shadowy place of plastic cups, underfunded projects, and memos querying expense claims for a taxi ride and a sandwich. This was what Nathan was going back to, and he would never see the Californian filtered sunshine, the swimming pools, or the money ever again.

Then Nathan noticed something strange. Plastic Tolstoy was still talking.

"I don't know, maybe I'm the only idiot in this town who pays for writers to tell me what he just said. Maybe it's a special talent I have. . . . 'That Tolstoy,' they all say behind my back, 'he pays for an echo.' They're laughing at me. . . ."

Nathan realized that the man had not even heard his outburst. Plastic Tolstoy had just kept right on going, happily developing his little comic theme, wallowing in the glorious sound of his own voice. As far as Plastic Tolstoy was concerned, Nathan only existed when Plastic wanted him to.

"Okay, so we've established what I want," said Plastic, having finally exhausted the particular well of sarcasm from which he had been drawing. "Now maybe we can find out what *you have."*

"Okay," said Nathan, momentarily emboldened by his close shave. "Mother Earth is always attacking the Claustrosphere Company because it claims that Claustrosphere people are hastening the end of the world. What our movie has to say is that Claustrosphere wants exactly the same things that all those greenies want, it just happens to be a bit more responsible about it—"

"This I *know!"* said Plastic, but Nathan barged on before Plastic could get going again.

"The biggest mystery about the Mother Earth lot is where they get the money from, right? I mean, I've seen these people, they have limos, incredible-tasting potatoes, everything. Some shadowy philanthropist is clearly bank-rolling them, but he just won't take the credit. Well, how about this? How about *we take it!* We say in our movie that it's *Claustrosphere that is providing the funding!* . . . I mean, what a great twist, right? All the time you've got these greenies attacking the very people who are paying for them to do it! But the Claustrosphere people just keep on paying, because they believe in the future of the Earth more than anybody, and think Environmental protest is important.''

Plastic Tolstoy stared at Nathan and for once he did not speak. He was thinking. Nathan blathered on, as writers do when met by producer silence.

"I mean it is *the* greatest plot twist, don't you think?" he said, trying not to sound desperate. "Like all through the picture, the greenies are trying to kill the head of Claustrosphere—we'll fictionalize him, of course—mean-time, they're filled with gratitude to this mysterious guy who makes it possible for them to continue the fight. Then at the end, they realize it's the same person! That Claus-trosphere is part of the Green Movement! That's when they learn the error of their ways. I mean, irony or what? You've got to admit it.''

For a moment, Plastic Tolstoy seemed to be far away.

"It's an extraordinary idea," he said finally. "You told anybody else about it?''

"Have I, hell! There are more plagiarists in this town than at an Elvis convention.''

Maybe it was the mention of the name Elvis, that hal-lowed and imperial American name upon which his moth-er's fortune had been based, that decided Plastic. He seemed to snap out of his reverie suddenly and make a decision.

"Okay. We'll run with it. It's a good idea. It's a great idea. Go write the script.''

*   *   *

Factory town.

Nathan virtually floated out of Tolstoy's mansion. Even the thought of Flossie could not puncture his delight. He nearly sang to himself as he touched his sports coupé into action. His idea had been accepted! He was going to be allowed to write the initial script for a genuine fullfledged feature. He knew it would only be the initial script, for it is a foregone conclusion in Hollywood that any feature will be written by more than one person. It has to be this way . . . so that the producer may remain in control.

Many artists working in Hollywood resent what they see as the factory mentality of the town. They consider it crass and wicked that their creative juices are seen as merely one ingredient in a cocktail that somebody else is mixing. They forget that Hollywood *is* a factory, and pretends to be nothing else. It has no sponsors, it receives no government money. Like a producer of canned food, it exists solely on the income it can generate in the marketplace. The Royal National Theatre of Great Britain may proudly commission plays that people don't like, written by tired old playwrights who don't like people, because it is generally considered to be a function of government to subsidize national culture. The New York Museum of Modern Art may be in a position to purchase an obscure arrangement of wire and pebbles from a talentless drug addict because some rich industrialist wants to cloak his brutal legacy with a veneer of culture. This is all well and good, and no doubt much to be encouraged, but Hollywood can count on no such indulgences.

When somebody commissions a film in Hollywood, they are spending money that somebody else has invested in order to make a profit, and unless the artist is a committed Marxist, then he or she has no real grounds for complaint. They may moan about artistic freedom, financial censorship, making room for ideas to grow, but in other industries the creative elements do not expect such indulgences.

The chefs at Heinz do not consider it outrageous that their bosses aren't interested in a fascinating new recipe they are working on for anchovy-flavored baked beans.

The Director Monster.

Some film writers accept these financial arguments, but still plead with producers to be given a chance to see a script right through to production. They promise that they will make the end product even more profitable than if the script were produced by committee. They are wasting their breath. If scripts written by individuals rather than a succession of hired hands were ever accepted, the writer's vision would be seen to have at least partially shaped the movie.

This can never be. For the ego of the Director Monster must be fed.

It is this gargantuan appetite that has come to shape the pecking order of the film industry. The self-esteem of the writer must be sacrificed, along with that of everybody else involved (barring that of the star, if very big), to satisfy the Director Monster's insatiable gluttony for credit and control.

The Director Monster, or Director, as he or she was once called, is the bloated queen bee at the center of an army of drones. It was directors who invented probably the most arrogant billing in the annals of human endeavor. It is they who, not content with the mere words "directed by so and so" at the end of a film, decided to insist on the phrase "a so and so picture" at the beginning of the film. The beginning of a film, it must be remembered, that will have involved the artistic commitment of literally hundreds of people. No other command figure feels the need to grab credit in this all-encompassing way. The President of the United States does not insist upon the words "a so and so country" prefixing any mention of the U.S.A. The D Day landings are not remembered as an "Eisenhower liberation."

Clearly there have been many great film directors of vision and ability. Some, perhaps, who actually deserve the credit they get. That said, a film must of course have a script. It also requires actors, who will wear costumes that must be designed and made. Those actors will perform within selected locations and on specially designed and constructed sets. The film will require a cinematographer to shape the pictures and lighting designers to provide the atmosphere. There will be sound engineers, special effects wizards, also an editor, the person who actually pieces together the thousands of disconnected shots to create the whole.

Of course, the director is in charge of all these things, but he or she does not actually *do* any of them. The director does not even have to ensure that the actors exit through the right door and look to the correct side of the camera during their close-ups. They have a continuity person to do that.

None of this is to run down the director's contribution. He or she is the boss, and since movies began, the director has been rightly respected as the principal *auteur* of any picture. But the cult has got out of hand. Ask some directors what they would like to be written on their gravestone, and the answer will be, "A so and so life." What else?

Happiness is a temporary thing.

Nonetheless, despite the knowledge that his script, when finished, would be handed on to other writers, Nathan was happy. Even though his self-respect would eventually be forcibly taken from him, he was thrilled. Yes, his vision would be pulverized and distorted . . . yet he was deliriously happy, for he had been green-lighted to write a script, and for a writer in Hollywood, breaks do not come any better than that.

"Yes," Nathan thought, "I am happy."

Then, of course, he remembered Flossie, and realized that he could not be happy, because he was unhappy. The little demons inside him reinserted the lead weights into the pit of his stomach and reminded him that to pretend that you are happy when you are, in fact, unhappy, is a contradiction in terms.

Pulling herself together.

As it happened, Flossie was thinking of Nathan. She had just had a very unpleasant experience, and it had led her to ponder her life somewhat.

For Flossie had just lived through the day of the Rat Run. The day on which the peoples of the world had acknowledged that normal life on Earth had finally become unsustainable and had hence retreated to their Claustrospheres. Although on this occasion it had not actually been the people of the world that had acknowledged this horror, but merely the people of Great Pew, a tiny village in Oxfordshire. A village in which Nathan and Flossie had once lived, and in which Flossie now lived alone, her brief, post-Nathan affair having ended some time before.

Flossie had awoken that morning with no suspicion of the momentous events that were about to unfold. What she had awoken with, however, was something of a hangover. Her supper on the previous night had consisted of a bottle and a half of red wine and an entire packet of chocolate biscuits. She was definitely feeling a bit rough as she staggered into the kitchen, still dressed in her nightclothes . . . a big nightie, baggie tracksuit pants, and large furry slippers. The half-full bottle of wine stood on the kitchen table where she had left it, but Flossie resisted the temptation to take a slug, and instead made herself a cup of tea.

The kitchen was a bit of a mess. The kitchen was, in fact, a lot of a mess. There was a huge pile of used tea bags on the edge of the sink, which had some mandarin peel in it. There were old newspapers and old tea towels. Empty frozen-food cartons, frozen-food cartons with a bit of lasagna still left in them, frozen-food cartons with a bit of lasagna and also a couple of old tea bags, some mandarin peel, and a cigarette butt in them. On the floor, beside the bulging kitchen garbage, there was a pile of pizza boxes. These would stay on the floor forever, because they would not fit in the garbage, even had it not been bulging. There were some moldy crumpets and a ketchup bottle that had all its ketchup on the outside. The floor needed sweeping, and the washing-up needed washing up.

It was not merely because she now lived alone that Flossie was living this dissolute existence. She had always been completely slack, domestically. But cigarette butts in the lasagna? A whole packet of chocolate biscuits for supper? Still in your nightie at eleven in the morning? Flossie feared that she was becoming a touch gross.

Sitting down with her cup of tea, Flossie decided that she really had to pull herself together. Of course, if Nathan were still around, he would have told her that. What's more, she would have been infuriated by his prissy attitude. She would have told him that the world would not come to an end just because a girl did not put her socks in the dirty clothes basket. Sometimes she had wanted to throttle him, the way his whole body had twitched with agony if she so much as made a ring with her coffee cup, or left the newspaper folded inside out, the way he seemed to follow her about with a damp cloth.

Now she felt differently; now she would have rather liked Nathan to be around to tell her what a state she looked. After all, it was not much fun looking a state if there was nobody there to tell you how beautiful you were, even when your hair was greasy. The bitter truth was that nobody was bothered whether Flossie looked a state or not. She could scum around the house all day in yesterday's underwear and an old nightie, and nobody would care. She could go naked if she wished, daubed only in cold

lasagna and fat scraped from the bottom of the frying-pan.
Flossie had only herself to please, and she hated it.

She decided that she needed to inject a little dynamism
into her life. She would pull herself together. She resolved
to have a bath, put on some proper clothes, eat a proper
breakfast, including fruit, and then do some work, which
in her case was dressmaking.

Just then, just at the very moment when Flossie had
definitely decided to get her life in order, pull herself together, and damn well get things sorted, the world came
to an end.

Midnight.

The Rat Run had started. That moment that had been
talked about for so many decades, around so many dinner
tables, and on so many talk shows had arrived. The dooms-
day clock that scientists had long used to illustrate the
Earth's close proximity with eco-Armageddon had finally
struck midnight.

Flossie first heard about it from her radio. People still
listened to the radio, despite the numerous technical innovations that, it was regularly announced, would supersede
it. Radio, despite being well into its second century, remained the only medium that one could enjoy while doing
other things. At the moment the Rat Run started, the other
thing that Flossie was doing was pouring another cup of
tea. This being the first part of the process of procrastinating, by which she would put off the moment when she
would begin getting her life in order, pulling herself together, and damn well getting things sorted.

The music that had been playing on the radio suddenly
stopped, and a stern voice announced an urgent news
flash, adding that all listeners should stand by for information of the utmost importance. Momentarily Flossie was
pleased. Here was justification indeed to put off pulling

herself together. The radio had actually told her to, and you couldn't get a much more official excuse than that. She sat down with her tea. Almost immediately the announcement came, and any sense of well-being that Flossie may have been harboring instantly left her. The news was truly and hugely terrible. The unthinkable had happened. The Rat Run was beginning.

It seemed that the mosquito infestations that had become such a familiar feature of the British summer had taken a dramatic turn for the worse. Years of exceptionally hot and wet weather, combined with ever-expanding swamplands and increasingly ineffective insecticides had produced breeds of skeeters with jaws like tigers, who could suck the sap out of a tree, massive, bodybuilding insects who drank DDT for breakfast and that one did not so much swat as wrestle. It used to be said that you could not get blood out of a stone; the truth was that these terrible airborne vampires probably could.

Now it seemed that they had decided to take over the Earth. The radio informed Flossie that there had been a sudden and catastrophic explosion in the insect population, and that they had swarmed. Vast clouds of virtually invulnerable bloodsucking monsters had appeared all over the northern hemisphere. It was a plague, similar in many ways to the plagues of locusts that crop up so regularly in the Bible, except whereas the locusts ate only crops, these mosquitoes ate people, a few drops at a time.

Within an hour or so, the announcement said, the Home Countries would belong to the insect world, soon all Britain and Europe. Therefore, it was suggested that everyone should get inside their Claustrospheres immediately and not come out until the following year, when the mosquitoes would have been destroyed by their own weight of numbers.

Flossie sat for a second as the message was repeated. She could not move, it was all too much. One second she was thinking about having a bath; the next, it's get in your

Claustrosphere for a year, or have all the blood sucked out of your body by billions of fist-sized mosquitoes. A siren outside in the street jolted Flossie into action. She went to her front door and saw an army truck, beside which stood an officer with a megaphone.

"Get in your Claustrospheres! Get in your Claustrospheres!" he shouted, as soldiers in protective suits rushed from door to door. One of them ran up the garden path of Flossie's little cottage.

"Haven't you heard?" the soldier shouted through his mask.

"Yes, but—" Flossie responded weakly.

"Then get in your bloody Sphere, you stupid cow! Quick! They'll be here in an hour! Norfolk's black with them, carpeted from the sea to the broads."

Flossie's next-door neighbor was at her door, nearly hysterical.

"But my husband's at the office!" she cried.

"Can't help that, madam," the soldier shouted. "He'll find a place in a municipal shelter all right. It's only a year, you can find each other then! Now get in your Claustrosphere!"

With that, the soldier ran on to the next house, where some of his comrades were helping an infirm old couple.

Feeling completely stunned, Flossie went back into her cottage, took up the half bottle of wine, and made her way into the backyard. She did not need the booze, there were plenty of drugs and dehydro wine in the Sphere, but she took it anyway. She tried to think of something else she might like to take, but couldn't. What was the point? The Claustrosphere was fully equipped, that was what it was for. The urgent commotion in the street was getting louder. Flossie could hear it even standing in the backyard.

"This is the last warning," the commotion said. "This environment will be lethal in approximately fifty-five minutes!"

Dressed in her nightie and slippers, Flossie went inside the Claustrosphere and closed the BioLock.

The black hole of Great Pew.

The geodesic shell of Flossie's Claustrosphere was non-transparent. All Claustrospheres were like that, the reason being that the outer surface of the dome was its energy source. Sunlight so dangerous that it could kill people was still a valuable source of solar power, and it was this solar fuel that made the BioCycle viable. There were not even any windows. So delicate were the ecological rhythms of existence within the dome, it was thought that the intrusion of a natural light cycle might imbalance the process. Besides which, no transparent material had yet been developed that could be guaranteed to filter all the harmful elements of naked sunlight. Many Claustrosphere psychologists argued that windows would be a bad thing anyway. They felt that, to the occupants, their Claustrosphere *was* their world, and to be able to look out at another might lead to their denying their new reality and failing to come to terms with their own world.

Therefore, once inside, Flossie was completely alone. Claustrospheres had no phones. The very fact of Bio-Sphere technology was based on the presumption that all life outside was over. Therefore, any factor that required maintenance, power, or organization from outside the Claustrosphere was, by its very nature, untenable. Some richer people had invested in expensive radio and solid-state land-line networks between small groups of friends, but any intrusion into the structure of the geodesic shell was frowned upon by the manufacturers. The whole principle worked on complete enclosure. A world apart. They refused to guarantee shelters in which the dome had been punctured. "Once you're in, you're in" was the cheerful slogan employed by the companies marketing the numer-

ous Claustrosphere accessories that ranged from Virtual
Reality sex-suits to worry beads. Flossie was in.

Now she knew how much she missed Nathan. She
missed him, to coin a phrase, with all her heart. In fact,
with all her heart and all of the rest of her body. She shook
with how much she missed him. She wept and she wept.
She was weeping when she realized that a light was flashing, and a recorded voice was speaking to her.

"Please activate LifeCycle immediately, please activate
LifeCycle immediately."

Flossie knew what that meant. She had to start the damn
thing up. Claustrospheres produced their own oxygen, and
if the occupant did not start the generation process within
approximately half an hour of closing the BioLock, the
available natural oxygen would be exhausted, and the occupant would suffocate.

Flossie seriously thought about ignoring the warning.
Why not? She was alone in a Claustrosphere! Alone, without Nathan, in the Claustrosphere that they had built together after endless debate and hand-wringing. True, it was
only for a year, but a year alone in a Claustrosphere? Could
she hack it? She looked around at the big TV screen and
the miniature rain forest that would be her only compan-
ions. She could not even turn the lights off because she
and Nathan had decided that they couldn't afford a nighttime cycle.

It was the thought of Nathan that made her turn on the
LifeCycle. If she loved him, and she knew now that she
did, she could wait a year. Where was he? she wondered.
In America; that was in the northern hemisphere, wasn't
it? Of course, it was. Would he make it into a Claustrosphere? He had faxed her a message to say that Plastic
Tolstoy himself had rented him a house off Sunset. It
would have a Claustrosphere, surely? Of course it would.
There was not a house in the U.S. without one. Flossie
tried to think of Nathan, sitting in some American Claustrosphere. She wondered if he was alone. She hoped not,

for his sake. Flossie found her own solitary prospects rather daunting. On the other hand, she rather hoped there wouldn't be any women with him. It could happen, if he had been forced to retreat into an L.A. municipal. He was a man with a development deal, possibly about to spend a year among secretaries, waitresses, and wannabe actresses. Flossie decided not to think about it.

The banging.

Flossie drank the rest of her wine and tried to adjust. She stood, she sat, she stuck an old film into the entertainment center. She could not settle, however, and the moments crept by. Without any light changes she had only the clock to tell her the time, and she was sure it was slow. She would look up at it, convinced that an hour had passed, to discover that only five minutes had gone by. Then only one minute. At this rate she felt it would not be long before time would stop altogether, and then she would never get out. What if time started to go backward? she asked herself. Would that mean that she could get out before she got in? Or would it only be going backward in her world? Would the world outside carry on without her? These were the thoughts of a woman all alone in the universe with only a bottle of wine for company. They were big thoughts, but they did not take long to think. Scarcely any time at all seemed to have passed.

The clock was getting slower. The silence was oppressive. After three or four hours, Flossie began to wish that she had not turned on the oxygen.

Then the banging started.

Flossie nearly jumped out of her skin. The banging was certainly worse than the silence. She should have been expecting it, of course, but somehow it had slipped her mind. There could be no doubt that this was the noise of those terrified, dying people trapped outside. Every Claustrosphere brochure warned of this development. It was obvious that there would be those who either did not have access to a Sphere, or who got caught too far away from home and, ignoring the public shelters, had tried to make it back. These were the people who were now hammering in terror upon Flossie's door. But she could not open it. The stern warning given out by the police and the Claustrosphere company alike was that, once you had closed your BioLock, under no circumstances should you open it again. If the poisons that were killing the desperate souls on the outside should once upset the delicate ecobalance on the inside, then no one would survive.

After about twenty minutes, Flossie could hardly stand it.

"Go away," she shouted. "I can't open it! You're not supposed to! I can't."

But she knew they could not hear her. The sound of a voice would not travel through the dome. The banging continued. Flossie could not bear to imagine the scene that was being played out in her own little backyard. Choking, dying people, gasping their last on her AstroTurf. It hardly seemed possible. Perhaps there were children? Some of the bangs seemed less hard than others. This thought was too much for Flossie, and she resolved to open the lock. She could not live with herself for a year, imagining the skeletons of tiny children clawing at her door outside. The little Eden Three that she and Nathan had bought could support four people, and she was only one. That was not right. Flossie felt that she must try and share, whatever the risk. Of course, the people outside might be a gang of adults, in which case she would perhaps die. She had no weapon, and if a desperate crowd wished to eject her, then there would not be much she could do about it. Nonetheless, she resolved to open the door. She could not in all conscience take up four Claustrosphere places while people, possibly children, died outside.

BioSting.

As Flossie opened the door of her BioLock, the police officers outside were just fixing a charge of dynamite with
which to blow it open. Claustrospheres were extremely
tough, but if you had the right explosives, you could get
into them.

"Good afternoon, Mrs. Hoddy," said the head constable.
"Glad you opened up. You're not supposed to, you know,
but it did save our ruining your Claustrosphere."

What had happened made the news worldwide. It was
a BioSting. A beautifully conceived and executed crime.
Great Pew was a very wealthy village. A couple of rock
stars had built studios in the surrounding manor houses,
and all the residents were London media people. The place
simply dripped with money. It was also very self-contained. There was only one road in and out, meaning that
a simple detour sign ensured privacy for at least at little
while.

The moment the residents of the village had been hur-
ried into their Claustrospheres, the thieves had removed
their army uniforms, switched off the radio jammer that
they had used to intrude on the local air waves, and
robbed all the houses. They were in and out in under an
hour; it took another two for anybody to notice anything
amiss; and it was midafternoon before the police began to
blast people out of their Spheres.

"What a beautiful idea," said Judy to himself when he
heard about it later. "I'm amazed that nobody thought of
it before."

17

The difference between Virtual Reality and actual reality

Delegation.

PLASTIC TOLSTOY MADE AT LEAST A HUNDRED MAJOR DECISIONS an hour. His colossal empire required a never-ending succession of split-second judgments. When he moved he had to move fast and he was always moving. This required delegation. Tolstoy was constantly giving orders. He was a general with a whole army of foot soldiers who scurried about the world, day and night, doing his will. He had development people, money people, management people, marketing people, and he was in virtual constant communication with all of them. Just occasionally, though, Plastic Tolstoy put them all on hold and gave orders to his killing people.

Boring door knockers.

The process of procrastination began anew. While Flossie was wandering around her Claustrosphere, Nathan was wandering around the nice little house off Sunset that Plastic Tolstoy had rented for him. He sat down at his computer console. He got up again. He walked around. Had a cup of coffee, played with himself. He flicked through the news input channels. Jurgen Thor had fully recovered from the explosions at the Euro parliament. Hitler's lawyers had pulled off a plea bargain whereby he admitted to the lesser offense of using intolerant and inflammatory language, and the court agreed to drop the six-million murder charges. He got a hundred hours' community service.

Eventually Nathan wrote something.

Scene one.

It was a start.

Then the procrastination began again. What style of computer font to employ? What type size? Word processing had increased the opportunities for writer procrastination considerably. Nathan was still playing around with his computer mouse fifteen minutes later, when the doorbell rang. He jumped up in delight. Here was a genuine diversion. Nathan had no idea who it might be, for he had told no one of his new whereabouts except Max, and of course Flossie in England, but it didn't matter. Anyone would do to get him away from his computer.

The world is full of quite awesomely boring people who knock on doors. Often they are religious zealots, sometimes political representatives, occasionally market researchers. Normally, the reaction that these sad door knockers provoke is one of brusque dismissal. Most people make it quite clear that they resent the intrusion on their privacy, and that they neither wish to be told what to think, nor asked what they think. Indeed, so thankless is the lot of the average boring door knocker that it is a mystery how they keep going. The truth, of course, is that every job, even door knocking, has its occasional rewards. Every now and then, not often, very rarely in fact, but sometimes, the boring door knocker knocks on the door of somebody who is pleased to see them. Somebody who, on being asked the question "Where will you be spending eternity?" will actually be prepared to give the matter some thought. Somebody who does not shout, "Rover, kill!!!" when faced with the announcement "Hi, we're talking with people today about faith." Somebody who is actually prepared to express an interest in current proposals to turn some parts of the north end of the south section of the main street into a no stopping zone. It is these seemingly generous, open-spirited souls who keep the boring door knockers going, for in them exists the great door knockers' illusion. The illusion that somebody out there appreciates them. Appreciates the fact that they have chosen to devote their lives to irritating other people with their fatuous prejudices or public-spirited obsessions. Alas, it is only an illusion. For the people who encourage them do so out of purely selfish reasons. For they are writers merely seeking further justification to procrastinate. Desperate people, every one, who would welcome a burglar into their homes as a happy diversion from having to sit down and do some work.

Welcome visitor.

Nathan was in for a pleasant surprise, for the person at the door was Max, which meant that he could put away the idea of work for the rest of the evening.

"I don't know, I just thought I'd come and say hi," Max said, walking in. "I know you're working, so I won't stay above a minute," he added, putting two six-packs of beer and a fifth of Jack Daniels on the coffee table.

"No, that's fine, stay as long as you like," said Nathan

eagerly. The arrival of a superstar definitely absolved him of all obligation to write. Particularly a superstar who was going to star in the film he was supposed to be working on.

"Nathan," said Max, cracking open the beer and the whiskey, "I've never felt like this before."

Max had been thinking about Rosalie. He just could not get the girl off his mind. Nathan was the only person he knew who had met her (unless you counted Tolstoy), so Max naturally gravitated toward him. Besides, Nathan too was unhappy in love; he understood how obsessive it was.

"I tried to get a lawyer in Dublin to send her a message, and it turned out that she'd escaped. Can you believe that? Already! What a woman. I just *have* to see her again."

"Even if you knew where she was, she doesn't want to see you. She said so."

"Girls say stupid things. All I have to do is find a really good reason to speak to her again. I need something to get back in her confidence. Like, if I could do something for her, you know? Like, if I could steal the plans to a nuclear plant or something and place them at her feet."

"They have all that stuff already, Max," Nathan said sympathetically. "That's part of Mother Earth's mystery, they're so well informed. I don't think there's much you can offer in the green stakes that would impress a girl like Rosalie."

"How about money? Supposing I got word to her that I wanted to fund all her bombs and shit?"

"They have money too," said Nathan. "You know that. Actually, it's the funding thing that our movie's going to be about."

There was an evangelical light in Nathan's eyes that Max had seen in the eyes of writers before. It meant that they were about to explain their idea.

"Nathan, I don't want to hear your movie idea right now. Please don't tell me about your idea."

"All right," said Nathan.

But he could not be stopped. Despite Max's protests and

efforts to get the conversation back on to the subject of Rosalie, Nathan explained his idea. It was understandable, really; he was far from over the excitement of being green-lighted by Plastic Tolstoy himself. When he had finished, Max could not help but nod with approval.

"It's neat," he said. "And you say Tolstoy liked it?"

"Well, at first I thought, not. The room seemed to simply reek of Brussels sprouts and gravy. Tolstoy went all thoughtful and didn't say a thing, which is a bit rare for him, you must admit. But it turned out he was just thinking about it, because he's told me to go ahead and write it."

"A full green light?"

"Absolutely, so I'm holed up here like a monk until it's done. No going out, no parties. I've only told you and Flossie I'm even here. . . ."

At the mention of Flossie, Nathan's face fell. He remembered that he had forgotten to remember that he was unhappy. Max could see what had happened and tried to cheer him up.

"Hey, looks like we're going to make a Tolstoy picture together, partner," he said, and they clinked glasses and drank. Then they did it again, and again, and for a moment they were both happy. Then the little devils that now lived inside both their stomachs reminded them both that to be happy when you are unhappy is a contradiction in terms.

They both sank back into love sadness and poured more drinks.

"She's so strong willed," they both agreed. "That's what I like about her, I suppose," they both assured each other. "Fucking women, eh?" They clinked glasses in a positive orgy of mutual understanding. The booze flowed.

"You know something, Nathan," Max slurred, "you are the greatest guy, you know that? I mean, do you *really* know that?"

"Listen, mate," the Englishman replied, "I love you; no, I mean it, I really do, I bloody love you, mate."

Where truth and fiction merge.

About two-thirds through the JD they decided to have a wrestle. This was not done in the old-fashioned method of grappling around on the floor and bear-hugging prior to being sick on the carpet. You did it via a Virtual Reality linkup that would even be sick for you if you liked. Max had picked up a couple of disposable helmets at a Hyper-Mart when he'd got the beer and whiskey.

"Let's fight it out, old pal," he said drunkenly, handing Nathan a helmet.

The game was called Trial of Strength, and it enabled a person to find out who was better at fighting, they or their friends, without getting hurt. What you did was put on a helmet that was linked to your opponent's. These helmets read the abilities of the people wearing them, and your pal's computerized likeness would become your adversary in a series of combat situations.

Half drunk, they shook hands, put the helmets on, and prepared to fight each other to the death from opposite easy chairs.

Inside the helmets they could both see two masked fighters facing each other. One was Max, the other Nathan. The first situation was unarmed combat. There was no contest; Max's hologram, imbued as it was with Max's strength and training, utterly pulverized Nathan's hologram, which was, of course, as wimpy as its controller. The Nathan figure thrashed about helplessly while the Max figure chopped it up, punching it, throwing it, stamping on its head.

From their respective easy chairs the two real people rocked with laughter at the thrashing that Nathan's thinkalike was receiving. The disparity in their abilities was so great it was comical. When the first round was over, a little voice inside the helmets announced that Nathan had better be better with a Ninja stick, or his ass was dead.

Nathan giggled, feeling for his drink in the real world, while inside the helmet his hologram picked up the unfamiliar weapon of two sticks connected by a chain. Max laughed, because it was clear how reluctant to fight the Nathan-hologram was. Max made his thinkalike demonstrate his powers with a stunning display of Ninja training, whirling and slashing the sticks about his head. They both roared with laughter and swigged at their drinks as Nathan's hologram did the only thing the real Nathan would have been capable of doing, which was to throw his sticks at the Max figure and launch a massive kick at its balls. The Max figure simply avoided the kick, spun around, and in a single sweeping movement hit Nathan's man so hard that the head was actually partially severed.

"Fuck! I bloody felt that," Nathan shouted out loud, laughing, although of course he could not hear himself inside the helmet.

"Looks like the English guy's a wimp," the little voice inside the helmet said. "Maybe he could use some firepower."

And inside the helmets the two holograms reappeared in a barroom situation, both armed with handguns. The two real men laughed as the Max figure raised his gun and fired. The Nathan figure shuddered with the impact and was propelled backward over a table and onto the floor behind. Max walked his hologram forward to finish the job as the Nathan hologram screamed. With one hand Nathan's figure grasped its wound, holding the other one up toward Max's figure, as if pleading with it to stop.

"These helmets are fantastic!" the real Max said into the real world. He was getting a genuine feeling of pain and panic from Nathan's figure. "Okay, kid, say a prayer," he said, shouting the way people do when they have earphones on.

Inside his helmet Max made his figure raise its gun as the wounded Nathan-hologram desperately tried to crawl away, whimpering in agony.

"You're really scared, aren't you?" Max laughed to himself. "Well, I can cure that." But as Max's hologram took aim, the prostrate Nathan figure shuddered horribly. It seemed to be convulsing and twitching with pain. Max laughed hugely at the writhing figure, took another pull at his whiskey, and poured computer-graphically generated fire into the hologram on the floor inside his helmet, finally putting it out of its misery.

"Eat lead death, limey redcoat colonialist scum," Max laughed. "That's for Yorktown. I'm a Yankee Doodle Dandy."

Then the holograms suddenly faded, and strange visions began to appear. There was a sudden wash of color, mainly deep red but with some purple in it, which seemed to fill the whole of Max's helmet. Max felt as if it almost filled his head. Half-formed images appeared and started to swirl about inside the color. Max could vaguely make out a woman's face and a little boy running, then a house. There were many much less clearly defined shapes. Max thought they might have been people, or perhaps animals . . . he could not make out for sure because all the time flashes of the harsh red and purple kept intruding on the vision. Max felt a great compulsion to understand the shapes, almost, he thought, to *remember* them, but he could not . . . the red kept getting in the way. A red that, although it filled Max's whole helmet, still managed to give the impression of being somehow jagged.

"Cool," Max murmured to himself, appreciative of the way the game makers had programmed such an intense and innovative graphics package with which to end the first part of the game.

The red wash began to throb. Max wondered if it was throbbing to the beat of his pulse; it rather felt that way. It was a sort of undulation, a very intense one, also very uncomfortable, but nonetheless extremely compelling. The jagged quality of the color intensified, as the woman and the other figures began to fade away. Max was sorry to see the shapes go. Although he had not understood them, they had felt very warm, nostalgic even. Max felt sad, he wanted to see them again. He knew that he could do this by simply restarting the program. And yet, somehow he felt that he couldn't, that the shapes or memories had gone forever, far beyond recall. As they faded away completely, Max felt an irrational sense of loss. Something was coming to an end. He knew, of course, that it was just the graphics program, but it felt like something much greater than that. Then, suddenly and with shocking violence, the face of Plastic Tolstoy burst into the helmet, the image one of blinding clarity. That is not to say that the face that filled Max's helmet and mind was a perfect likeness of Tolstoy, it just *was* Plastic Tolstoy. For a moment, the helmet almost seemed to *be* Plastic Tolstoy. But only for a moment . . . the face disappeared as quickly as it had come, but while it had remained, there had been a palpable sense of outrage inside the helmet. The Tolstoy face wasn't outraged itself; it was more that it was surrounded by outrage and suffused by it. Tolstoy and outrage seemed to be part of the same thought. Max felt the outrage inside himself, deeply and personally, also a sudden surge of furious anger. Then immediately after that, so quickly, in fact, as to be almost at the same time, the sadness returned, a kind of desperate, hopeless sadness that brought tears to Max's eyes, which he hoped would not short-circuit the helmet.

The red throbbing returned, but now it was faded and slow. It went from crimson to pink, and then, in a moment, it was gone altogether, although as it went Max felt again the face of the woman that he had seen when the display began. After that he knew that it was over.

"Intense, man. That was *weird*," said Max out loud.

He sat back in his chair and waited for the next combat situation, which was scheduled to be machine guns in a cityscape, although he doubted that anything could beat the display that he had just seen. Nothing more appeared, however, and the helmet informed Max that his opponent

had wimped out and was now disconnected, hence Max
was the champion.

With a whoop and a holler Max dragged off his helmet
and let his eyes readjust to the mundane reality of the
room. Nathan was not in his chair. Max presumed he must
be in the bathroom or something. He called out, but received no answer. Then he realized that he could smell
gunsmoke. He had smelled it inside the helmet and
thought it was part of the sensual graphics package. But it
was still there.

Then he saw Nathan's foot; it was poking out from behind the chair. He jumped up and ran across the room.
There behind the easy chair lay Nathan, facedown in a
pool of blood. Almost exactly as the hologram-Nathan
had been.

"Shit! I killed him," Max whispered, desperately trying
to unfuddle his brain. Max could see an exit wound at
Nathan's shoulder and an entry wound in the back of his
neck. Nathan had clearly been knocked over the chair by
a bullet in the chest and had been trying to crawl away
when the second bullet in the neck had killed him.

Actual reality.

Max sat for a while thinking. Sobering up and thinking.
He had not killed Nathan; Virtual Reality was not actual
reality. Nathan had been alive when he had put the VR
helmet on, and he was dead now. Max had not moved
from his chair in that whole time. At first he was tortured
with vague fears that somehow, in the heat of the game,
he had in some way managed to get hold of a real gun and
had instinctively fired it. But there was no gun, and besides, Max had certainly not pursued Nathan across the
room and shot him in the neck.

Max knew that there was only one explanation. Nathan
had been murdered while playing the VR game. The mur-

derer, or murderers, had entered the house while Max and Nathan were preoccupied inside their helmets, and Nathan had been killed without ever removing his. He had not seen the murderers. He had died not knowing who had killed him, or why.

Max could remember the way the hologram had writhed and shuddered. That must have been the computer attempting to transmit an image of the thoughts Nathan was having while being shot and propelled backward over the couch. Then the holographic figure of Nathan had jerked and slumped, which was clearly the computer's mind picture of Nathan being shot a second time while blindly and desperately crawling away. It was then that Max had made his hologram fire imaginary shots into Nathan's hologram to finish the game.

After that had come the visions. Those were the thoughts that Nathan's helmet had been transmitting, and which Max's helmet had attempted to visualize, after Nathan had been shot in the neck. At that point, the killers, whoever they were, must have known that Nathan was breathing his last.

Max had actually watched a computer graphic representation of Nathan's mind as he had died.

18

Reading a dead man's mind

New recruit.

ROSALIE SAT LOOKING AT JUDY. THEY WERE IN THE CELLAR OF A
Mother Earth safe house on the outskirts of Dublin.

"So how do I know you're not an FBI plant?" she
inquired.

"Do I look like an FBI agent?" replied Judy, who was
quite capable of using his nerdiness to his advantage, if it
suited him. One of the few genuine perks of being a member of an oppressed minority is that you can choose when
and when not to play the card. One minute, objecting to
being defined by one's religion, race, or whichever orifice
you choose to take it up. Then the next minute, claiming
special debating rights at dinner parties on the very same
grounds. Sometimes this trick can actually be pulled off
in the space of a single sentence.

"As a Buddhist cat-sodomizer, I deeply resent the way
you seem to constantly categorize people by their religion
or sexuality."

Hence Judy, who had spent his life challenging the idea
that wimpy-looking people are crap, was now attempting
to turn this prejudice to his advantage. Unfortunately for
Judy, Rosalie did not suffer from quite such knee-jerk prejudices as most of his colleagues.

"You got me away from the airport," she remarked.
"Awfully impressive, I thought. Maybe you really do turn
into Superman when you get in a phone booth."

"Look, I've told you, I'm a clerk with the Bureau, I have
been for fifteen years. I do the green stuff. . . . Other clerks
cover commies and God-botherers, I do green. I'm the guy
who writes your diary. I know about everything Mother
Earth ever did, and why you do it. Like, how about this?
You remember the guy you knew as Shackleton? You cut
a transmitter out of his arm in the middle of Death Valley
before you hit DigiMac? I briefed him. All the environmental stuff he knew? I told him."

Rosalie sat silent. She was of two minds about this fellow.
Not so her colleague Saunders, who was pacing about behind
Judy. He wanted none of this inconvenient little American.

"Look, I don't know why we're even talking to this
bloke, right?"

Saunders was a tough Liverpudlian who wore a bag over
his head after having lost his face through radiation exposure. Saunders claimed that the exposure had been so bad
that he could not have his face replaced, due to the need
for constant treatment. There was, however, some suspicion among other Mother Earth activists who knew Saunders well, that he had rather got to like carrying such
gruesome battle scars.

"He might be straight, he might be a plant, right?" the
Liverpudlian stated. "Either way we'll never be sure, so
let's dump him now."

"If you dump me I'll get picked up in hours, and I'll do
fifteen years minimum for saving your team boss here from
twenty-five to thirty in a U.S. jail," Judy said angrily. "Listen, I didn't plan this, I just did it. They sent me over

here with the actual agent to ensure Rosalie Connolly's identification. Like I say, I'm the expert on you guys. Well, I've been thinking about changing sides for years. . . . For Christ's sake, I know more about how close we are to eco-Armageddon than even you people do."

Judy paused to consider the reaction he was provoking. Saunders was openly hostile; Judy could not tell about Rosalie. One thing was certain, though. Like Max before him, Judy would be very glad when those fierce green eyes were drilling holes in somebody else.

He persevered.

"You can't look at what's happening to the planet every day like I have to without being affected. Eventually, you get to thinking that maybe you're on the wrong side. . . . Ever since I heard they were going to pull Ms. Connolly here in for the DigiMac hit, I'd been kind of feeling bad about it, and when they put me on the assignment . . . Well, I didn't know what I'd do, but in the end what I did was drug the same agent stupid in his hotel and pick you up myself. And that's it, I'm a criminal now. I can't go back, and I don't want to. I want to join you, I'm switching sides, and I reckon I've earned a place in your team."

"Earned a place!" Saunders shouted, his big fists clenched in anger. "*Earned* a place! Jesus Christ, you don't earn a place with us typing letters for the FBI. I'll show you how you earn a place with us, mate!" And with that, Saunders whipped the bag off his head to reveal his complete absence of face. The man's eyes bulged out of the livid pink flesh, his teeth stood forward, stark within the lipless hole that had been a mouth.

Judy would have liked to have greeted this sudden revelation with a cool and steady stare. He nearly pulled it off. Apart from being instantly and hugely sick, he showed almost no emotion whatever. It wasn't that Judy was particularly squeamish—he had seen many shocking things in his time as an agent—it was just the shock. Judy had presumed that Saunders was wearing a mask for security reasons, and to be suddenly presented with what was to all intents and purposes a living skull was something of a surprise.

"Ha! Wants to fight with us!" Saunders sneered. "The man's been sick on his shirt."

"Oh, for heaven's sake, Saunders!" said Rosalie. "You really are the limit sometimes. Now put your bag back over your head and shut up, or I'll have you counting dead seabirds in the Shetland Isles."

Saunders, although a decent enough chap at heart, was a colossal embarrassment to Rosalie and indeed her whole unit. He seemed to see the entire environmental destruction of the Earth as nothing more than global justification for him to stamp about the place, proving how tough he was. It was very difficult to sack a person, though, who had given their face for the cause. Besides which, Saunders was a dedicated and brave fighter, and that had to be respected. Still, Rosalie was not going to be overconcerned when he got himself shot, as he inevitably would sooner or later, being such a complete lunatic.

"Look," said Judy, after he had cleaned up the vomit a bit. "I know one hell of a lot about your organization. I also know plenty about the FBI and its attitude toward you. I think I can be of use. Besides which, as I say, I rescued you, Ms. Connolly."

Rosalie studied Judy for a long time. Judy thought to himself that just because she could go for ages without blinking, it did not intimidate him, but this was not true.

Finally she said, "If you're lying to me, I shall find out, and I shall definitely kill you."

"And I'll kill you as well," said Saunders, which completely ruined the effect.

Telephone voice.

The phone rang, jerking Max out of his reverie. He had been sitting deep in thought for a long time. All the whiskey was gone, but Max could not remember finishing it.

Nathan's Ansafone clicked into action. Max listened briefly to the voice of the dead writer. Ansafones had been around since before anybody still alive had been born, and yet people still felt the need to offer the age-old instruction "nobody's in, leave a message," etc. Max had never realized quite how English Nathan sounded, except, of course, that this was just his telephone manner. The English always adopted a telephone manner, Max thought. As it happened, so did Max, except that instead of effecting a more "proper" voice, like Nathan, he instinctively tried to appear laid back. His own Ansafone message was a low growly drawl, sounding as if nothing really mattered and life was something of a drag anyway.

"Uh . . . Hi, yeah . . . Okay, it's the machine, right? But you knew that. Listen, um . . . leave a message, don't leave a message . . . live, die, it's all the same dream, right? . . . Bye." And you can't get much more telephone-mannered than that.

It was a woman on the phone. Her voice followed Nathan's recording. It was another English voice, but lighter and more relaxed than Nathan's rather stilted message.

"Nat," the voice said. "Nat, it's me."

And Max knew that he was listening to Nathan's gorgeous and unobtainable Flossie.

"Look . . . I don't know, I think we should talk. I got all your letters, but I haven't rung before because I've been thinking a lot. . . . You know, about us. . . . Something happened today, it was just so weird, anyway I want to . . . Oh hell, look, I'm not going to discuss it with your bloody machine . . . but phone me . . . soon . . . I really do think we should talk. Bye." There was a pause and then, softly . . . "I love you, Nat. Glad you still love me."

Well, irony did not get much more painful than that. If the poor dead bastard behind the chair could have just stayed alive another hour he would have got his girl back.

On the other hand, Max reflected, three months from now he'd probably have been just as annoyed about the underwear on the bathroom floor as he'd ever been.

Chasing girls.

Max decided to leave. He was very sorry for Nathan, but there was nothing he could do for him now. It was best to get out. With the exception of the murderers, who were unlikely to come forward, Max was the only person who knew that anyone beside Nathan had been at the house that evening. Max would just walk away. He had no desire to get caught up in the police investigation. Besides which, he was going back to Ireland. He had something to tell Rosalie.

Max had decided that Plastic Tolstoy had ordered Nathan's murder. His reasoning was clear. Nothing had been stolen, and Max, who had been in the room when the attack happened, had been spared. Whoever it was, wanted to kill Nathan Hoddy and Nathan Hoddy alone. No implications—like dead movie stars—just an unknown, unattached British writer, dead, a long way from home. They knew what they wanted to do, they had done it and left. But who had sent them? It had to be Tolstoy. Nathan had only moved into the house the previous day, no one even knew he was there. All he had done since returning to Hollywood was pitch his idea to the great man.

His idea! That had to be the key. Nathan must have stumbled upon the truth! It was the only explanation for his swift, clinical dispatch. Max pondered the story that Nathan had forced upon him only a few hours earlier. He had not really listened very hard, because writers telling you their ideas is generally a pretty dull experience. He remembered the basic point, though . . . it was such a wild idea he could scarcely forget it. The idea that the Claustrosphere Company was funding green terrorism. This was the thesis that Nathan had pitched to Plastic Tolstoy and that Tolstoy clearly did not wish to see developed. This was the thesis that, Max believed, had killed Nathan.

Max knew that he was not the first person to draw this conclusion either. In his final moîtal moment, Nathan had instinctively guessed at the identity of the man who had ordered his death. It was Plastic Tolstoy's image that had come in fury into Nathan's mind and that had from there found its way into Max's helmet. Outrage at Tolstoy had been Nathan's last thought on Earth, excepting for perhaps a fleeting sadness, when Flossie had reentered his mind at the point of extinction.

There was only one conclusion to be drawn from this. Nathan's idea was more than fantasy. Max could not imagine why, but the Claustrosphere Company was funding Mother Earth. Rosalie was in Tolstoy's pay.

Max wished he had not drunk so much. His head was spinning with the size of his suspicions. It was madness. Even Max, who had little time for current affairs, knew that if Mother Earth could close down every Claustrosphere in the world then it would do it in an instant. It would blow them all to bits, and kill the people who made and sold them. For Claustrosphere to fund Mother Earth was like the chickens feeding the fox.

Max was suddenly filled with a sense of purpose, which was a strange sensation for him. A point seemed to have arisen in what was becoming an increasingly pointless life. The old drunk, silly, dilettante Max was being replaced by a new Max, a Max who wanted to know what Tolstoy and Claustrosphere were up to and why Nathan had had to die. A Max who, more than ever, wanted to talk to Rosalie. He had been looking for a reason to see her again, now he had one. How would she react to his suspicions? Could she possibly know already? Of course not, she hated Claustrospheres more than anything, all Mother Earth people did.

Max knew that he had to disappear. He could not be

sure how Plastic Tolstoy would react to the news that he had been at Nathan's house on the night when the murderers had done their bloody deed. Would the killers have recognized him under the helmet? He did, after all, have a very fine and distinctive chin. All in all, Max decided that he would like to be away from Hollywood for a while. Ireland seemed as good a place as any.

Except for the fact that he had, of course, only thirty-six hours earlier, been ignominiously ejected from that country and had his visa revoked.

Max was thinking straighter than he had done in nearly a decade. Before leaving Nathan's house, he took Nathan's passport from where it lay on the desk. He also brought a knife from the kitchen and gently scraped a little of the congealed blood from the corpse's neck into a small envelope. He did not like doing it. No amount of Virtual Reality blood had prepared him for the real thing—it was much stickier for a start. However, he had no choice. He had to get past passport control, and he intended to use a trick that had been employed by a character he had recently played. Max hoped it would not turn out to be just the stuff of fiction.

Lost in L.A.

Max drove home and raided his makeup box for a few small items of disguise: facial hair, nose putty, latex. Max was rather proud of still owning his own makeup box, despite enjoying the services of the best facial synthesizers in the business. Like all actors, when he wasn't dwelling on how wonderful and different being an actor was, Max liked to think of himself as nothing more than a worker, an artisan who did an honest day's labor for an honest day's two or three million dollars.

"It's a craft, that's all," he would say, "and these are the tools of the trade."

As it happened, the only time Max ever used his makeup box was when he wished to avoid being recognized, which, since he was an actor, was not very often. However, as he ordered a cab to take him out to the airport, Max felt that on this occasion some effort at disguise would be sensible.

This was not because he was fearful that the holographic photograph in Nathan's passport would give him away, but merely because he knew that he had to travel incognito. Nobody ever looked at the photos on passports anymore; the DNA cellular print was foolproof. The traveler inserted his or her passport into a scanner followed by the forefinger of either hand. The machine then took a single-cell-thickness laser scrape from the finger and checked that the DNA from the scrape matched that listed on the passport. The system could not be cheated, unless, of course, a passenger happened to have an envelope full of dried blood belonging to the person from whom he had stolen the passport, in which to dip his finger before sticking it into the machine.

The cab took nearly five hours to reach the airport. This was not because Max instructed the driver to dawdle, or visit the low dives and houses of ill-repute, but simply because that was how long it took for the man to stumble upon the correct destination. London is the only city in the world that really takes its taxi driving seriously, and considers it a genuine profession for which a person must be trained. All other cities treat the art of people-moving with various degrees of contempt, ranging from mild to utter. In Los Angeles it goes beyond that. It is almost as if being completely lost all the time is a qualification for the job.

In truth, the only actual job qualification to be a cab driver in most cities is being able to drive (sort of). If you can drive a car, you can drive a cab. That's it, no special skills are required. In L.A., people often take up the profession on their first day in town, simply in order to get in from the airport. It's a curious situation; no other profession takes such a relaxed view as to what is required to enter its ranks. The fact that a person is able to work a stove does not mean they can readily find employment as a chef. Most people are capable of lifting a scalpel and, no doubt, would be equally capable of plunging it into somebody else's flesh, yet this is not generally considered sufficient justification for allowing them to practice as surgeons. But cab driving insists on no such niggling restrictions. If you've got a car and can turn it on, then you're off.

By luck, endless references to the map, appeals for help over the radio, and shouted suggestions from passersby, Max's driver eventually managed to get him the six miles from one of L.A.'s premier residential districts to the airport. Max always gave cab drivers the same tip.

"You're in America," he said and entered the departure hall.

Into Africa.

The passport trick worked at LAX, and after the rigors of the cab ride, Max hoped that he was finally on his way. Unfortunately, the flight took a little longer than expected. It was a suborbital, which normally involved a vertical takeoff, a brief suspension in the stratosphere while the Earth spun beneath it, followed by direct dropdown to your destination: two hours on the schedule. But as Max's flight commenced its descent into Dublin, it got hit by a pressure drop and blown out of alignment.

This sort of thing happened all the time. The weather hadn't been right since they replaced all the real forests with acidic little fern numbers. Billions of Christmas trees just didn't get the job done. Areas of high and low pressure drifted all over the place, and the average conventional flight was punctuated by more altitude variations than a roller coaster. Passengers would, without warning, find their planes dropping thousands of feet in seconds, causing their backsides to shoot upward and hit the compartments above them. Some aeronautical experts claimed that there had been instances where terrified passengers had actually managed to crap on top of their own heads.

Anyway, a huge squall over Europe meant that nothing was landing for a while, and Max's flight got diverted into North Africa to wait out the weather. It was a bad day to land in Addis, Ababa. Sensational news had just been leaked. The locals had discovered that the vast debt-funded constructions to the north of the city, which, it had been popularly presumed, were hospitals, power plants, and food research centers, were nothing of the kind. What had in fact been built was a vast armored Claustrosphere complex, into which the government and its business friends would scurry should the Rat Run ever occur.

This type of centralized Claustrosphere "town" was becoming increasingly common in the poorer countries of the world. Countries where there was no question of universal ecocover, but still plenty of rich and powerful people around who didn't want to die. Obviously, in the event of Earth death, isolated elite ecoshelters would be extremely vulnerable to terrified dying people. The answer was, of course, collective security.

The Ethiopian president had tried to reason with the angry crowds. He had been disarmingly frank.

"Come on!" he said, his voice full of genuine surprise. "What's the problem? Some of us are rich, some of us are poor. What's new? I've got a car, you haven't. I've got enough food, you haven't. That's always been the case; it didn't make you riot then. Why riot now? It's bloody obvious that anybody who can afford a Claustrosphere is going to get one. Just the way anybody who can afford decent housing and medical care has always got it. There's no difference. What's all the fuss about?"

It was a powerful argument. The furious masses paused for thought, and the president pressed home his point.

"Besides which, the honkies and the Japs won't lend us

any money unless we use it to buy their products. Well, we don't want any more dams, do we? The ones we've got turned the country into desert. We've got enough guns and helicopter gunships, surely? So I bought Claustrospheres. What did you want me to do? Turn *down* the money! Say no to billions and billions of dollars and ECUs and yen? Are you stupid or something?"

The disturbances did not actually reach the airport where Max's suborbital was waiting. The populations of the poor countries had been so decimated by decades of ever-encroaching land death that there weren't that many of them left to riot, and those who did were not overfit. In the latter parts of the twentieth century, world leaders had been greatly worried about what they saw as the ever-increasing population. They predicted that pretty shortly there would be tens of billions of people wandering about the world wondering why they should be the ones who were starving to death. Great barriers were erected in anticipation of the day when the majority of the world's population would arrive uninvited at the door of the minority of the world's population and ask to stay for dinner. The Mediterranean Sea became a battle line, all guns facing south. The Panama Canal was similarly armed, as were the Ural Mountains and the borders of the nations of the Pacific rim. In the end, however, the problem never arose. Deforestation, salination, and desert growth provided a solution. As large areas of the Earth died, so did the population who had lived upon it. The much feared south-north population shift withered on the vine.

Scenic route.

When Max finally arrived in Dublin, he hired a car and drove straight out of the city, heading northwest.

He had, of course, only the vaguest idea of where he was going. If only he had taken a little more notice of the journey he had taken with Rosalie in the back of the Garda truck. On that occasion, however, Rosalie's stare had absorbed his entire attention, and his one clear memory of the trip was a pair of fierce green eyes drilling into his soul. Beautiful and splendid though those eyes were, they were of little use as a landmark, and Max had little else to go on. The only thing he could remember for sure was that Ruth and Sean's cottage was about three hours' drive from Dublin, and that the route ended in a dirt track.

Sitting in the plane on the tarmac at Addis, Max had tried to get his thoughts together. He made a rough guess that the police convoy would have averaged about thirty-five or forty miles an hour over the entire journey, which suggested a distance of between 110 and 120 miles from the city. Max had studied the map of Ireland that he found among the perfume ads at the back of the unbelievably dull airline magazine. Ireland was a fairly small place, and it was clear that unless the Garda had driven by an extremely tortuous route, which seemed unlikely, Max's goal lay on either the west coast or in the southwest of the country. He knew he could dismiss the north, because it had been the Garda who had arrested him, not United Nations forces. Due to the powerful Irish Catholic lobby in Congress, all Americans, even party animals like Max, knew that the UN kept the peace in Northern Ireland, or attempted to, and had for decades.

Taking up the little vanity bag with which he, as a first-class passenger, had been presented, with compliments of Aer Lingus Orbital, Max removed the drawstring. Using the scale on the enclosed map (one inch to thirty miles), he measured the string to approximate the 120-miles radius that he guessed would be the area of his search. Then, tying a pen to one end of the string and pressing the other end onto Dublin with his thumb, Max drew a semicircular line on the map. The line ran approximately from Sligo in the northwest of Eire, down through Galway and then Limerick, ending up in Cork on the south coast. Max resolved to begin at Sligo and weave his way down the country along this line, in the hope that he might pick up a clue or landmark that he recognized.

At the airport, a nice Avis car-rental lady asked Max where he was off to.

"Sligo," he replied, suddenly feeling rather daunted by the task he had set himself. Certainly, Ireland was small compared to the U.S.A., but it was pretty big compared with one not very large person. For a little while Max's spirits drooped, and as he negotiated Dublin's urban sprawl he pondered whether he might not be on something of a fool's errand. He did not even know whether Rosalie was still in the country . . . she was on the run, after all, and he himself had met her in California. On the other hand, Max was pretty certain that if she wasn't in Ireland, her grandparents would know where she was.

Once he got away from the city, Max felt better. The bulk of the countryside still operated under "daytime," on account of the European-funded orbital sunscreen, and despite the ravages of acid rain, the landscape still looked green and blooming. What's more, the winds coming in off the stewlike Atlantic created a real (albeit false) impression of fresh air. Max, who had lived all his life in a riot-torn super city, had scarcely realized that real green pastures existed anywhere outside of old movies.

"Now this is cool and indeed righteous," he said to himself as he drove along with the roof down. Had he happened to have a Geiger counter, he might have felt differently. But what the eye doesn't see, the heart doesn't grieve over, not until fist-sized tumors start popping up all over it, anyway.

Having arrived at Sligo and wandered around the bay for a while, Max headed off slowly toward Galway. He did not really know what he was looking for as he traversed hither and thither along the little roads of West Ireland. He hoped that perhaps something he saw might trigger some recognition. At first, he had presumed that people who looked as disgustingly old as Rosalie's grandparents would be pretty notorious, but as he drove through village after village he realized that craggy faces and hairy ears seemed to be quite fashionable that year among the more mature citizens.

Suddenly, though, Max no longer felt in any particular hurry. Despite all the global disturbances that had become a part of daily life on Earth, there was something about this part of the world that soothed the soul. It was possible to relax among the ancient villages and hills. Max discovered new delights, like lunch, for instance. Max could not remember the last time he had eaten lunch, merely for the simple and private pleasure that could be got from it. In Max's world, lunch was a thing with which you cloaked your real intentions; getting laid, getting a job, firing a close friend. To rediscover the delight of lunching *alone* was a pleasure indeed. To be simply sitting with some bread, cheese, and pickle, pondering the trivia quiz on the back of a beer can was a genuine thrill. The pace of life was so much slower than in L.A., although Max wondered whether in the long run any less actually got done. Probably, he thought, which was a very good thing.

Of course, not everything about the Irish countryside is so relaxing or idyllic. Socially, things can sometimes get a little more pressurized. It is not so relaxing in this quiet world if you happen to want an abortion, or a divorce, or to screw somebody other than your lawful spouse and perhaps adopt a position other than the missionary. Max fell into none of these categories as he meandered from one gorgeous view to another. Certainly, he would have liked to have screwed Rosalie, and in any and every position she cared to favor. However, since he was not in a position to do this, he confined himself to drinking, eating, and enjoying the scenery, and, hence, was made welcome wherever he went. This was Max's kind of country. You could get a pint of beer in a post office, and the licensing laws merely served to confirm the Irish reputation for writing good fiction.

"What time do you close?" Max had inquired on his first evening in Galway.

"Well, we close on the dot of midnight," the landlady had replied, "but you'll be all right for a drink until three or four."

The pub lock-in is a grand old tradition in rural Ireland, which the Garda often seem to see as their duty to protect. As Max was shown out of the back via the cabbage garden, he wondered whether he might not have found his spiritual home.

19

Sexual situations

Rendezvous.

IN THE END IT WAS NOT MAX WHO FOUND ROSALIE, BUT, AS BEFORE, she who found him. Gossip travels fast in the country, and on Max's fourth day back in Ireland, Rosalie's grandparents heard word that a rich, mad American was driving from village to village, asking about an old couple called Ruth and Sean who had great taste in vegetables. They, of course, guessed who it must be and sent word to Rosalie.

She found him in a bed and breakfast in County Cork.

"Will you get up now, Mr. Kennedy?" (for such was the name Max was traveling under) "It's half past eight already and there's a young person to see you."

The voice of his landlady brought Max struggling to consciousness, and it was a struggle, for this was a big hangover. He conducted his usual morning reconnaissance, moving his tongue about to see what he had slept in. Crisp, fresh, linen. Not bad, he thought. A sheet, that sounded hopeful. Then a worrying idea occurred to him. Maybe it was a shroud. No, it couldn't be a shroud, he was facedown, they don't bag you facedown, surely, not in a Catholic country. No, Max decided, he definitely wasn't dead, although he felt as if he *had* died and was now being unceremoniously dug up. He tried to recall where he was, and more importantly where he had been. A linen sheet, that must mean a bed. Slowly it all began to come back to him. The fiddler and the guy with the weird drum that you hit with both ends of the same stick . . . the singing, his spirited rendition of "Yankee Doodle Dandy" . . . the eight pints of Murphy's and eight Paddy chasers. That's right, he was in Cork, and he was looking for a beautiful girl.

"What in the name of goodness have you come back for! Shouting about my granny and grandad all over the bloody country? I ought to shoot you where you sleep, that I should, you stupid American bastard."

That beautiful soft lilt. Music, even on a hangover. He'd found her.

Rosalie walked into the bedroom and closed the door behind her. The landlady had been slightly scandalized about letting her go up, but short of physically restraining Rosalie, there was not a lot she could do. Max turned over under the quilt to face her as Rosalie drew back the curtains. The light was blinding.

"Please, you'll rupture my pupils," Max protested, grabbing for a pair of shades. Rosalie threw open the windows.

"Jesus, the stink of booze in here is disgusting." She stared down at him with a pitying expression.

"You still mad at me?" Max inquired.

"Of course I'm still mad at you. Gracious, you make me think you've saved me from the cops, and then it turns out you've completely messed it up. Wouldn't any girl be angry?"

But despite herself Rosalie could not restrain a smile. He did look cute, she thought, lying there in bed, blinking behind his shades like a startled rabbit. The fact that she had so far escaped prison had rather softened Rosalie's attitude to Max's disastrous attempt to help her elude the Garda. He had *tried,* after all.

"My God, the state of it," she continued. "Can it think? Can it talk?"

Max found her tone a little patronizing and felt the need to assert himself.

"Excuse me, but it takes more than eight pints of stout and eight Paddy's Scotches to leave me without the use of my faculties."

He had said the wrong thing. The process of European Federation had quickened the already relentless pace of cultural conformity, and Rosalie was big on maintaining Irish icons.

"Paddy's is not a Scotch, you ignorant philistine. Paddy's is an Irish. Scotch is Scotch and Irish is Irish, and if you can't tell the difference, then you should stick to whatever foul designer poisons they call drinks in Hollywood."

"Well, pardon me and six Hail Marys."

Max lit a cigarette. One of the smaller ironies of the complete degradation of the environment had been the revival in the fortunes of the tobacco companies. It was extremely difficult for health experts to get overconcerned about the long-term prospect of lung cancer when the mere fact of breathing was giving people respiratory disorders. Besides which, lung cancer held few fears for anyone with even a modest income, since a new lung could be bought virtually for the price of installation. The development of "zipper surgery," plus the fact of millions upon millions of people starving around the world, had meant that the price of "dual organs" (i.e., those of which the body is supplied with two) had dropped to a pittance. Solo items had, of course, maintained their price. It is difficult to persuade even a desperate person to part with their heart. A human kidney, however, could often be obtained more cheaply than properly force-fed duck liver.

"You've no idea how revolting that cigarette smells,

mixed up with the foul fug you seem to produce naturally."

"Listen, it's morning, I've been drinking for days. If I smelled good it would be weird."

Rosalie decided to let it go.

"I asked you why you were here."

"Well, it's partly social, you know? I thought we were starting to have fun."

Rosalie let this go. "And the other part?" she inquired.

"It's kind of connected with what we were talking about before," said Max.

"I've told you," Rosalie snapped, "I wouldn't get involved in your stupid pal's stupid film script if you were to—"

"Nathan is dead," Max interrupted, rather expecting the drama of the situation to pull Rosalie up somewhat.

"Who's Nathan?" Rosalie replied, spoiling the drama.

"He's my stupid pal. The one who hid under the table at your granny's place."

"Oh," said Rosalie. "Well, what's that got to do with me?"

It was not that Rosalie was a callous person, but she had seen many things die, and she could scarcely even remember what the film writer had looked like.

"Just before he was killed, he pitched a screenplay concept to Plastic Tolstoy. I think Tolstoy had him killed because of what that concept was."

"I heard that film was a cutthroat business," said Rosalie dryly.

"Nathan was going to base his story on the idea that it is the Claustrosphere Company who secretly funds Mother Earth."

During the previous few days, Max had often wondered how Rosalie would take this idea. He had feared that she would laugh right in his face. Had she done so, he had planned to take her through his reasoning, explaining how Nathan had died, how only Tolstoy could possibly have arranged it, how only Tolstoy had heard Nathan's idea, how Tolstoy had been the object of the final, furious thoughts in Nathan's life. But Rosalie was not laughing. She was thinking. A bell was ringing somewhere far away in her memory. A bell that she did not wish to answer.

"Sounds awful stupid to me," she said, but hesitatingly. "I wouldn't pay to see a thick film like that."

Max could see that he had hit a nerve.

"What's so stupid, Rosalie? Nobody knows who backs you. It's been thirty, even forty years. You'd think somebody would have taken credit by now, wouldn't you?"

Pick up.

Rosalie was remembering a night five years previous. A night she had spent with Jurgen Thor. . . .

She was twenty and had joined Natura two years before that, after failing to turn up for her first lecture at Trinity College. It was not long before her qualities of courage and intelligence were noticed, and she had been discreetly recruited into Mother Earth. There followed a grueling eighteen months of training, toward the end of which she had met the great man.

She and fifteen other trainee combat activists were attending a secret political briefing at which Jurgen Thor was speaking, and he picked her up; it was as simple as that. There were seven young women in the group. Thor had chosen her, and she had let him. She hated to admit it, but her role in it had been that passive. The moment Thor entered the room he was clearly deciding which of the girls he was going to screw, and he had picked her. All women know when they're being looked over, and Jurgen Thor made virtually no attempt to cover it. As the world's premier environmentalist, he was often accused of wearing his heart on his sleeve. Anyone who had ever met him knew that it was another organ altogether.

Rosalie was rather irritated by this casual, arrogant sexuality, and when, after the briefing, one of Thor's aides told her that the boss would like to see her, every instinct said she should tell him to stuff it. But she didn't. She was completely thrilled. Jurgen Thor was the Green God. The man to whom all environmentalists looked for leadership and inspiration. The one person with the authority to face down the world's leaders and get things done. Ever since she was a girl, Rosalie had admired Jurgen Thor above all people. She had also, like millions of other women, wondered what it would be like to make love to him. She still wondered. He was the strongest, most handsome man she had ever seen, and even though he came on like sleaze, he still had more sex going for him than a brothel on Watership Down. Rosalie did not normally fancy big men, but Jurgen Thor was not just big, he was magnificent.

And so, when her weekend leave came up, instead of going home to Ireland to see her grandparents as she ought to have done, Rosalie flew with Thor in a Natura helicopter to his magnificent home in the Swiss Alps. A home perched on a cliff so high it actually still had snow and ice upon it, despite the disappearance of such stuff elsewhere in the mountains.

Icy passion.

The stairway down from the rooftop helipad led straight into Jurgen Thor's bedroom, where a bottle of schnapps was warming over a candle. Rosalie was utterly knocked out. It was a room of such splendid sexiness, just being in it could have dropped the drawers on a concrete nun. The room occupied the entire top floor of the house, and every wall was glass. For 360 degrees all that could be seen was mountain range. The huge snowy white bed stood dead in the center of the room, and from there it was possible to make love on top of the world.

"I do not bring many women here, yes?" Jurgen Thor had said. "This place is very special to me."

"I'm not surprised," Rosalie had replied, looking about in awe.

Jurgen was an expert. He enfolded Rosalie in his arms and seemed almost to kiss her clothes off. At least, she could not remember his unbuttoning her blouse, taking off her shoes, or undoing her trousers, and yet there she was, lying on that huge bed in her underwear as Jurgen Thor knelt beside her, looking down and smiling. Even on his knees he towered above her.

"Jurgen, you'll take it easy, won't you? . . . I'm new to this."

"It is perhaps . . . the first time?" Jurgen inquired gently. Rosalie did not reply, and Jurgen knew that it was.

"There is no need for the worrying, please," he assured her calmly. "For me there is only pleasure in the pleasure of the woman. I make love to make women happy. That is the only reason I do it."

He meant it too. Nothing feeds a man's soul the way a woman can feed his soul by telling him that he just made her eyes roll and her loins melt. Jurgen understood that the greatest thrills could be found, not in losing oneself, but in inducing abandon in another. To take a woman to the peak of pleasure, to see her forsake her control. To see her hovering between ecstasy and despair. To hear her *plead*. That was sex. Domination by breathless consent was what turned Jurgen on. To be the catalyst, whereby a strong woman or a nervous girl or, indeed, as in Rosalie's case, both, surrendered her body to his passionate manipulation. Here lay the route of his relentless sex drive. He was a sensual imperialist. Any fool could bend another to their will by force or payment, but to make a woman beg you to do as you please, to have her offer herself up that you might take her and keep her as long as you wished, now that was worth going to bed for.

Jurgen took especial care with Rosalie. A virgin's sigh

was tribute of the highest order. No better proof could be found of a man's sexual and spiritual power. To overcome her pain and bring her to a celebration of her abandonment, that, truly, was a triumph of lasting splendor. For she would always remember that first sigh, and all other men would be measured against it. In a way, whoever could do that for a woman would own a part of her for life.

Such was the logic of love to a control freak. Jurgen tolerated no moment of abandon in himself. He could not bear for a woman to begin to work *her* wiles upon him. Should she start to stroke or touch his body beyond the simple return of his kiss, he would clasp her tight until again it was he who was charting the course of their passion.

At twenty years old, and dazzled by his power and glamour, this was all fine by Rosalie. Seldom can a woman have been deflowered under such splendid circumstances. Long before he actually entered her, Jurgen's skills had induced a climax of an intensity that was new to Rosalie. His smooth, smooth face between her thighs (Jurgen always waxed his chin for special occasions such as this) made her back arch with joy, and when the time came to fully consummate the night, big though he was, Jurgen had made her ready.

Afterward she lay exhausted on the bed for some time. Jurgen Thor got up and, taking his drink, sat naked on some cushions and watched as the sun dipped behind the glorious mountains outside the window, and turned his body to a silhouette. It was then that the full splendor of the situation enveloped Rosalie, and for a moment she almost swooned, an experience she had never had before or since. She did not swoon, however, because something was preventing her from fully glorying in the luxury of the situation. Something felt very strange, in fact, felt wrong.

"Jurgen," she said.

"My darling, you were wonderful," he said, still staring at the setting sun.

"Thanks, but that wasn't what I was going to ask."

"What, then?"

"Who pays for all this?"

There was a tiny pause.

"It's not so very expensive."

"A house built on top of a mountain with a helipad. That's *quite* expensive."

Jurgen turned to her. For the first time, there was a touch of irritation in his manner.

"We have friends who believe that what we do is of some worth. What *I* do is of worth."

"I know that, Jurgen." Rosalie pulled a sheet over herself. "I was just saying that this is pretty amazing, that's all."

"I'm a world leader, you know that, don't you? A *world* leader."

"Of course I know that, Jurgen."

"Natura fights elections in every democracy on Earth. Do you begrudge me some trappings of office? A house, a helicopter? Perhaps I should arrive at summit meetings by public transport."

"Well, maybe you should." Rosalie was now a little annoyed herself. "We all know what the private car is doing; if everybody in the world used public transport that alone would probably save the—"

"I *know* that, Little Miss Idealist! I knew it before you were born, damn it all, man! But there are practical considerations for a man in my position. People try to kill me, you know! I am also a bit too busy to be waiting for buses!" For a moment Jurgen Thor seemed almost hurt. "Oh, my sweet naive little almost-virgin, how I would love the luxury of your innocence. To be twenty and to judge every little thing by what is right. But I have to lead, and it is the leaders who have to make the tough decisions, yes, and then live with themselves afterward. You could not imagine the awful truth of some of the compromises I have made in pursuit of what I believe. So be careful what you ask, tiny girl. You might get the answers that you don't want to hear!"

Jurgen stopped, the fire in his eyes dying as suddenly as it had been kindled. He got up, and big and naked though he was, his expression was that of a little boy. He crossed back to the bed, his tone suddenly sad and conciliatory.

"Forgive me, little funky beautiful babe. Sometimes even I get tired, you know? It's a tough game you're going to be playing. You must be careful that your dreams do not betray you. Idealism is a wonderful thing, it got you into this, but it is pragmatism that will keep you alive. There are many things we have to do that we don't like. Compromises that must be made. When we set off a bomb, we do not like the damage it does, but we like even less the thing that we seek to destroy. Let's not talk any more. I spend half my life talking."

And he, of course, spent the other half fucking, which is what he proceeded to do until both he and Rosalie fell asleep.

Later though, and for some time afterward, Rosalie thought about this conversation. He had seemed so moved, he had actually been hurt and angry. She could not escape the feeling that Jurgen Thor had been talking about more than his house and his helicopter.

Further adventures in cross-dressing.

"Hey, you want to get a coffee or something?"

Max's voice intruded upon Rosalie's thoughts. Bringing her down off that mountain in Switzerland and back across the years. Jurgen's bitter little speech had occasionally returned to her, tainting the memory of what had been a wonderful night. What had he meant about compromises? Why had he seemed so sad? So angry? Surely what Max was suggesting could not be true? Claustrosphere funding

Mother Earth? The idea was insane. Then again, the fact that the human race was happily destroying the planet on which it lived was insane, everything was insane. But this? It was impossible.

"Max, I have personally led teams that have destroyed four plants that make Claustrosphere components. We attack them all the time. They can't possibly be funding us."

"All I know is what I've told you. Maybe it's all bullshit, but Nathan definitely got knocked off after meeting Tolstoy, in a house hired by Tolstoy, and it was a professional and clinical hit with no robbery involved. I can't think of a single motive other than the one I've suggested."

"Maybe he had other enemies?"

"Come on, he'd only ever spent two weeks in L.A., in a hotel room. Who's going to kill him for that? Besides, nobody but me, Tolstoy, and his wife in England even knew where he was."

"It's insane."

"Well, maybe it is. I don't know. Why don't we go ask your pal Jurgen?"

Just then the beeper that Rosalie was wearing went off. She stepped to the window and looked out.

"Garda . . . Oh dear."

Down in the single street that was all the village consisted of, Rosalie's lookout had been arrested. By an unhappy stroke of poor luck, the local Garda were being particularly vigilant at that time, looking for Republicans from the North who were believed to be lying low in the area. Rosalie's comrade, hanging about as she was, had been routinely DNA-scraped by a constable and immediately identified as a member of a Mother Earth unit known to be led by Rosalie. Instantly, the Garda had dropped all thoughts of boring old Republicans. Rosalie was an escapee, somebody who had seriously embarrassed the force. If she was in the village, she would make a grand catch indeed. This was why the Garda were now knocking on doors at both ends of the street and a helicopter was clattering above the houses.

"They're searching every house," Rosalie said from her vantage point at the window. "My God, why did you have to come back? They've got me now for sure."

Max was thrilled. Here was his chance to redeem himself.

"Look," said Max, "I know I didn't do too well last time but—"

"Don't tell me you want to pretend to be me again. That story will have been all over the force—they're hardly likely to fall for the same trick twice."

"Variations on a theme, man. Will you trust me? Ask the child inside."

Rosalie had little choice; there were no avenues of escape remaining to her. As far as she was concerned, within ten minutes she would be under arrest.

"What did you have in mind, then?"

"On the dressing table, there's a mustache and some cosmetic putty—bring them over here."

Rosalie nearly just gave herself up there and then.

"I will not. If I'm to be arrested, I shall do it with dignity."

"Rosalie! We only have moments left," said Max, and leaping out of bed, he grabbed his makeup bag. Rosalie would have protested further, but she found it difficult to speak because Max was sticking a false mustache to her upper lip.

"This time you get to be a man," he said.

"Max, you're insane! I have a bosom."

"Not by Hollywood standards, you haven't. . . . You said you'd trust me, well, trust me! What do you have to lose?"

He pulled Rosalie's hair back tight into a ponytail.

"Okay, you'll have to strip, completely, I'm afraid. Come on, come on, we don't have much time."

"Max, I'm a *woman!*"

"I *know* that. Now strip!"

Scarcely knowing why, Rosalie stripped naked, and Max instructed her to lie on the bed, her head propped against a pillow. He draped a crumpled sheet casually across her breasts, but left the rest of her body exposed.

"Okay now, legs together . . . casual, come on, you're drunk, you've passed out, you're asleep." Max raised one of her knees slightly, while making sure that her thighs were still clamped together. Then, even as they heard the Garda outside in the street, Max rolled the fleshy putty into a small sausage.

"I don't believe . . . !" gasped Rosalie, looking down.

"Lie still!" Max barked. "You're unconscious! You've got to *think* unconscious. You've got to *act!* A lot of people think acting is easy, but it isn't, it's a *damn tough trade.* Now remember, you are not a wild woman on a mission to save the planet, but a drunk Californian homosexual on holiday with his lover, okay? It's complex, it's delicate, it's *acting!*"

"Well, what do I do then?"

"Just close your eyes and try to snore a bit."

And with that, Max gently buried one end of his little putty sausage into the mound of Rosalie's pubic hair and draped the length of it delicately across one of her thighs. Rosalie's legs twitched at his touch.

"Keep them together, for Christ's sake," Max urged, "I can't do balls at this speed, I'm not Michael-fucking-angelo."

Rosalie's legs lay still. Max could hear the landlady conversing with the Garda downstairs. He knew he only had moments left. Rosalie already had the slightest downy snail-trail running from her pubic hair toward her belly button. Max took some ash from the ashtray and darkened the hair slightly, considered attempting a shadow on the chin, but knew he would smudge it in the rush. There was a half-empty Paddy bottle on the bedside table, and he laid it on the bed placing the neck of the bottle in Rosalie's hand. He checked again that the sheet across her chest was sufficiently rumpled to disguise the small rise of her bosom, then he gathered the undersheet together on either side of her thighs in an attempt to disguise the feminine curve of her hips. Rosalie's slim waist, he could do nothing about. It would just have to do; acting came down to bluff, and that was up to him. He whipped off the jockey shorts, which to his shame he had been wearing in bed, and just as the Garda began to hammer on the bedroom door, he draped himself completely naked across the bed, his head on Rosalie's stomach.

"Open the door!" a stern voice demanded from outside.

"Ugh!" Max moaned as if from a deep sleep.

"Open the door or I shall kick it open!" the voice shouted.

"What? . . . Hey, who the hell is . . . ?" Max knew how to act half shit faced, he was that way most mornings. The door burst open, and two uniformed officers rushed in. Max gave them a split second to take in the whole scene before jumping up, naked, drawing their attention to him.

"My God! Oh no! *Scream!!*" he shouted, affecting a fey campness that would not have gone down very well with those members of the homosexual community who object to such stereotyping.

"Nathan, wake up! It's a bust! Don't tell me boy love is still illegal in this country! It's not! I know it's not! I checked with the travel agent. How dare you burst in here . . . you . . . you damn caveman! Wake up, Nathan! . . . Oh, my God!" Max pretended to notice Rosalie's nakedness for the first time. Giving the Garda officers just a moment with which to follow his gaze and see again the pale, soft, feminine, but unquestionably equipped with penis, body on the bed, Max grabbed a coat and hurled it over Rosalie, before seeming to notice his own nakedness for the first time and to cover himself with a towel.

"We were told there was a woman in here," the constable stuttered, not knowing what to think.

"A woman! Don't be *disgusting!*" Max screeched.

"The landlady said there was a woman in here." The policeman was getting out of his depth.

"Darling, I fear that in Mrs. Mop's tiny world, when two people are fucking like rabbits and making the china shake in the parlor, they are, by definition, a man and a woman. No other couplings would occur to her. Wake *up,* Nathan . . . !" Max shouted at Rosalie's prostrate form as he marched over to the dressing table and grabbed both his own passport and that which had once belonged to the actual Nathan. "Look. There're our ID's, I'm American, he's British, and we're both *men,* thank you very much. I can assure you, I would know! . . . Wake *up,* Nathan!" The officer flicked nervously through the two passports. Max, fearing the man might study the photos, attempted to partially obscure Rosalie's face by bending over to shake her, taking care not to disturb either the mustache or the rumpled sheet over her breasts. Rosalie, who was beginning to believe that Max might pull this off, groaned and dribbled, distorting her features as much as she felt she could get away with.

"My God, that Paddy's *Scotch whiskey* is *lethal,*" Max shrieked.

Max had judged his man well. The constable shuddered slightly. He was not a great fan of the love that dare not speak its name at the best of times, but when the homosexual in question also turned out to be a complete whoopsie who thought that Paddy's was Scotch, then the less time spent with him the better.

"Well, sir, as I say, I was informed that you had a woman with you, but since it's a fellah, I suppose . . . that's all right, isn't it?"

Max allowed his eyes to moisten and his voice to quiver with emotion.

"Officer, may I remark that that is the single most lovely thing I have ever heard a policeman say."

"Yes . . . well . . . sorry to have bothered you then." The

policeman had got himself a little confused. "Um, I hope your . . . friend . . ."

"Lover."

"Yes, well, I hope he recovers. . . . Good day to you, sir . . . and sir," and with a slight nod at Rosalie's prostrate form, the constable and his companion left.

As she heard the door close Rosalie opened her eyes, and they shone with wonder and excitement. In all her experience of living the life of an outlaw, in all the daring stories of escape she had heard around campfires—or while bobbing about in inflatable boats, or sitting waiting in the bellies of helicopters—none had ever come close in audacity and flair to the trick in which she had just been a part.

Max was at the window.

"They've drawn a blank. . . . I think they're going to chuck it. Don't break character yet, they may decide to bring their pals up for a laugh at the gay guys." He stood watching for a while, watching the cops in the street, while Rosalie watched him.

"They're bringing their truck up. . . . Man, they're going!" Max spun around to face her, completely thrilled, triumphant. "We did it!"

"You did it, Max." Rosalie was a fair-minded girl and gave credit where it was due. "I can't believe it, but you did. What a concept! What a performance! You saved my neck, and you were completely bloody wonderful."

Yes, he had been wonderful. Max could scarcely demur, it had been a masterpiece of aggressive bluff, and what, after all, was great acting, but bluff?

Rosalie's eyes, which had been fixed upon Max's face, dropped slightly. She could not help but notice that Max was reacting to his own brilliance in his customary manner. Max followed her gaze. Beneath his towel was a stiff you could have flown a flag off.

"Oh dear," said Max, genuinely embarrassed. "I'm not

really such a vain guy . . . honestly, not in normal life. . . . It's just, when I do a really great show I . . ."

"Hey, Max," Rosalie said, and her soft, soft Irish voice would have made lush green pasture of a desert, "don't apologize. You were great, and if anyone's entitled to a celebratory hard-on, it's you."

This was it, and they both knew it. The excitement of being so nearly busted, the adrenaline rush of escape. The intimacy that the need for survival had already forced upon them. It was so right. They were even already naked, Max would not even have to take his socks off.

"I've got a laminate spray in my bag. Would you get it?" Rosalie said, and as the gentle music of her voice drifted out of the open window and into the street, all the milk in the village turned into rich butter. Max found the spray.

"I use it to seal my gun in wet weather," Rosalie added.

"No woman should ever apologize for carrying protection," said Max.

"Yes, well that's all very well, but as a rule spontaneous lovemaking is not my style."

"Nor mine," said Max, spraying on the stretch laminate. He sort of believed himself too, for he had given all that up now. He made a mental note to tell Rosalie about his past sometime, but not now.

He got into bed. They embraced.

"Would you mind removing your mustache?" Max inquired.

Rosalie removed the offending disguise, and they embraced again. Max's hands stole down Rosalie's naked body.

"Would it be okay if I took your penis away as well?" he said, having encountered the little putty tube that had served them so well.

"Okay, but don't spoil it," Rosalie said. "I want to keep it. No prick has ever done me better service."

Max knew he could not equal that, but he resolved to do his best, and he and Rosalie made love.

It wasn't like in the movies, there were still elbows to get stuck under backs and hair to get in mouths, but suddenly that didn't matter. There can be few things better on Earth than to go to bed with the someone you have been dreaming about. Someone for whom you have been yearning. Max had imagined himself kissing and touching Rosalie's small, soft but hard body a hundred times. Rosalie, although otherwise occupied, and somewhat less of a drip than Max, had also been thinking of him. Scarcely even realizing it, they had fallen in love, and now, in each other's arms, they acknowledged it.

20

New lovers, old lovers, and screams from beyond a rocky grave

Limping out.

JURGEN THOR SAT NAKED ON HIS CUSHIONS, SIPPING HIS PEACH schnapps. The sun was dipping down behind the mountains, and his tanned blond skin was growing shadow dark. A young woman lay on the bed. She too was naked, her body as near perfect as Jurgen's. A golden couple, silent in the setting sun. It was as it had always been. The stunning surroundings, the young, starstruck beauty. The man, great and good, unlocking the door to her heart and letting the passion out. It was as it had always been, a thousand seductions, a thousand grateful girls. Just the same. Except it was different. More different than Jurgen could ever have imagined, for instead of the sounds he usually heard emanating from the bed on these occasions—sometimes breathless, coy, half-finished sentences filled with wonder, sometimes gentle sobs as emotions became too much—instead, Jurgen heard something he had quite literally never heard before.

"Please don't worry about it," the young woman said, "I hear it happens to all guys sometimes. Really, I don't mind."

Jurgen struggled to maintain his self-control. That this *little girl* should be trying to comfort him! Assuring him that she did not *mind!*

"My penis was recently blown off by a bomb, you know," he said, trying to seem casual. "That bitch of a surgeon must have sewn it back on wrong."

"Yes, that's it," said the girl, whose name was Scout. "She must have sewn it on wrong."

But they both knew that the surgeon had not got it wrong. Jurgen had been fine and upstanding during the protracted foreplay. He had undressed Scout in his usual accomplished manner, her clothes disappearing as if by magic. He had deposited her, near naked, upon his great bed. Stayed her hand as she made to remove her bra, because, as with all things sexual, he liked to do it himself . . . the removal of underwear being something that he particularly liked to dwell over. Yes, everything had been running along familiar lines. As usual he had knelt down on the bed beside her, feasting his eyes upon her while he spirited away her flimsy final garments, and all the while the surgeon's work appeared to be holding up superbly. His erection was as proud and vertical as it ever was; you could have chucked horseshoes at it. Scout's eyes had grown wide with nervous but eager anticipation as she contemplated the miracle of natural engineering upon which she was about to allow herself to be impaled.

"Good Lord," she had remarked, her voice betraying a childhood spent at a posh English girls' school. "You will take it easy, won't you, sweetie? The last time I saw anything hung like that, it had just won the three-thirty at Epsom." Scout snorted with laughter. She was a jolly girl, and like many English girls of her class found demonstrative passion a bit foreign and embarrassing. She found sex altogether easier to cope with if it was treated as something of a joke. This could, of course, be rather disconcerting for any poor fellow nervously attempting to engender an atmosphere of lustful abandon. Nothing spoils a grunting, groaning, bed-wobbling approach to climax like a loud giggle followed by the comment . . . "Sorry, I was just thinking how *funny* we must look from behind."

But Jurgen had encountered slightly gauche English girls before, and it was not horsey giggles that had led to his surprising sexual collapse. Far from it. He usually liked this type. He knew very well how a really grown-up rogering could quickly wipe the silly grin off these girls' faces. He had, in fact, been hugely looking forward to seeing Scout's nervous jollity turn to that look of complete surprise that comes when a girl realizes that all of her inhibitions have been expertly removed and are now lying in distant corners of the room along with her underpants and her hair clips.

"There is no need for the worrying," Jurgen assured Scout, as he assured all the girls. "For me, there is only pleasure in the pleasure of the woman. I make love to make women happy. That is the only reason I do it."

"Oh, don't worry about me," Scout said with a jolly snort, "you just carry on. The only place I ever get an orgasm is in Louis's Pâtisserie in Hampstead."

But it looked as if tonight was going to be different. Because as Jurgen applied his considerable skills, Scout's body began to respond in a manner entirely new to her.

"Oooh," she said as Jurgen played delicately with her breasts. Stimulating them in a manner that was very different to the maulings that chaps had given them in the past. So different, in fact, that had Scout not been absolutely sure, she might have imagined that Jurgen was caressing a completely different pair of tits altogether from the ones she normally wore to bed.

"Gosh," she gasped as Jurgen's smooth jaw slid down between her thighs, his lips upon hers. How she shivered as he kissed her where previously she had only been gobbled, and even then, rarely, since Scout had always harbored a vague feeling that vaginas were things into which no chap had much business sticking his face.

By the time push came to shove, so to speak, Scout could not have been any hotter if Jurgen had set fire to the bed.

"Go on, then, fuck me," she astonished herself by saying. Up until now, the most passionate comment she had managed at this stage of the game was, "I suppose I don't mind if you really want to." Now, however, she wanted to be fucked, and she said so. Jurgen Thor needed no further prompting. He sprayed on the laminate and plunged in.

"Wow!" Scout shouted in gay abandon, unaware that she had such hidden depths . . . and then only moments later, a muted, "Oh."

The seemingly impossible had happened. For the first time in his life, Jurgen Thor had gone the way of all flesh. For a moment, confident in his conquest, he had allowed his mind to wander. Having realized that his mind was wandering, Jurgen had reflected that he had better concentrate on the job at hand or else the unthinkable might happen. At which point, of course, the unthinkable did. Jurgen discovered, later than most men, that once you start worrying about it, you've lost it.

Reflections on erections.

Jurgen sat on his cushions in moody contemplation. His mind had wandered. Why? It had wandered a lot of late. He was becoming more and more distracted, and he did not really know why. Except, perhaps, that times were changing, and even his legendary energy, both physical and mental, must surely ebb someday. It was a curious sensation for Jurgen to be so bothered about something. Very little affected him emotionally in his life, nor had much done so for years. He had lived for so long with a full and profound knowledge of the real extent of planet death that conventional emotion had been rather lost to him. Every single day, he was confronted with statistics so terrible that he had become numb. Jurgen found it difficult to care about anything very much. But he did still value his sexual powers. To Jurgen, virility was a symbol of life in a dying world, and now even that was collapsing. A sense of mortality cloaked him like a contraceptive laminate. The end was nigh. Even his beloved mountains had changed forever. There was no snow or ice at all on them now, not even on the highest peaks. The last ice had melted five years ago, and it would never return.

Dirty snow.

Jurgen had always loved the cold. Snow and ice appealed to him far more than sun and sand. But it was gone. The only ice remaining lay at the poles, and Jurgen knew better than most how soon that too would disappear. It was not because of the famous greenhouse effect that the ancient ice was finally giving up the ghost, but by dint of something much less complex. Straightforward dirt was in the process of liberating four-fifths of the world's fresh water. Airborne pollutants had begun to dirty the shimmering white that lay at the hub of the world. Darkened as it was, it no longer reflected the sun's rays with the efficiency it had once done. Soon it would actively absorb them, and soon after that it would be possible to go surfing in St. Louis.

The Claustrosphere Company, recognizing the problem, had begun to fit Spheres located in low-lying regions with diving gear. Being hermetically sealed, a Claustrosphere could offer complete protection against submersion as long

244

as you did not open the door. This was fine for a while, except that the whole point of the Claustrospheres was that the human race would survive to walk again on the surface of the planet. It would be a shame if your children's children were to emerge from their long captivity and immediately drown. Hence the scuba tanks.

Jurgen was distracted from his somber musings by the distant sound of an approaching helicopter. He was at once on guard. He had invited no other guests, and as the world's premier greenie, he had many enemies. Jurgen suggested that Scout get dressed, and calling to his servants to arm themselves, he took his gun and climbed up the spiral staircase that led to the helipad.

The sound of the helicopter grew louder.

An old lover was returning.

From Galway to the Alps.

After leaving the little village in Galway where they had had so much excitement, Rosalie and Max had rejoined Rosalie's unit in the mountains, where they were preparing for their next action, an assault on the toxic waste convoys that converged in Belgium on their way to Britain.

Saunders, Rosalie's bag-headed colleague, was his usual inhospitable self.

"So now we've got a bloody poncey actor to add to our FBI man," he had sneered through the hole in the front of his bag.

"This man saved my bacon in that village raid," Rosalie snapped. "We lost Hilary down in the street, and without Max here, I'd have been caught as well, for sure."

"Oh, so he saved your bacon, did he? So now we have to cart around *two* Yanks who've saved your bacon, do we?" Saunders said, referring to poor Judy, who was sitting under a tree, wrapped in a blanket. Judy looked miserable, which he was. He was not well suited to the life of a guerrilla fighter and was missing his down quilt and hot chocolate. The sneer that Saunders directed at Judy's bedraggled form could be felt even through his bag. "Jesus Christ, Rosalie, if we have to take on every bastard that saves your bloody bacon, it looks like we're going to end up with quite a crowd."

But Saunders did not really mind. He was actually quite impressed to have someone as famous as Max Maximus join them for a spell. He had long thought that *The Man With No Face* would make a terrific subject for a movie, and here was just the person to talk it over with.

"What I was thinking, right," the Liverpudlian said, buttonholing Max, "was that you could play me before I got contaminated, and I could play me after. That way we could save money on makeup. What do you think?" And with that, Saunders whipped his bag off.

"Potentially, it's huge. I'd suggest we do lunch, but I don't think I could keep it down." Max looked around, hoping that Rosalie would come and save him from the lunatic. Rosalie, however, was nowhere to be seen. She had asked Judy to accompany her on a little stroll, and they had wandered off together out of earshot. They were now sitting on some rocks, deep in conversation. At least Rosalie was sitting on the rocks. Judy, who suffered occasionally from hemorrhoids, was trying to avoid sitting on any cold, damp surfaces, which is kind of a difficult thing to do if you happen to be living on the side of a mountain.

Rosalie was questioning Judy about Mother Earth funding.

"Surely the FBI must have investigated it?" she asked.

"I'm sure they did, but either they drew a blank or else they covered up their findings, because I asked many times. Not one of my superiors admitted to having any idea whatsoever about where your cash came from."

"What about you, did you try to find out? Did no hint ever come out in all the files you had to work on?"

"I never saw the slightest thing. It's too well laundered.

Sometimes I wonder whether even Jurgen Thor himself knows who pays."

But Rosalie felt that he did know. The memory of Jurgen's tired cynicism on that night in his sex den all those years ago kept returning. Rosalie knew that Jurgen Thor held the only key to the mystery.

Sad reflections.

Despite the absence of snow and ice, the Swiss Alps still presented an awesome sight when viewed from the air, and as she and Max approached Jurgen's lair in the helicopter Max had hired, Rosalie was remembering the last time she had flown over those mountains. On that occasion she had been filled with excitement, nervously anticipating the adventure that she had let herself in for. Now she felt a strange sense of foreboding. She could not explain it, but the mountains that had appeared so inspiring before, with their glittering peaks, now seemed somber and unforgiving. Of course the sun was setting, and the great craggy shadows that blackened the landscape would surely have dampened the lightest of spirits, but it was more than that. Rosalie could not shake a strange sensation of defeat and sorrow. Her spirits were sinking with the sun.

Perhaps it was because it had been among these mountains that she had first begun to lose her innocence. Not sexual innocence, although she had lost that here too; Rosalie attached no great significance to virginity. She knew that there was a first time in life for all things, and a last. Rather it was her spiritual innocence that had been so sadly eroded since she had last left these mountains. Since then she had seen so much horror. Horror that she had never dreamed of as an idealistic girl. Dead forests, dead lakes, dead species, dead communities. Everything she ever saw or touched was dead or dying. Rosalie was a naturally spirited person, and the planet's agony was her agony. She honestly believed that she felt it, just as some people's bones ache when the weather changes.

As Max piloted the helicopter through the gloomy sunset (he had starred in the fourth remake of *Apocalypse Now*), it dawned upon Rosalie that it was here that she had first begun to understand how unutterably and indescribably sad humankind was. Jurgen Thor's little lesson in compromise had proved horribly prophetic. She was a terrorist in a terrible world, and like a black crow struggling in a stormy sky, she could not be distinguished from the environment in which she did battle. The passion that had brought her to the struggle against planet death had been replaced by what was merely a grim refusal to take the inevitable lying down. Only a fool could have seen the things that Rosalie had seen and remain an idealist. She had long since given up any thought of fighting for a better, more beautiful world. All her life meant, now, was a struggle, to prevent the most gruesome excess of a situation that was, and always would be, disastrous.

"Anything wrong?" Max asked.

"People are shit, the world's dead, and everything is pointless."

"Oh, good, I was worried something was bothering you."

Rosalie smiled wearily.

"I was just thinking, that if your theory about Claustrosphere and Mother Earth is correct, my entire adult life has had no point whatsoever."

"Well, you're only twenty-five. Plenty of time to throw it in and do something else."

"Perhaps I should."

She wanted to turn around. She was losing her nerve. All they had, after all, was the stupid hunch of one dead screenwriter, and an English one at that. On the strength of this they were preparing to invade the great man's privacy, entirely uninvited, and confront him with the extraordinary suggestion that the forces of environmental protection were in fact in the pay of the planet's number one enemy.

"He'll laugh at us," said Rosalie as Max maneuvered the craft down on the helipad.

"Laughter would be fine," Max replied. He could see Jurgen and a couple of minions waiting on the deck, heavily armed and ready to shoot.

The pragmatist concludes his lesson.

"We have to speak to you, it's important," Rosalie announced as the clatter of the helicopter blades began to subside.

"Why not?" Jurgen shrugged. "It must be pretty important, okay, for you to interrupt your preparations for the toxic convoy raid. Yes, babe?"

Jurgen loved to show how he was party to all Mother Earth actions. He knew Rosalie as an activist; he also recalled their previous intimacy. Max Maximus, he recognized, of course, but if he was surprised at the arrival of a famed media star, he did not show it. Jurgen, of course, mixed constantly with world leaders in every field; he was more than used to celebrity. Besides, he himself was a bigger star than any Hollywood actor.

Dismissing his servants, Jurgen led Max and Rosalie downstairs into the house. They descended through the bedroom, which, as Rosalie recalled, covered the entire top floor of the house and offered the only access to the helipad. Scout was still there as they passed through, and Rosalie experienced a small sense of déjà vu. Pausing for a moment on the spiral stair, she took in the proud, slightly defiant face of the pretty young woman and glanced at the huge white bed and crumpled sheets.

Jurgen Thor made his excuses to Scout and led Max and Rosalie down into his study. There, on the wall, they were astonished to find the mounted heads of animals belonging to several species that were basically extinct, except, of course, for a few genetically recreated specimens in zoos.

There was a tiger, a lion, even an elephant, its expression one of inconsolable sadness . . . as indeed it might have been, considering its head had been cut off and stuffed with straw, its natural habitat had been totally destroyed, and its race had disappeared from the face of the Earth. Jurgen noted the surprise and indeed revulsion that convulsed the faces of his guests as they took in his macabre interior decor.

"They keep my anger alive," he said, by way of an explanation, although it fell a long way short of convincing either Max or Rosalie. They could not help feeling that there were perhaps more sensitive ways of maintaining one's commitment to wildlife than displaying the severed heads of dead life-forms above your writing desk.

"So what is it that is so important that you fly all the way to the highest mountain to talk to me about?" Jurgen inquired.

Max had convinced Rosalie that if Nathan's idea was correct, the only hope of getting Jurgen to come clean about it was to catch him off-guard, to confront him directly and with confidence. It was a risky plan because if they were wrong, Rosalie, in particular, was going to look something of an idiot. She was, after all, an environmental activist, and it was pretty big stuff to accuse the biggest green hero of all of sleeping with the enemy. Max, however, was confident that they were not wrong.

"Mr. Thor," he said. "We have come here because we know that the Claustrosphere Corporation funds Mother Earth, and we want to know why."

Jurgen could not prevent a flicker of shock from crossing his handsome, granitelike face. He had not expected this, and for a moment it seemed that he would hurl their accusation back in their faces. Then he sighed. He had been feeling that events were beginning to approach their end. This surely was just one more symptom.

There was almost a hint of relief in his voice when he

asked, "You ask me why? I would have thought the answer was patently obvious."

Despite his somber mood, Jurgen enjoyed the effect he had on Rosalie. He might have failed to get it up Scout, but he was certainly still capable of making a beautiful woman gasp and roll her eyes.

"How did you find out?" he added, casually stroking the head of a monkey, whose jaw served as a tobacco pouch.

"It isn't true!" Rosalie shouted. "Claustrosphere pays us! Pays me! It's madness, they're the enemy. They hate us. . . ."

"Of course, they hate us, and we hate them. That doesn't mean that we can't do business, does it?"

Rosalie was speechless. She could not begin to imagine what Jurgen Thor was talking about. It was nonsense, it had to be. Except, of course, that it wasn't, it was just business, as Jurgen went on to explain.

"Think about it, Rosalie. Why do people buy Claustrospheres?" Neither Max nor Rosalie offered an answer, which was fine by Jurgen; the floor was his and he was holding it. "Because they fear that the Earth is dying, of course. And who is it that tells them every single day that they are right? That the Earth *is* dying! Why, us, of course! It is Natura and Mother Earth whom people look to for the truth, and, my God, do we give it to them. We tell them the truth. We show them the truth. You, Rosalie, personally risk your life most days to confront people with the truth. And the truth is that the planet is getting dangerously close to being incapable of supporting human life. We tell them this in the hope that people will wake up! That they will start to nurture their planet. That they will adjust their lifestyles. Boycott the products of polluters, lobby their politicians, *save the earth!* That is why we tell them the truth. But what do most people *actually* do when confronted with the unanswerable evidence that we hurl before them every day?"

"Buy a Claustrosphere," said Max. "I know I did."

"Exactly. Buy a Claustrosphere. Of course you did," said Jurgen. "It would be madness not to. If the dear, conscientious, idealistic old greenies are right, and planet death is upon us, *which it is,* what else can one possibly do?"

"Yes, but . . . ," Rosalie blurted, but for the time being she could do no better than that. Her mind was reeling.

"Exactly," said Thor. "Yes, but . . . what? Yes, but nothing, darling, okay! I have spent half a lifetime searching for that elusive 'yes, but,' and not one sniff of it have I had. We are trapped by our own beliefs. Prisoners of the truth that we must tell. We say that to own a Claustrosphere is in itself the greatest act of planet treason you can commit, because by owning a Claustrosphere, a person accepts that the death of the Earth is survivable. How, then, are we to stop people from taking this terrible step? We must warn them of the consequences of their actions! So we shout that buying a Claustrosphere will hasten the demise of the Earth. And what does that warning make people do?"

"Buy a Claustrosphere," said Max.

"Exactly." And for a moment Jurgen Thor even seemed to smile. "Everything that we do sells Claustrospheres. We are their greatest advertisement. No wonder they fund us."

Rosalie spoke as if in a dream. "But what you're saying is that it would be better for us to do nothing, to say nothing."

"Believe me, I have often considered it," Jurgen continued. "Because if every environmentalist on Earth shut up, then Claustrosphere sales would plummet. But if we did that, then planet death would surely occur without even a protest, without even a small effort to stop it. That must never happen; we will not die on our knees! And so we are caught, Rosalie, caught between the devil and two hard places, you dig? If we are silent, the Earth will probably die; if we are the shouters, the Earth will probably die. I am a man of action, and so I prefer to be a shouter."

"But that Claustrosphere should pay for it!" Rosalie was struggling not to give way to despair.

"Who else would support us so generously? Who else would supply us immediately and without question with everything we need? Once I have decided to fight, I would be a fool to deny myself the best weapons simply because I did not like the arms dealer. I don't like any arms dealer. Would you like me to turn them down, to say, no, I will blow up this waste ship with a poorer, cheaper, but somehow cleaner bomb?"

"You don't have to have such a bloody nice house."

Suddenly Rosalie was furious. It was the calm logical way he described it, and he did seem to do so damn well out of it.

"Why the hell should I not have a bloody nice house, goddamn!" Jurgen too was angry all of a sudden. "I'm happy to spend as much of their money as they care to give me. I once told you, Rosalie, pragmatism in all things. Would one less Claustrosphere be built if I denied myself beautiful things? Will one more flower grow? No, of course not, I would be cutting off my nose just so I could have some spite on my face."

"That is a totally corrupting argument."

"I *am* corrupt, Rosalie. The nature of leadership requires that I be corrupt. If I were not corrupt, you would have no guns! The nice ladies who send out our mailings would have no envelopes. My corruption pays your wages."

"No, I don't believe it, we have subscriptions, fund-raisers."

"Jam and bazaars while the enemy has the combined wealth of total world exploitation. Would you have our people face a lion with the shooter of peas?"

It was an unfortunate image. There was a lion, or at least a part of one, as silent witness to their debate. Rosalie felt an overwhelming sense of revulsion, against Jurgen, against herself, against the mere fact of being alive.

"I'm going to blow the whistle. This is wrong, it can't go on."

"If you do that you will sell another ten thousand Claustrospheres in an hour. If once the dreadful truth emerges, that the human race is so utterly damned that its only defense must be financed by those who seek to destroy it, then surely there will be a panic of the soul. Even those who still hope, who still harbor some small semblance of responsibility to themselves and others, will give it up. They will say, if even Mother Earth is part of the process of planet death, then it is over, the planet *will* die. I saw it in your own face a moment ago. It's hopeless, you thought! What is the damn point, you thought! Well, if that is your reaction to the truth, to the natural logic of human madness, then how will the less concerned react, the less *pure?* What do you think they will do the day you tell them that Mother Earth sups with the devil?"

"Buy a Claustrosphere," said Max.

"Stop *saying that!*" Rosalie shouted at him. Her eyes were filling with tears, for she knew that Jurgen Thor was right. On learning the truth, a terrible dark fiend of despair had taken her by the throat and brought her to the ground. She had been utterly overwhelmed by the hopelessness of hope. Anything other than bitter cynicism seemed completely naive. Others would feel the same, and worse. The truth would provide the ultimate justification for cynicism. That must never be. She could not tell. In order to continue to fight for the truth, she and Mother Earth must continue to live a lie.

"Why doesn't the Claustrosphere Company itself blow the whistle," asked Max thoughtfully, "if it would sell so many units?"

"In the short term it would, but the shock would wear off. People would learn to live with this revelation of human frailty as they have with all the others. With us green fools gone, Claustrosphere would lose its greatest propaganda tool It would have destroyed us, but in doing

so it would cripple itself, and the Earth would stagger toward death with neither defenders nor exploiters. For
without environmental protest, how can it market the end
of the world? We are the shit against which it must kick.''

"Market the end of the world! My God, listen to yourself!
You sound like Plastic Tolstoy.'' Rosalie could not bear
the way Jurgen Thor seemed to glory in his pragmatism.

"You pay me a handsome compliment.'' Jurgen smiled.
"For Plastic Tolstoy is a genius. It was he who first understood what a splendid marketing tool we are for Claustrosphere. It was he who approached me with the offer to
fund us. Believe me, if we could market ourselves with
the skill with which he has marketed Claustrosphere, the
planet would be healthy indeed.''

"You can't market responsibility! It's not a packet of
fish fingers.''

"Exactly. What we offer is painful truth and difficult
decisions, both of which are bloody difficult to sell, you
dig? Which is why I take Tolstoy's coin. No one but he
would support such a hopeless cause with such generous
commitment.''

Rosalie sank into a chair made out of stag antlers. She
was drained and weary.

"So what am I supposed to do?'' she asked eventually.

"Do? Why, nothing. You continue as before. You go back
to your unit and organize the raid on the toxic waste convoy. Very few people know what you know. Myself, some
senior figures in the movement, and of course our opposite
numbers in the Claustrosphere Company. If you ever did
decide to break the confidences I have shared with you, I
would of course deny them utterly. If necessary, I would
have you silenced permanently; because if you were believed, then Mother Earth and Natura would be finished,
and the last barrier between us and the Rat Run would
be gone.''

"I won't tell,'' said Rosalie in a hollow monotone. "As
you say, it would do more harm than good.''

"Remember what I once told you, Rosalie," said Jurgen. "Be careful what you ask, tiny girl. You might get the answers that you don't want to hear."

There was nothing more to say.

"Come on, Max, let's go," said Rosalie wearily. "Thanks for being so honest with us, Jurgen."

"It was nothing, baby, okay?" Jurgen replied. "My congratulations at having discovered the truth for yourselves. Every day I expect the whole world to wake up and figure it out, but they never do."

Jurgen offered them dinner, but they declined politely. Rosalie didn't want to talk anymore, she just wanted to leave. One thing was still bothering her though.

"If the Claustrosphere Company are your friends, how come they tried to blow you up in Brussels?" she asked as they made their way up to the helipad.

Suddenly all Jurgen's masterly charm deserted him. His face flashed with fury. Rosalie thought that he would hit her.

"They are not my damn *friends,* you stupid fucking bitch!! Haven't you been listening to anything? I take their money because I hate them! I take their money because I want to fight them with the best weapons I have. I take their money because if I do not stop them they will destroy the Earth. They pay me, and I try to kill them. It's a simple business transaction."

"And they try to kill you."

"Of course they do. At the moment, I am the leader of our movement, but there are others, there will always be others. Perhaps one day you, Rosalie; you are very highly thought of in our movement. I am valuable, but expendable. That is why they tried to kill me. Why they try to kill me now."

"Why now?" Now Max was curious.

"Because Claustrosphere is in a minislump. Everybody already owns one. Tolstoy must mount a new marketing drive. He wants to institute a massive and completely pointless upgrade of existing technology. My death would be a tremendous boost for him. Can you see the headlines? GREEN GOD DEAD! LAST SANE MAN ON EARTH MURDERED! ENVIRONMENTAL MOVEMENT IN TURMOIL! It would sell ten million units. Tolstoy has been saving me up for this."

Rosalie was about to enter the helicopter. She turned and looked at Jurgen.

"So they pay us, we work for them, our goals are diametrically opposite, and we want each other dead."

"Of course, isn't it obvious?"

Dominant fantasy.

Jurgen Thor watched as the helicopter containing Max and Rosalie disappeared into the distance. They had been lucky, he thought. Really, he should probably have killed them for what they had discovered. But somehow, he preferred to let Rosalie stew in it. He knew she would not tell, and Jurgen rather enjoyed the knowledge that beautiful, dedicated little Rosalie, one of the prides of Mother Earth, should have been tainted by the terrible truth. Or at least a part of the terrible truth. Jurgen could not really explain it to himself, but he felt that by sharing at least some of his dark secrets with Rosalie, he had somehow *soiled* her, and that made him feel good. It made him feel strong and bad. He had forced that sweet, pure little girl to descend partway into the mess of compromise and deceit that he lived in every day. She was dirty now, like him, and he had made it so.

One day, perhaps, he would tell her the whole truth, then she really would have something to cry about.

Within his loins Jurgen felt the stirrings of the erection that had eluded him earlier in the evening.

"How do you feel now, little virgin?" he shouted after the lights of the distant helicopter. "Now that you're in

Jurgen Thor's world? Do you feel good, huh? I said, do you feel good?" But Jurgen knew that she didn't feel good; he knew that she felt sad, and compromised. He could picture her, sitting in the passenger seat of the helicopter, miserable, small, confused, and . . . dirty. That made Jurgen happy. It filled him up and satisfied him. Except it didn't, because now he wanted to screw her. If only she hadn't brought that shitty little movie star, he told himself, he would have screwed her too.

Then he remembered that Scout was still in his bedroom. Now there was a treat indeed with which to end his sad, dark day. Why not? he had earned it. He would go downstairs and fuck that young idealistic little idiot's brains out . . . what brains she had, anyway. There would be no collapse of manhood this time, Jurgen told himself. For he was Jurgen Thor, and he was standing on top of the world. The chill wind of the night whipped at his long blond hair as he glared angrily into the darkness. His chest thrust out, his legs foursquare, and his face set with ugly defiance. It was as if he was challenging whatever God watched over him to damn him for the things he had done. For the things he had still to do.

Before retreating to the bedroom for his reward he watched until the lights of the helicopter disappeared completely.

Yes, one day he might give himself the pleasure of telling sweet little Rosalie the whole truth, and she could come with him to hell.

Fatal idealism.

Jurgen Thor turned and went back down the staircase into his bedroom. There would be no protracted foreplay this time, no gentle pursuit of the female orgasm. Jurgen Thor intended to tear the clothes off young Scout and bang her till he was finished, that was all. Then he would drink all night and bang her again as the dawn came up.

His fantasies of domination were brought to something of an abrupt conclusion, however, when he found himself facing the barrel of a gun.

"You disgust me," said Scout, her lips trembling with emotion.

"Excuse me, baby?" Jurgen inquired, genuinely shocked.

"Don't 'baby' me, you limp-willied hypocrite!" Scout shouted. "I was listening at the door to everything you said when you were downstairs."

"You listened?" Jurgen Thor was a little concerned by this.

"Of course I did! Coo, you don't get many chances to hear Jurgen Thor talking with huge movie stars. I thought it would be exciting, a bit more exciting at least than things have been with you so far, anyway. I thought it would be inspiring, that Max Maximus must be a secret activist and that I'd hear wonderful things about the fight against Claustrosphere. What do I hear? The most disgusting compromise there could ever be. I still can't believe it. You, me, all this, paid for by Plastic Tolstoy! It makes me bloody sick. I've wasted two whole years of my life training to be a hypocrite, and I think it's absolutely off."

"Give me the gun, Scout," Jurgen said.

"Like hell, I will. Crikey, you've got some nerve, still thinking you can hand out orders to me."

"So what is it you want, then?"

"I'll tell you what I want, chum. I want a full confession from you on videotape. This bloody charade has gone on long enough."

Scout was just too young and idealistic to swallow the kind of pragmatism with which Jurgen had persuaded Rosalie to maintain her silence. She had not gone through the five years of pointless struggle that Rosalie had gone through, had not watched everything she tried to defend die. She was still a young girl who believed the world could be saved by people acting decently. She also believed fervently in that old Mother Earth dictum that

259

Claustrosphere was planetary treason—in fact, she had a poster of Jurgen Thor on her bedroom wall that said exactly that. How often had she lain on her bed, staring into those gorgeous eyes, dreaming of how one day she would follow the Green God into battle against Claustrosphere. Now it turned out that those eyes had lied, that Jurgen Thor and Plastic Tolstoy were just two sides of the same coin. Scout was too young to accept that nothing was sacred and that even idealists must make compromises. She was discovering all at once just how wicked the world was and what a terrible thing it was to be human. She could not take it.

"I don't care what it does to Mother Earth, I'm going to make this nightmare public," she said. "In the long run you can't build anything lasting and decent on lies."

"That is not so, my love. Lies are as important as truth, for without lies, the truth is worthless," said Jurgen.

"Now that's just bloody twaddle, and you know it. You don't like being called a hypocrite, that's all. But that's what you are, and I'm going to tell, so just get downstairs; you must have a video camera in your study."

And so Jurgen Thor returned to the study where he had been so recently conversing with Rosalie and Max, only this time he was not the masterful one, secure and in control. This time he was the prisoner of someone he considered scarcely more than a child. That was what Scout thought, anyway. As it happened, Jurgen was about to regain control in spectacularly brutal fashion. He did not want to kill her, so he made one last attempt to reason with her.

"Scout, you're making a big mistake here. No good can come of this, for you or the Earth. Are you catching what I'm saying here, babe?"

"Listen, Mr. Thor, either you're going to tape a confession about Claustrosphere and Mother Earth, or I'm going to shoot you and hang the consequences. I feel sick of everything, and I don't care anymore."

"So be it," said Jurgen Thor sadly.

It was a simple matter for Jurgen to maneuver Scout into the position he wanted. She was maintaining the maximum distance she could from him, so in order to get her to stand against the wall he required, he merely had to stand against the opposite wall himself. Of course he could have disarmed her. Jurgen was as sure as anything that Scout would not shoot if he called her bluff. But what then? He could scarcely let her go. This was one girl that he could not guarantee would keep her mouth shut. She would blab and blab and blab, and even though no one would believe her, hers was a story that Jurgen simply did not want told.

The house was built on the actual peak of the mountain. The top floor, which made up the bedroom, was parallel with the mountaintop, and the lower floors were built out from the steep rock that fell away from the summit. This meant that underneath the bottom floor, which was Jurgen's study, there was nothing but the supporting poles that jutted out of the rock face. In order that these support poles might be periodically maintained, there was a trapdoor in the study floor. It was over this trapdoor that Scout now stood.

Jurgen Thor had always loved that trapdoor. He sometimes opened it at night and sat at the edge, dropping lighted coals into the dark chasm beneath, watching as the bright embers disappeared into a grim crack in the rock hundreds of yards below. He had even had a trapeze fitted. His friends could scarcely believe it, but Jurgen Thor sometimes *swung* from beneath the trapdoor. With no safety harness or line of any sort, he would hurl himself through the air, back and forth, back and forth, nothing but rushing air between him and the chasm below.

"Scout," he said, "you are about to experience something truly strange and unique. Something I have always wondered about. Try to stay conscious and aware as it happens, for it will be a fine and a triumphant end for a brave but stupid girl.''

Even as a moment of nervous doubt and concern flitted across Scout's face, Jurgen crossed to his desk in a single stride and pushed a button. The trapdoor fell away beneath her feet, and with no more than a gasp of surprise, she disappeared into the cold darkness.

Jurgen went to the edge of the deadly hole and peered out. There was nothing to be seen; Scout was long gone, and the velvet night had enveloped her. She could still be heard, though. The scream, which had found its voice moments after Scout's deathly descent began, rang around those dark and terrible rocks, invisible in the blackness, but awesomely present all the same.

Scout screamed for a moment or two, even after she died. The drop was a long one, and the speed of sound is no respecter of the dead. As the last echoes of her short life faded into the stillness, Jurgen Thor closed the trapdoor. To his surprise, he found that he was crying, as much for himself as for Scout. He was truly sorry that he had had to kill her. Repentance would do him no good, though, he knew that. If there was a God, then Jurgen Thor was damned, and a few idle tears would not wash away his sins.

21

Betrayal and disaster

Traitor in the midst.

THE POLICE COULD ONLY STAND BACK AND WATCH AS THE FIRST
of the mighty tanker trucks pulled onto the grand mosaic-
covered piazza at the front of the European parliament.

In a Land Rover leading the lethal procession, squashed
in between Rosalie and Saunders, sat Judy, his mood
swinging from misery to elation with every bump in the
road. He was miserable because he was cold and wet and
his backside was sore. Judy had loathed camping and adventure holidays as a child, and the intervening years had
not changed his attitude at all. The lifestyle that the
Mother Earth activists had chosen for themselves was one
that, as far as Judy was concerned, they could keep.

Despite the cold and the damp, however, he was also
feeling pretty pleased with himself. Here he was, at the
very heart of a major Mother Earth action. He had infiltrated further into the organization than he could have
dreamed possible, further indeed than any of his more fa-
vored colleagues had managed in a very long time. True,
he was acting entirely on his own initiative, and had de-

serted while in the line of duty in order to do it; but Judy hoped that if he achieved the result he was looking for, then all would be forgiven.

He shifted uncomfortably in his seat.

"Keep still, will you!" barked Saunders, the man with no face.

"Sorry. I was just thinking that I may have developed hemorrhoids."

"Ha! You hear that, Rosalie?" Saunders sneered. "A noble wound, eh? Give the man a Purple Heart, he's got a sore arse. Some of us have got *real* battle scars."

One of Saunders's hands left the steering wheel and began to tug at the buckles that secured his head-bag at the neck.

"Leave it alone, Saunders, and drive the bloody car!" snapped Rosalie.

She too had a lot on her mind. Despite the fact that the raid had so far been a colossal success, Rosalie could take no pleasure in it, knowing as she did that the whole thing had been financed by Tolstoy . . . who was, to all intents and purposes, the Antichrist. She was certainly in no mood to deal with Saunders's bombast.

"Don't even think about taking off your bag, Saunders," she went on. "I'm in no kind of mood for it. Just leave Schwartz alone to worry about his bum."

It was not, in actual fact, hemorrhoids that had made Judy shift uncomfortably in his seat. His reflections on how successful he had been so far had reminded him of the unpleasant fact that his success had been obtained at the expense of deceiving Rosalie. Judy was not at all happy about this. He admired Rosalie and knew that it was only because of her recommendation that the Mother Earth leadership had agreed that he remain with the unit at all. Let alone be allowed to take part in a mission.

"He saved me from a life sentence," Rosalie had said while pleading Judy's case. "That means prison for him if we throw him out. I think we owe him the benefit of the doubt. Besides, if he is what he says he is, then he could be very useful indeed. Let me keep an eye on him, I'll answer for it."

Judy was keenly aware that Rosalie had chosen to trust him and that he intended to repay that trust by betraying her. This did not make him feel good about himself. However, it was Judy's opinion that Rosalie was about to commit a ruthless and wicked crime that he had to stop. He did not doubt that she would be acting in accordance with her own sense of what was right and just, but then every murderous zealot in history had claimed to have God on their side.

Celeb status.

Rosalie had also sought to get Max on to the team, but at this, a line had been drawn. It was felt that famous media stars could prove something of a liability while trying to hijack toxic waste shipments. Autograph hunters would only get in the way.

"If he wants to join Mother Earth," the leadership had said, "he can start at the bottom, just like anybody else."

Rosalie could see their point. Terrorist raids were not social events; lovers and boyfriends could not be included. Max was less understanding. In fact, he was mystified.

"But I'm a *major celebrity,* man!" he had exclaimed. "Most people kill to have my puss in their hood."

"Max, Mother Earth is a guerrilla army, not an L.A. nightclub or a video launch. We don't get better results because we have famous people along."

Max said that he understood, but he didn't really believe it. He had lived for too long in a world in which fame was the ultimate credential. A world where there was literally no activity, neither business nor pleasure, that was not deemed the better for having a celebrity attached to it.

"Okay, okay," he said, trying not to sound offended. "I'll

just sit on my butt in Paris and get wasted. You know, really get in touch with my excessive side. That's what I like to do anyway. Party, right? Your mission is to save stuff, mine is to party. I was only trying to be cool." There was a pause, then Max gave himself away by adding, "You're *sure* you told them it was me?"

"Yes, I did, Max. I'm sorry, but I think that made it worse."

Now Max knew there had been a mistake. He attempted to absorb what Rosalie was suggesting, but he simply could not, it was too alien a concept. His name had made things *worse?* Impossible.

"Listen," he said, "it's kinda clear there's been a fuck-up at their end, but don't you worry about it, okay? Just let it go. *Walk away.* I'll have my office check it out with these people and we'll have the crummy little no-names crawling to us on their knees in a day or two."

Rosalie took Max's advice and let it go. Reminding herself always to remember that even though hers and Max's world may have collided, they were still worlds apart.

Waste disposal unit.

The mission, on which Max would not be going, was to hijack the convoy of waste that regularly crossed the English Channel from mainland Europe for what was inaccurately called "disposal" in Britain. Then to take the captured convoy to the center of European administration in Brussels and dump it.

Britain was Europe's waste disposal unit, and indeed the world's. Anything that could not be illegally dumped in the poverty nations, Britain took. As far as Britain was concerned, dumping other people's crap, or "processing and disposal," as it was called, was actually a desirable industry that had been quite deliberately developed over many decades.

"Waste is an inevitable by-product of growth, and what is growth?" the Prime Minister had inquired of the faithful at a recent Party conference.

"Growth is good!" the faithful had thunderously replied.

"How often is it good?" the Prime Minister shouted.

"It's always good!" came the nearly evangelical answer.

"Exactly," said the PM, calming down. "And we should be proud of the amount of deadly poisons lying around in Britain, as it is proof of our important role in the growth cycle."

There was much to be proud of. Every nook and cranny in the British Isles was crammed to bursting point with hamburger boxes, old condoms, and nuclear waste. From disused mine shafts to condemned housing projects, the waste "disposal" companies proved endlessly ingenious at finding new ways to "dispose" of the undisposable. And they needed to, for more kept arriving every day. Sometimes the garbage was comparatively benign. Many American cities, for instance, banned from using up any more of their own environment as landfill dumps for domestic garbage, paid the British to take it off their hands. Often, though, the garbage was more sinister. Nuclear waste "disposal," for instance, was a major industry in Britain. Every day the thousands of power stations, with which the French kept the European Grid alive, produced copious quantities of radioactive waste that the British then "disposed" of. They did this by sealing it in concrete tombs. Tombs that they then covered in alarming symbols, in the hope of dissuading as yet unborn civilizations, thousands of years hence, from tampering with that which would surely kill them.

Such is progress. The Egyptians left tombs that thousands of years later yielded up treasures of indescribable beauty, testimony to the glory of their civilization. The British, who have produced so many things that could serve as splendid witness to a great society, leave only deadly poison to be remembered by.

Target.

Then there were the industrial toxins. Those embarrassing by-products of economic activity that could kill a river or poison a sky. Toxins that were taken once a month by convoy from the industrial centers of Europe to be "processed" in Britain. It was these toxins that were to be the target of Rosalie's raid.

The convoys had long been the focus of much peaceful protest. The Natura argument was that at any point in the lengthy "disposal" process, a terrible disaster could occur. The authorities argued that such a disaster could not occur because the safety precautions employed were foolproof. Eventually, the Natura leaders decided that this complacent attitude must be exposed. It was decided that Mother Earth should demonstrate the convoy's vulnerability by hijacking it before it reached the Channel Tunnel and diverting it to Brussels.

"We will mount a terrorist raid and capture the whole thing," the Mother Earth strategists had said at their secret planning meeting, "in order to demonstrate how easy it would be to mount a terrorist raid and capture the whole thing."

Once the convoy had been taken to Brussels, the plan was that the entire cargo would be dumped outside the thirty-five-chambered Palace of Peace and Profit. (The thirty-sixth chamber had been destroyed by the bomb attack on Jurgen Thor.)

"We will see just how dangerous those Euro bastards think this stuff is when they have to climb over it to get to their cars!"

The Founding Beardies.

That Rosalie's group should have been chosen to carry out the hijack showed the great respect in which she was held at Mother Earth. It was an enormous responsibility, toward which Rosalie would normally have been looking with a thrill of excitement. However, she could not get the grim discovery of how Mother Earth was financed out of her mind. Jurgen Thor's little lesson in pragmatism had changed her attitude to her work entirely, and it was with weary resignation that she had made the final preparations for the action at hand.

The hijack was, in fact, to be Rosalie's first direct action as a unit commander, or "Group Facilitator" as the rank was known within Mother Earth. To have become a Group Facilitator was a tremendous leap for Rosalie. There were only fifteen Groups worldwide, and Rosalie would be the youngest Facilitator by far. Rosalie did not like being called a Facilitator, any more than her second-in-command liked being called a "Facilitator's Friend," or her superior liked being called a "Team Enabler." These rather horrid titles were generally felt to be a total embarrassment. They could not be dropped, however, because they were part of the Mother Earth tradition and held dear by the very oldest activists, veterans who had been so overexposed to toxicity during the early days of struggle that there was really very little left of them anymore but false teeth, boring anecdotes, and a seemingly insatiable desire to inform people of how things had been in the early days.

Before Jurgen Thor had formed Natura, there had been a terrible period when mainstream environmental politics were the preserve of naive, idealistic old hippies and, perhaps even more gruesomely, witches and "new pagans." These greenies were nice (some of them, anyway) but a bit stupid, firmly believing that if they and their friends pretended that something was so, then it would be so.

"If we want to change the world, we must first change ourselves," earnest people with beards and big sweaters and the occasional pointy hat assured each other. "You cannot destroy a structure by creating a structure."

"But surely this makes no sense and could in fact be

described as full," the odd brave soul would say, only to be told that their hostility proved the point.

The bearded and sweatered ones (the ones with pointy hats having by this time walked out in disgust and gone off to celebrate a convenient solstice) claimed that since it was power structures that maintained the polluters in their positions of authority, then those structures should not be copied.

"We will not caricature the methods of those we wish to destroy!" they said. "We will reinvent a non-exploitative structure, to bring about a nonexploitative world. We must *be* what we stand for! Otherwise we will be hypocrites."

Whether they were hypocrites or not was a matter of opinion; what was beyond dispute, however, was that they very soon became a complete joke.

Having rejected the concept of leadership, their position was presented by an ad hoc committee of occasional speakers, which meant, of course, that they completely failed to communicate with the outside world. The truth (as everybody knew but no one had the guts to admit) was that an argument, no matter how good, if delivered by an ad hoc occasional speaker was always going to be less convincing than an argument, no matter how bad, delivered by a fiery and charismatic media star.

"If you consume a resource without making provision for its replacement, it will eventually run out," mumbled an occasional speaker.

"So what? Let's party," shouted the well-oiled, highly geared media campaign organized by those who profited from resource exploitation.

When Mother Earth was formed, it was recognized even by the stupidest Big Sweater that you can't have an army without commanders. However, the Founding Beardies, as they were already becoming known, remained opposed to aping the structures of the forces against which they would be called upon to fight. Hence, Mother Earth soldiers were called "activists," which was fine as far as it went, but who was to tell the activists what to do? The answer the Founding Beardies came up with was "Catalysts." Catalysts would tell activists what to do and would be the rough equivalent of sergeants. Unfortunately, as the common structure grew larger and more complex, the Beardies soon ran out of credible alternative terms to describe the various posts that were being created. Rosalie had risen to the rank (or NHL, which stood for Nonhierarchical Level) of Catalyst by the age of twenty-one. Since then, she had been a Suggester (whose "suggestions" had to be obeyed by both Catalysts and activists), a Coordinator, a Facilitator's Friend, and now she was a Facilitator. If the Earth and she were to survive long enough, Rosalie might eventually hope to rise to the exalted Nonhierarchical Level of Number One Equal Person, which was Jurgen Thor's post and meant Commander-in-Chief.

Nice work if you can get it.

The hijack took place at Lille in Northern France, which was the rendezvous point for all the great toxic convoys of Europe. It was here that the colossal transports coming from the industrial regions of Germany met up with those arriving from Italy, France, and Spain and made up a supergarbage convoy that would then make its way on up to Ostend. It was at Ostend that the mouth of the third (and least leaky) of the Channel Tunnels was located.

Taking control of the convoy had been absurdly easy. Even the terrorists, who had only embarked upon the hijack in order to prove how stunningly easy it would be, were stunned at how easy it actually was. They just walked in, pointed a gun or two, and drove the tanker trucks away. Of course, they should not really have been surprised at the ease with which the crime was executed; the world was far too overloaded with poison for governments to get very excited about its transportation anymore.

For well over a century, the stuff had been shifted around the world endlessly, on trucks, boats, railways. It was, as they say, as common as mud.

"I don't know, I thought they'd have hidden guards or security locks or *something,*" Rosalie's Facilitator's Friend had remarked to her as they took control.

Someone to watch over us.

The fact was that the cynics in Mother Earth had been as naive as everybody else in the world about the nature of government. The basic presumption of modern society is that "they" (that vague, catchall term for the powers that be) are at least *attempting* to look after our best interests. That there is a logical and at least partially benign force that watches over us and for which we pay our taxes. Certainly, we all think that "they" are, in the main, a bunch of hypocritical bastards on the make, but deep down we presume that at heart they want what's best for us. "Surely 'they' wouldn't let us drink polluted water?" we say to ourselves. "Surely 'they' would tell us if the food was poisonous. Surely 'they' would never haul people in for crimes those people did not commit and put them away for twenty years without appeal?"

But most of the time, of course, either out of malice or incompetence, "they" would do these things. They would also, and have always, left nuclear missiles lying around behind wire fences, allowed radioactive materials to travel on ordinary trains, and, as in the case of the Lille convoy, allowed toxic waste to be trundled around the public highways, protected by poorly regulated private security companies whose only reason for being in the "business" at all is to make a profit from it.

The dreadful suspicion.

And so the terrorists drove the tanker trucks away. Brussels was only about forty minutes' journey from Lille, and by the time "they" (in this case the police) knew that any-thing was wrong, the convoy had already arrived in the suburbs of the capital city of Europe. At this point there was nothing much that the police could do. They could not risk confronting or attacking the tankers, for every one of the transports was a Pandora's Box, filled with hellish poisons. The only course of action open to the bemused police was to wait for the hijackers to stop and do what-ever it was that they planned to do.

It was very late at night, and so there was little traffic as Rosalie led her cargo of death through the streets of the city. Brussels, being home to all the politicians, had an orbital filter, so of course it still operated on daytime. In the darkness of the cab, Judy was trying not to shift about too much on his hemorrhoids. He did not wish to provoke Saunders's anger, partly because he was scared of Saun-ders, and partly because Saunders was very noisy when roused, and Judy needed peace to think.

He was very tense. He knew that at some point he would have to act, but he did not know when. For Judy was con-vinced that Rosalie planned to poison the heart of Brus-sels, and he knew that it was his duty to stop her. It all fitted; the same sequence of events that he had followed on so many previous occasions was happening again. Ex-cept that this time Judy was not piecing it together after it had happened, he was actually there, right at the heart of it. He could prevent it.

Judy believed absolutely that this operation would not be a mere demonstration; he knew that Rosalie's team would not simply dump the convoy at the Palace of Peace and Profit and then disappear, as they had said they would. Judy believed that there would be a far, far more spectacular protest than that. There always was.

Stealing a glance at Rosalie, he reflected on how little one could ever tell about a person from his or her appear-ance. Rosalie did not look like a villain, like a person capable of coldly murdering hundreds, perhaps thousands, of people to further her own political agenda. Not that Judy doubted Rosalie's aggressive commitment to the environmental cause, but it had seemed to him that her principles were based on a love of life and a respect for other living things. She seemed an unlikely murderer. Yet unless Judy had made the most monumental miscalculation, Rosalie was about to render Brussels, and possibly the whole of Belgium, temporarily uninhabitable; and Judy knew that he had not miscalculated. The disasters always occurred where Natura was best placed to exploit them, and the shadowy hand of Mother Earth was always detectable. It was the same as before; all the elements were in place.

This was why Judy had infiltrated the radical Green Movement. He had become convinced that a dreadful, black propaganda war was being fought. From the wealth of evidence that he had assembled over the years, Judy had concluded that Mother Earth must have become frustrated with the complacency with which the public viewed the environmental destruction of the Earth. It had therefore decided upon a most terrible course. Planning and executing a colossal double bluff, whereby the public might be shocked out of that complacency.

Judy had concluded that Mother Earth was creating set-piece disasters in order that it might then protest against them.

Hidden agendas.

The poison convoy quickly arrived at the Piazza of the Palace of Peace and Profit and came to a halt among the sculptures and the fountains. As the noise of the engines began to die away, Judy knew that he had to act. The plan as described to him was that, at this point, the convoy drivers would disable their tankers and scatter into the night to take refuge in safe houses around the city. The piazza was huge, and all the floodlighting had been knocked out by an auxiliary unit. Besides which, the police were keeping well clear, being unsure as to what the hijackers intended to do with all the poison. The activists would simply melt away, having proved the vulnerability of the toxic waste disposal system.

That was the plan, as Judy had heard it, but he did not believe that the transporters were going to be merely disabled. He believed that they would be sabotaged, which was why he had to act.

Judy produced the inflatable handgun that he had kept secreted about his person since infiltrating the unit (he rather suspected, in fact, that this was the source of his aggravated hemorrhoids). He held it to Rosalie's head.

"Ms. Connolly. I am an FBI agent, and I demand that you order the immediate withdrawal of your people from the scene of this operation."

"Judy, you—" Rosalie blurted out, but Judy was in a hurry.

"*Now,* Ms. Connolly! I mean it. I suspect that you are intending to poison the city, and I shall certainly kill you to stop that. Order a withdrawal *now,* or I fire!"

Rosalie thought that Judy had gone mad. However, mad people are perfectly capable of pulling triggers, and Judy looked serious. Rosalie shrugged.

"The operation's basically over anyway; disabling the trucks was just a bit of mischief." Taking up her radio, she gave the order to withdraw. "Take no further action," she recited on Judy's orders. "This operation is terminated."

Through the window of the Land Rover, Judy watched the activists scatter.

"You too, Saunders. Run," he said.

"I'm going to find you one day and I'm going to kill you," said Saunders, leaving the truck.

Once they were alone, Judy faced Rosalie in the darkness

of the deserted piazza. He silently flipped on the little audio recorder in his wristwatch. What he needed now was a confession. Having of necessity stopped the sabotage before it had occurred, he wanted proof that it was to have happened. This would require very careful handling. The police would soon begin to edge their way forward, so Judy had only minutes in which to coax from Rosalie that which he already knew. He had little experience of interrogation, but he did know that the first rule was to show confidence. Lead with the presumption that everybody knows exactly what's being discussed.

"I'm curious, Rosalie. How were you going to do it?" he asked.

"I have no idea what you're talking about, you two-faced little worm."

"It would have to look like an accident, wouldn't it? Corrosives, I suppose. Rusty tankers finally giving way? Is that it? You rupture the tankers yourselves and then claim that you've *uncovered* the criminal negligence of the toxic waste industry. Of course it's quite a coincidence that the 'accident' just happened to occur during a Mother Earth hijack, but so what? Coincidences happen and who would ever suspect the saintly environmental movement of dirty tricks? Not with lots of nice Natura people all set up and ready to scream about the nasty corrupt government. Do they know, Rosalie? Natura? Do all those pretty little hippies know what you do? I don't think so, they're as big a bunch of patsies as the public they preach to."

The gist of Judy's theory was beginning to sink in.

"Are you suggesting that Mother Earth *causes* environmental pollution so that Natura can kick up a fuss about it?" Rosalie seemed genuinely flabbergasted. Sufficiently flabbergasted for a tiny doubt to appear at the back of Judy's mind.

"You wouldn't be the first to play that trick," he said, "the Bureau uses agents provocateurs all the time."

There was a silence. It was strange to be in the middle

276

of that great city, at the very administrative hub of a vast, international federation, and yet hear a silence. Not a deep silence, there was noise in the distance as the police cleared the area surrounding the piazza, but in the cab of the Land Rover there was a genuine pause in proceedings. Finally Rosalie spoke.

"I have never been so insulted in all my life," she said, and ignoring Judy's gun, she punched him in the mouth. Judy dropped his weapon, and Rosalie produced hers.

"Come on," she said, "I'm going to hand you over to Saunders."

They left the Land Rover and began to make their way across the huge, dark, empty piazza. It was about two hundred yards to the edge, and they crossed it slowly and carefully. Rosalie was nervous, lest some brave police officer had finally decided to make his or her way toward the silent convoy.

She was, however, still pretty stunned by the nature of Judy's accusation and could not resist further comment.

"I still can't believe it," she whispered, pushing her gun into Judy's back. "It's got to be a joke, hasn't it? Surely you're not going to tell me that the FBI actually believes *we're* causing environmental disasters?"

Judy's confidence was evaporating fast. His theory was suddenly beginning to look a bit stupid. There had, after all, been no disaster, and Rosalie's indignant surprise seemed worryingly genuine.

"As a matter of fact," he confessed, "it's my own private theory. Everybody else in the Bureau laughed at it."

"You amaze me," said Rosalie with bitter sarcasm.

Then, just as they reached the edge of the piazza and were about to disappear into the deserted streets beyond, they heard a noise. It was a sort of huge hiss. It came from the toxic waste tankers that they had so recently left. Judy and Rosalie turned to see what appeared to be steam of some sort emanating from the side of one of the tankers. Then the smell hit them; it was horrible, enough to shrivel the hair on the inside of their noses, and both Rosalie and Judy retched in disgust. Just then the steaming, hissing tanker seemed to buckle . . . it just gave way in the middle. There was a splash, and the ground surrounding it began to froth and burn, quite literally, as if the stone had been melted.

Anyone with the slightest knowledge of what that buck-led tanker contained could see that a major environmental disaster was about to occur. Both Rosalie and Judy had that knowledge. It was like being there at the moment the bomb doors opened.

"It's going to spread to the other trucks," said Rosalie. "The whole bloody lot will go."

Judy was completely astonished. This was exactly the thing that he had just prevented, and yet here it was, hap-pening anyway.

"Rosalie," Judy said. "You didn't do this, did you?"

"For God's sake, man, of course I didn't, you mad idiot!" she replied. "This is the bloody stuff we try and stop."

The fire and the corrosion around the ruptured tanker was beginning to take hold. Pandora's box had definitely been opened, and all the evils of the world were flood-ing out.

"I think we should run," said Judy. But Rosalie did not hear, she was already gone.

22

The penny drops

The minister replies.

JUDY PUSHED HIS WAY THROUGH THE TERRIFIED CROWDS AND
shouting policemen and away from the scene of the ruptured tankers. He would have liked to have hailed a
cab, but of course there were none to be had. Only endless emergency vehicles screaming and wailing, hurtling
through the streets, hurrying toward yet another stable
from which the horse had well and truly bolted.

The toxins were in fact heading out from the piazza
more quickly than Judy himself. Within minutes, they had
hissed their way across the piazza floor, poured straight
down the storm drains, and into the water system. In doing
so, they had, as it happened, brought about one positive
result amid all the horror. They had destroyed the much
loathed and completely incomprehensible symbolic mosaics that covered the whole Euro piazza. Although, interest-
ingly, the chewing gum that covered the mosaics remained
unaffected, no toxin in the universe having the power to
remove chewing gum once some antisocial bastard has decided to drop it.

Even as the burning poisons poured into the storm drains, BioSuited Natura scientists were on the spot, addressing the media.

"All tap water in Belgium will very shortly be undrinkable," the principal spokesperson stated to the robot news cameras that surrounded him.

"Now hang on, hang on, hang on, things are nothing like that serious," said the relevant junior minister, who had been sent out to attempt a little damage control, and who was wearing a BioProtection outfit the size of a bus. "Let's not be alarmist about this now, shall we? It isn't that the water will be undrinkable, you *can* drink it, of course you can drink it . . . and if you're a fit person with no history of liver disorders, and if you remember to induce vomiting immediately after swallowing, well, then you should suffer nothing worse than a mild, or perhaps severe case of the runs. So you see? The word *undrinkable* scarcely describes the situation at all, and alarmist generalizations, of which my radical friends here seem so fond, are really no help to anyone."

"All rivers and streams leading out of Belgium must be damned at the frontiers," the Natura spokesperson insisted. "Also infants and the aged must be evacuated. The atmosphere will be lethal to them and to anyone with respiratory difficulties for at least a month."

"Now hang on, hang on, hang on," said the relevant junior minister. "Let's just get our terms straight here, shall we? Bandying words like *lethal* about is really no help to anyone. What exactly do we mean by *lethal* exactly? Hmm? If my alarmist friend here means that breathing the air will kill babies and grannies, well, then, yes, perhaps there is some foundation to the basis of his remarks, but really it's much too early to be counting bodies, surely? And as for sealing the borders of Belgium, may I remind my sanctimonious chum that it was his terrorist pals who dumped the damn stuff in Brussels in the first place."

"Perhaps the minister would rather that the disaster had

happened in Lille? Or Ostend? In the English Channel, maybe?"

As it happened, the minister, who lived in Brussels, would definitely have preferred that, but he did not say so.

"The point is that the rupture of the tankers has happened. As for years we have been warning that it would. If it had not happened on this trip, then it would have been next time, or the time after. The people of Europe should be thankful to the activists of Mother Earth who diverted this deadly load into the very seat of government. At least now those whose greed, idleness, or complacency have led to this terrible disaster are having to stand face-to-face with the results."

"Well, now, you see that's absolute nonsense," the relevant junior minister said. "As I can make perfectly clear by explaining to you seventeen simple points. Let me take the second point first, because it relates partly to the first, and partly to the third. I shall, of course, return to the first point in due course before proceeding with my other points."

The relevant junior minister was very good at damage control. He had scarcely got halfway through his points before the cameras had been switched off and everyone including the Natura spokesperson had given up and gone for a drink.

No direction home.

Puffing and panting and generally making heavy going of it (Judy's asymmetric legs were not at all suited to this type of thing), Judy arrived at a small café that was situated on the corner of a tiny square at the crossroads of four little streets.

All the bottled water had, of course, been sold, so Judy had to settle for a hot chocolate with whipped cream, warm cognac, and a great big double-chocolate brioche.

281

Holding a handkerchief over his face between swigs and bites, he sat down to collect his thoughts, some of which had sunk so low that he had to fish them out of his pants cuffs. Assessing his situation, he recognized it for what it was, which was not good. The crossroads upon which the little café stood offered, Judy thought, something of a metaphor for his life, for that too was at a crossroads. Unfortunately, it was crossroads off which all the roads were dead ends. Look at it from whatever direction he might, and Judy tried them all, even standing on a table in the corner of the room to do it, he was in something of a pickle. A solitary pickle, alone, despised, and unloved, the sort of pickle that is normally only found in a hamburger and that has to be fished out in order to render the burger edible.

Which road should Judy take? The road back? It would not be easy; his old colleagues in the FBI no doubt considered him a traitor and a snitch, and who could blame them? Judy had, after all, assisted in the escape of a suspected terrorist from a foreign police force, thus disgracing the entire Bureau. All things considered, the road back looked rocky. Judy searched for an alternative route.

Could he take a road forward? No obvious ones sprang to mind. His new colleagues in Mother Earth would no doubt now also consider him a traitor and a snitch. Again, this could scarcely be described as unreasonable. He had, after all, not only attempted to arrest their Facilitator, but had also accused them of going about their business with a callous and cynical immorality that made Machiavelli look like Julie Andrews.

How on earth had he got himself into such a fix? How had he managed to alienate absolutely everybody and achieve absolutely nothing?

Judy rehearsed again in his mind that series of suspicions and conclusions that had brought him to the lonely position in which he found himself. He had burned his bridges at the FBI because he had believed he had sufficient circumstantial evidence to conclude that the Mother Earth activists were agents provocateurs. Nobody at the Bureau would take his conclusions seriously, so he had been forced to act on his own. He had successfully infiltrated a Mother Earth unit and correctly predicted that during their next mission a massive environmental disaster would occur.

After that, sadly, his theories had collapsed. Rosalie was innocent, he was sure of that. Her surprise at his accusations had been genuine, and besides, both she and her unit had been well away when the disaster occurred. What had happened? Could they have carried out the sabotage before Judy had intervened? It was not possible; the convoy had been flying along the highway only moments before Judy had made Rosalie order a withdrawal. Could there perhaps have been a second unit involved, of which he knew nothing? Perhaps, although Judy could see no obvious reason for an extra terrorist presence. Had he not intervened, Rosalie's unit would have been quite capable of carrying out the sabotage. But he had, and they didn't.

Was it sabotage at all? Could it possibly have been a coincidence that made the first tanker rupture? A genuine accident? No, Judy would not believe it. He had come to Europe predicting exactly what had happened, and it had happened; the fact that he seemed to have erred on who the culprits might be did not detract from the fact that, yet again, the pattern had been maintained.

Somebody had sabotaged that convoy, and since Judy no longer believed that it had been Rosalie's unit, that meant that it had been tampered with before they had seized it. What was going on? Judy did not realize it, but the clue was staring him in the face.

Soap internationale.

There was a TV on in the corner of the café bar. Judy's eye was inevitably drawn toward it, reminding him momentarily of his finest hour, his achievement in getting

Rosalie away from her Garda escort. Quite a stunt to have pulled off, and for what? Nothing. He had completely lost the trust he had gained, and he was no closer to the truth.

The TV was tuned to the omnipresent Tolstoy system. A simulcast soap internationale was playing. These were dramas that were made in English, in Los Angeles, and then simultaneously dubbed into literally hundreds of languages by means of a computerized, voice-sensitive translator. The computer "heard" the American actor speak, and then, using a synthesizer with a vast vocabulary of words and phrases recorded by actors from other countries, it created new dialogue. Once an actor had comprehensively loaded his voice into the synthesizer, it was possible for him or her to dub shows forever, without ever being there, or in many cases even still being alive. Thus everybody in the world could now watch the same soap at much the same times, also the same news and the same talk shows. Everybody now heard and saw the same things. Even the French had all but given up on attempting to defend cultural boundaries. It was simply impossible to legislate against the myriad global ways in which information and imagery could be delivered.

The key to the mystery was about to be beamed into literally billions of homes in hundreds of different languages, just as that key had been beamed in countless times before. Somebody had to work it out sometime. That somebody was Judy, who was about to make a very big discovery, although not quite as big as the consequences would be.

Global marketing.

Judy idly began to count the "product placements" that were featured within the soap internationale drama. Soft drinks, designer clothes, cars. Some of the items outside manufacturers had paid to have featured, others were actu-

284

ally made by companies owned by Tolstoy and his associates. The term *conflict of interest* had long since become an obscure footnote in legal history. As Plastic Tolstoy himself had said during one of the last great court battles to prevent insider trading: "Hey! If a conflict of interest bothers you, just let me buy everything, you won't see no conflict then."

These days, product placement was considered an art form in itself. There were annual awards in which the drama directors who had most copiously featured their bosses' products were honored. It had got subtle enough for negative placement to have become a commonly used technique.

"Did you see how every time the Slasher killed a girl with a broken bottle I used a Pepsi bottle?" the proud young director of *Slasher 23* would boast. "But the *cops* only drink Coke."

"No, I didn't notice that," the proud young director's friend would say.

"Exactly!" the proud young director would shout in triumph. "You didn't *see* it, but it was there, and believe me, in your subconscious, Pepsi ain't so wholesome anymore."

Judy noted that one of the groovy young characters in the soap internationale that he was watching wore a Claustrophobe T-shirt. Claustrophobe was a clothing company set up by Tolstoy to exploit the cynicism and bleak humor that young people had developed about being potentially the last generation on Earth. They marketed jeans and T-shirts with ironic slogans on them like "Better a live rat than a dead self-righteous bastard" and "Listening to greenies won't help you live longer, it'll just seem longer."

It was a source of near despair to Natura that its constant appeals to adolescents to consider that the end of the world was nigh had actually served to create a "Well, fuck it" attitude among kids. In fact, that was one of Claustrophobe's best-selling lines, a sweatshirt depicting a slimy dead Earth with the simple phrase "Well, fuck it" embossed underneath.

Tolstoy's clothes on Tolstoy's TV show. Judy had a vague suspicion that it might still be illegal to so blatantly self-promote your own products, but, short of shooting down satellites, the law was impossible to enforce anyway, so the matter was entirely academic.

His mind was wandering. Judy knew that he should be concentrating on planning his next move, but the TV continued to exercise its mesmeric effect on him. The commercials came on, as they did every ninety seconds at this time of the day. First up there was an ad for the very clothes that Judy had just been musing over.

"They're getting cheeky," Judy thought to himself as the sexy Euro kids cavorted on the screen in Claustrophobe T-shirts and hats. "That bastard Tolstoy just can't lose. The ads are just an extension of the program. Control the information, control the ads, and sell anything you want."

Hard on this thought came a newsbreak. The terrible toxic spills in the European capital were, of course, the top story, and Judy forlornly watched the footage in the ludicrous hope that some clue as to the source of the disaster might emerge. He saw none. After the news there was another commercial break, and suddenly, while he watched the first ad, Judy got his clue. The penny finally dropped.

Unwelcome prodigal.

Judy now knew which road he had to take. He drained his cognac, finished his brioche, and went off to make his peace with the FBI.

He did not relish returning. He had had no contact with them since absconding with Rosalie at Dublin Airport, having avoided any form of communication on the not unreasonable grounds that if they had known where he was, they would have instantly arrested him. However, Judy was pretty certain that he had finally worked out what was going on, and he needed the Bureau's resources to prove it.

The preparations that Judy made before facing his old boss were both thorough and unpleasant. He dropped all of his IDs down a drain, a drain now so filled with dangerous poisons that the chances of the documents ever seeing the light again were zero. Next, Judy rolled around a bit in the wet gutter in order to give himself a disheveled appearance, then, finally and most painfully, he selected the toughest-looking fellow in the toughest-looking bar he could find and threw a glass of beer in his face.

Crawling out into the street ten minutes later, his eyes blackened and his nose broken, Judy was soon picked up by the police.

"I am an FBI agent who has just escaped from terrorists. I demand to see the American consul."

And so it was that Judy made his way back to the U.S., where the FBI placed him under arrest and asked him to explain himself.

It did not go down well.

"You're actually trying to tell me," Klaw bellowed, "that this *woman* dragged you onto the luggage conveyor, off the luggage conveyor, through a huge crowd full of soldiers and cops, and yet you were unable to stop her!"

"That is correct, sir," said Judy through his puffed and swollen lips.

"No, Schwartz," Klaw insisted, "it is not correct. I do not believe it. Not even you could fail so spectacularly in your duty. I believe that for reasons of your own you helped this girl escape."

"Reasons, sir? What reasons could I possibly have for helping a terrorist?"

Klaw hurled the photos of Rosalie down upon his desk.

"Pale skin reasons! Green eyes reasons! Cute little tits and ass reasons! You wanted to get laid, didn't you, Schwartz?"

"Sir, I—"

"Don't argue with me! You saw that you had one chance in your life to pork a really fuckable piece, and you took it. Look at you! You're disgusting. A deformed, half-crippled little nerd. When did you last get any? Never, that's when. What kind of life is that? Then suddenly you're chained to some dream pussy. And I'll bet she was putting it out, wasn't she? Baiting the honey trap? Of course she was. She knew a contemptible, inadequate piece of shit when she saw one. You weakened, didn't you, Schwartz? You followed your nasty little dick, and it's going to lead you straight to the cage. Now what have you got to say?"

"I'm gay, sir."

"Nothing! Like I thought—" Klaw paused for a moment as the statement sunk in "—say what?"

"I'm gay, sir; what's more, I've been legally bound to my husband for twelve years. We were married in San Francisco. It's all in my file, sir."

Klaw scrolled furiously through Judy's computer file. To his horror, it turned out that Judy was right.

"I didn't know we took you guys in the Bureau."

"Sir, the FBI has been legally obliged to employ a representative quota of homosexuals for over sixty years now."

"Oh . . . yeah, I did hear that, actually."

"Besides, sir. Hoover was gay."

"That's a damn lie!"

Klaw was rather shaken. He had thought he had Judy's case all sewn up, and now it appeared that he would have to think again, something he hated doing. In fact, he rather disliked even having to think the first time, let alone having to do it again. It had never occurred to Klaw that Judy was gay, nor had it seriously occurred to any of Judy's other colleagues. He never mentioned his private life while at work, so people just made the usual presumption of heterosexuality. The bullies who taunted him as a "queer" did so because they were dimwits, not because they had an astute eye for people's sexual preferences.

Judy seized on the moment of Klaw's confusion to press home his version of events.

"Ms. Connolly managed to lift my gun, sir. She threatened to shoot both myself and any bystanders who got in the way. We were in a crowded airport, sir, I thought it best to accede to her demands." Judy was hoping that Klaw had heard no reports of Judy's shouted allegiance to the Elitest Church of Christ the Crew-Cut. Klaw's silence suggested that he had not, and Judy felt safe to carry on with his story. "She had people at the airport, and I was effectively a captive of Mother Earth from that point on. They kept me with them in the hope that they might learn something of Bureau policy toward them from me." Judy paused for a moment and then remarked with casual stoicism, "As you can see, sir, their methods of persuasion were not of the gentlest."

Klaw eyed Judy's wounds. They certainly looked painful.

"What did you tell them?" Klaw inquired.

Judy tried to look shocked.

"I am a Federal Agent, sir. I told them nothing of either our policies or agents. In fact, they got nothing from me at all."

Judy got away with it. Klaw had no proof of wrongdoing, could find no motive, and the fact that Judy had returned voluntarily did not correspond with the idea that he had absconded. The Bureau was forced to accept that he had genuinely been captured in the line of duty. Which meant, to their horror, that they had to give him a Purple Heart for his wounds. They made it clear in the citation, however, that he had utterly disgraced the whole organization by being captured by an unarmed woman while he had the support of two police officers. Judy, who had never been popular in the Bureau, was now a marked man. He never ate in the cafeteria, never used the men's room, and locked any office in which he was working.

The lonesome trail finally gets warm.

Judy had no time to get distressed about his ostracism. He cared not one jot for the opinion of the majority of his colleagues anyway. The cold, lonesome trail that he had been following for so long was finally beginning to warm up a little. Judy set himself the task of finding out which commercials had followed which news bulletins for the last twenty or thirty years. He wanted to know what products were being pushed when environmental disaster was the top story. Day after day he plowed through the records of the broadcasting companies, the copyright libraries, and indeed the FBI itself, which monitored all electronic media.

"Sounds *absolutely fascinating,*" Judy's husband, Roger, said to him as he dabbed calamine lotion onto Judy's swollen eyes the evening after his return to work. "Being a secret agent must be just so incredible."

"I can't really tell you what it's about, Roger," Judy apologized.

"Can't tell me about thirty years of commercial breaks? How will I ever get to sleep!"

23

The lull before the storm

Tired and emotional.

WHILE JUDY WAS FERRETING OUT A TRUTH THAT WOULD shortly put both Rosalie and Max in mortal danger, Rosalie had joined her lover at the George V Hotel in Paris. She was in a funny mood.

"I want a holiday," she told Max after the laminate had been duly stretched. "I want a holiday a lot."

"Cool," said Max, who was pretty much on holiday all the time anyway.

"I'm tired, and I need a rest," she said.

"Anytime is party time for me, babe. Let's raise hell."

"I said I need a rest, and don't call me babe," said Rosalie.

Had she been able to see into the future, Rosalie might have been even more anxious for a break. The gift of foresight would have shown her how much more limited her travel options were soon to become. She could not, however, see into the future. What's more, she had suddenly become very confused about her past.

"I don't know what I've been doing, Max. I look back, and it just doesn't seem to make any sense."

"Welcome to my world, girl," said Max, "I feel that way nearly every morning."

But Rosalie was crying.

The toxic waste action had been something of a watershed. It was bad enough, having one's first action as a Facilitator degenerate into a massive environmental disaster, without the FBI popping up in the middle of it all and accusing you of the most extraordinary and horrendous things. That, coupled with the revelations that she had heard at Jurgen Thor's house, had so utterly thrown Rosalie that her idealism and determination seemed suddenly to have deserted her. She had been on active service for an unbroken five years and was entitled to some leave.

It was to be the lull before the storm.

Language barrier.

She and Max headed southwest and took a little room in a small village in Provence. Its sweet-smelling linen-covered quilt and little vase of flowers on the hand-painted dresser reminded both of them of the room in which they had first consummated their love. It made Rosalie feel a little lighter of heart. Max too felt good. A European tour with the person you love is something many a young American has dreamed of, and Max had always wanted to see the real France. He had found Paris a little snooty. He did not speak French, and on a number of occasions, while desperate to get his bearings, he had approached a Parisian and made the apologetic appeal, "Excuse me, but do you speak English?" only to be met by the infuriating riposte, "Yes, of course. Do you speak French?"

Nothing irritates the French cultural elite so much as the fact that, because of American economic hegemony after the Second World War, English became the dominant world language. The lingua franca, as it is called, as if to add insult to injury. It is a source of constant pain to the educated French that, but for a couple of unlucky results in the battles of the late eighteenth century, the United States would have been known as *Les États-Unis,* McDonald's would be selling *Grands Macs,* and rock 'n' roll would be known as *rocher at petit pain.* It is an understandable gripe for which Quebec and New Caledonia are no consolation at all.

Max had soon had enough of being patronized for being monolingual. His pride stung, he retreated to his hotel and holed himself up in his room, desperately cramming the French language. Virtual Reality had, of course, made learning the basics of a new language much easier than it had been in the past. It is universally acknowledged that the best way to learn to speak a foreign tongue is to plunge in among the natives. With a decent Linguafone VR helmet, it was possible to do just that in an extremely intense manner. Max spent days inside his helmet, visiting *boulangeries,* ordering *café au lait,* and buying bus tickets over and over again.

A *day in Provence.*

By the time he and Rosalie headed south, Max was very proud of his new skills and insisted on employing them to conduct all negotiations.

"Vous avez une chambre pour la nuit, avec une salle de bain?" he said, giving it plenty of Gallic intonation and pantomimic hand motion. All to no avail, as it happened. Max was a very good actor, but even he could not mime a bedroom with private bath. He was met with a blank stare.

"I'm awfully sorry," the house agent said in a plummy English voice, "I'm afraid I don't speak French."

Rather disappointed, Max was forced to negotiate for their pretty little room in English.

Having settled in, and then settled in again in a different position, they set off to explore the village. It was not as much fun as they had hoped, confined as they were to hot, dusty little BioTubes. Provence, having long since given up any pretense at agriculture in order to concentrate on tourism, was not granted the convenience of orbital sunscreening. Since this meant that strolling outside was as hot and stuffy as staying inside, Rosalie suggested they drop in somewhere for a drink. This was an idea that Max never turned down, and they made for a little cockneystyle pub called the Dog and Duck.

"Deux verres de vin rouge, s'il vous plaît," Max said firmly. Only to be met again with a noncomprehending look.

"Nobody speaks French here, Max," Rosalie explained. "This is Provence. The whole area became completely English-speaking over fifty years ago. They even drive on the left." She bought a couple of pints of bitter, and they sat together, alone in the smoky lounge.

Decent proposal.

Max was looking rather uncomfortable, a bit sheepish. There was something on his mind.

"What's up, Max?" Rosalie inquired.

"Oh, it's nothing," he said. "Well, hey, that's not true, it's definitely a vibe, you know, if you think these things are important, which I think I do, it's a vibe. . . . I was just wondering if, well, basically, if you would marry me?"

Rosalie was caught rather off her guard. Her eyes stared, and her face colored to a deep blush. Green does not, on the whole, go with red, except maybe on apples and in this case on Rosalie, at least as far as Max was concerned. Staring into her eyes, Max felt that he had never seen anyone or anything look lovelier. Feeling that his proposal had done little or nothing to reflect the heart-stopping beauty of its object, Max dropped to one knee and tried again.

"Rosalie, I love you. I would lay down my life for you

in a heartbeat. Your eyes are like emeralds, and your skin, when you aren't blushing the way you happen to be now, is like ivory . . . with freckles. You care about stuff, and your voice is smooth as Irish cream or something, and you can fight and handle a gun and I love you and you've got to marry me." Max paused, then added with a flourish, *"Je t'aime."*

"Lord Almighty, Max," said Rosalie, much taken aback. "That's something to throw at a girl. . . . You'll have to give me time to think about it."

"Of course, of course. I understand."

"I've thought about it. All right, I'll marry you."

That evening, over a celebration meal of traditional Provençal roast beef and Yorkshire pudding, followed by treacle pudding and custard, they discussed their wedding plans.

"Only close friends," said Max firmly. "This is going to be a real wedding, not some Hollywood stunt. We charter only *one* jumbo suborbital. That's it, the limit, *capisce?* Two hundred and fifty guests from America, max. It'll mean offending some people very dear to me, but I ain't marrying them, am I? And *no press!* Just those we invite. Two magazines, two tabloids, and any quality newspaper that wants the story, obviously. Now, who do you want to do your dress? I think it would be a nice move if we used a Dublin designer."

"Max," said Rosalie, "I'm a criminal wanted in Europe and America. If we get married, it will have to be in total secrecy. We can't have any press, we can't bring anybody over from America."

"No one?" Max asked, slightly stunned.

"No one, I'm afraid, unless you want to spend your wedding night visiting me in jail."

"Okay, so no one it is. Just my agent and my publicist then. Gee, that's weird."

"No one, Max, not even your agent and your publicist. In fact, especially not them."

Max chewed a ruminative mouthful of irradiated beef. The meat had been expertly reflavored using only the finest chemicals, and yet he scarcely tasted it. He was trying to get his head around the concept of doing something as big as getting married without his agent or his publicist. Who would handle the press? The fans? The cops? His mother? Then it dawned on him that none of these people would be there.

"You actually want me to get married *alone,* don't you?" he asked.

"Well, not entirely. I need to be there."

"Is it *legal* if the press don't witness it? I mean, I kind of thought they had to be there."

Rosalie gave Max's hand an encouraging squeeze.

"It'll be all right, Max. No need to be nervous. People do things that haven't been arranged by their agents and publicists all the time. In fact, most people don't even *have* agents and publicists."

Max was vaguely aware that this was the case, but after eight years as a supercelebrity he found it rather difficult to imagine. Eventually, though, he accepted Rosalie's argument.

"Okay, there's a church in the square, let's go visit the padre."

"Are you out of your mind, Max? This is *Provence!*"

"So?"

"Every church within twenty miles of here is *Church of England!* Sure, I'd rather get hitched in a witches' coven."

Nocturnal nuptials.

They left the little English carvery at about ten and headed north in their rental car. Rosalie drove, Max having had most of both of the bottles of wine they had ordered.

"It isn't always going to be me who drives, okay?" she said. "I like a drink too, you know."

"Fine, sometimes we'll take a taxi."

After passing through several villages that were quite nice, but only quite, they came upon the perfect church in a little village called Donzère, about eight miles south of Montélimar. Despite its being nearly midnight (country time) they called upon the priest.

"Father. We want to get married, and we'd like to do it now if that's all right with you," Rosalie said in passable schoolgirl French.

"Well, it is not," the priest replied in English. "Are you mad, coming here at this hour? I've a good mind to—"

"Father," Rosalie interrupted him, "I'm a wanted terrorist, and I can't get married in the normal way. Now I've got a gun, and my fiancé here has suitcases full of money. Either one of these things is going to persuade you to marry us right now. Which is it to be?"

"There's nothing in the world wakes a man up like the sight of young love," said the priest. "How much are you prepared to pay?"

The deal done, the priest hastily put on his robes and led the excited couple through the churchyard to his darkened church.

"You know it won't be a legal marriage, don't you?" he said. "Without the proper papers it can only be symbolic."

"That's all we care about," Rosalie replied.

And so the priest spoke the marriage service in the little church, lit only by a few candles. Neither Rosalie nor Max were particularly religious people, but where Rosalie came from you got married in a church, and that was the end of it. She could not imagine it any other way. Max sensibly neglected to mention his two divorces.

The road to Damascus.

Despite the fact that Rosalie was still very much wanted by the FBI, they decided to return to the USA. A new identity was a comparatively easy thing to obtain if you had Max's money and Rosalie's contacts, and she entered the country without trouble.

Rosalie had decided to resign her commission in Mother Earth. Plastic Tolstoy could pay somebody else to alert the world to the need to buy more Claustrospheres. She was fed up with it. She had been fighting almost continually for five and a half years and had achieved nothing. You couldn't breathe the air anymore, and you couldn't drink the water, walk in the sunshine, or enjoy the rain on your face, and Rosalie had no energy left to be bothered about it.

She had made the decision while flying the suborbital to L.A. with Max. Having got over the excitement that her first-class seat actually had an armrest on *both* sides, she had tuned into the news channel. She had been looking for an update on the situation in Belgium, but discovered to her astonishment that the disaster had already been dropped from the broadcasts. Three days down the track, and the poisoning of an entire country was old news.

Rosalie was not on the road to Damascus, she was on a flight to L.A., but at that moment she saw the truth as clearly as the apostle Paul had, on his journey.

People had got used to the planet dying.

They didn't care anymore; it had been lingering on for too long. The Earth was like some aged and slightly disgusting relative that just got sicker and sicker and yet refused to die. Requiring more and more attention, growing bigger tumors, bursting nastier sores, and soiling its sheets ever more often. An embarrassment and an inconvenience, a constant reminder of family guilt. It was almost as if, now that people had their Claustrospheres, they *wanted* the world to die. To get it over with. Everyone had lived with the imminence of planet death for so long that they really could not get excited about it anymore.

A young man was coming down the corridor from the bathrooms. He was wearing the famous Claustrophobe sweatshirt, slightly sanitized for general display. A picture of a slimy, dead Earth and the legend, "Well, f*** it" embossed beneath it.

Rosalie looked at the shirt, unconsciously quoting the slogan.

"Well, fuck it," she said to herself.

Except, in fact, she said it to at least the ten people closest to her. Rosalie was wearing earphones in order to hear the news. She had forgotten, as so many people do, that you lose control of the volume of your voice when wearing earphones. The stewardess approached and leaned across to Max.

"Would you mind asking your companion to moderate her language, please, sir. There are children on board."

The lull before the storm.

Few people are immune to the seduction of luxury, and Rosalie was under no illusions about her own delight in a bit of pampering. She did rather surprise even herself, however, when she moved into a house that had a Claustrosphere attached to it. A Claustrosphere, what's more, that was the size of four or five tennis courts.

"Do you like it?" Max had asked with genuine pride. "It has a pool, you know."

"Max, I've spent five years blowing these things up."

"Well, don't blow this one up, or I'll divorce you. It has state-of-the-art leisure facilities, and its fish cycle includes caviar. Come on, Ba . . . I mean, um . . . darling, we're on our honeymoon."

Max could see that Rosalie was torn; it was all very well leaving Mother Earth, but frolicking in a Claustrosphere was a big leap.

"Listen," he said, "husbands and wives are supposed to share each other's interests, right? Well, I've tried to get involved in your whole green thing, haven't I? Now you have to get into my stuff."

"Which is?"

"Partying, girl. You *know* it makes sense."

And suddenly she did. A huge weight seemed to lift from Rosalie's shoulders. It dawned on her that if she wanted to pack it all in for a while and have a good time, then she could. It was up to her.

"You're right," she said. "Bugger it, it isn't *my* fault the bloody Earth's finished. I didn't do it. I'm on holiday."

And to her astonishment, on the very first morning that she moved in with Max, Rosalie found herself lying by the Claustrosphere pool, wearing a bikini and sunbathing, something it had been impossible to do outside for over thirty years. Max suggested that since they were married and entirely alone in a hermetically sealed private world, Rosalie might like to dispense with the swimsuit.

"Maybe in a while," Rosalie said. She was readjusting fast, but there were limits. Being inside a Claustrosphere was one thing, wandering around it stark naked was another.

Slowly, though, throughout that first day, she relaxed. They both did, it was a honeymoon. They swam, they played tennis in the game-suits, they got a little drunk, and they made love in the soft, lush grass.

"I suppose this is what life must have been like in the real world, before it all got spoiled," Rosalie said as she lay in the quiet meadow, her hair mingling with the daisies and buttercups.

"If you were an outrageously overpaid movie star, yes. I believe it was tougher for the little guys," Max replied.

They did not return to the house that night, but stayed where they were, outdoors but indoors, naked in a tiny meadow, as the light cycle turned to velvet darkness and the fireflies in the forest area began to glow.

There was even dew in the morning when they awoke, a little chilly, at around five A.M., and Max brought cushions and blankets from the living area. They made love again and then watched the false dawn slowly turning

THIS OTHER EDEN

their little private world from darkness to cold gray. Rosalie felt a fine drizzle on her face.

"It's . . . it's raining," she said, astonished.

"It does sometimes," said Max. "You never know when till it happens. Just like the real thing, huh? The precipitation cycle is regulated according to seasons, but apart from that it's random. What do you think?"

"It's beautiful, Max. I had no idea these things could be so beautiful."

Of course Rosalie knew that not all Claustrospheres were as luxurious as Max's. The vast dormitory-style municipal complexes of the English Home Counties, for instance, or those in Long Island and New Jersey or underneath the Mediterranean Sea, could not boast quite such opulence, but they too had tennis courts and swimming pools, albeit public ones. They too were, in their way, beautiful.

"But it is obscene, you know that, don't you?" Rosalie said at last, trying to remember how much she hated the very idea of Claustrospheres.

"Yeah, yeah, sure, we all know that, but what can I tell you? You have to allow yourself some time off from yourself, you have to get out of your own way." And with that, he gathered Rosalie up in his arms, carried her to the pool, and jumped in, kissing her all the while.

To start the day with a dip in your own pool is a splendid thing, but to do so in the knowledge that you have nothing whatsoever to do after breakfast is doubly so. Rosalie shrieked with joy. She had not felt so lighthearted since she had been a girl.

All that day and the next, and the next until they lost count, Rosalie and Max swam and played and made love, never once leaving the Claustrosphere. This was the beginning of their lives together, and they did not want the beginning to end. Each afternoon Max worked out in his little gymnasium and watched videos, while Rosalie spent lazy hours by the pool with the ElectroBook. The ElectroBook was an extraordinary invention and a joy to behold.

It placed all the writings of the world in the palm of your hand. Of course, it had long been possible to condense all literature onto a disc or two and read it on a screen, but people had never really taken to this method of reading, because curling up with a laptop computer was just not as nice as it was with a book. The ElectroBook solved this problem of sensual aesthetics, for it was a real leather-bound book with hundreds of pages made not of paper, but of wafer-thin, flexible, fiber-optically-fed screens. Onto these screens, which could be folded, bent, screwed up, and read upside down in a hammock, would appear anything that had ever been written at the simple touch of an index.

One day, Rosalie and Max were lying in the meadow together. She was on her back, while Max lay with his head resting on her stomach. She had put aside her Elec-troBook, upon which she had been reading *David Copperfield,* and was staring up at the great geodesic dome above her. How splendid it looked, with its soft light and the delicate mists that floated up toward the roof. Rosalie was suffused with a wonderful feeling of well-being. All her life she had worried about the world, and now here she was in a perfect one. She had achieved that which she had always most desired: She was living in a perfect world. Outside its near-impregnable walls was the rest of the universe, filled as it was with other planets, Mars, Neptune . . . Earth. Planets that had nothing to do with her. Why should she worry any more about the dying Earth than she did about the frozen corpse that was Mars? Neither planet was her world. She had a Garden of Eden all of her own.

She found herself half-quoting some Shakespeare she had heard long ago. " 'This royal throne of kings, this sceptered isle, this earth of majesty, this seat of Mars, this other Eden . . .' "

"Richard the Second," said Max, who had done a lot of acting classes.

"I thought it was an old Claustrosphere commercial," said Rosalie.

"That too. Good choice, don't you think? It certainly sums up this place."

There was a long silence, broken only by the soft buzzing of the bees, special bees that could make honey out of old toenail clippings, lived for fifteen years, and had no sting.

Finally Rosalie spoke again.

"Max. Let's close it up."

"What do you mean?"

"You know what I mean. Let's shut the BioLock."

"It is shut, darling. The cycles don't work unless it's sealed."

"No, let's shut it properly. Put it on the time-safe."

"You mean . . . with us on the inside, don't you?"

Rosalie did not reply, instead she took Max in her arms and kissed him. It was a long kiss, passionate and committed, but with also just a hint of sadness, perhaps even despair.

Time-safe.

All Claustrospheres were equipped with a time-safe lock. This was because people feared the constancy of their resolve. Once faced with a lifetime inside a small shelter, they suspected that their will might crack after a while. That they might be tempted to ignore the numerous indicators and gauges with which their shelters were equipped, and open the door to have a look outside to see if things were really as bad as they were being told. If they did this while the outside environment remained poisonous, then those poisons would enter the Sphere and hopelessly compromise the ecosystem within, killing everybody inside. It had therefore been decided that when the Rat Run finally came, the authorities would issue an estimate as to when the environment might be safe enough again for people to emerge. It might be one year, it might be a hundred. Whatever it was, the occupants of a Claustrosphere would set their timer for that duration. Once set, the BioLock would not open under any circumstances until the time had elapsed. This system was thought particularly necessary in the case of the big community BioShelters. People recognized that it would only take one crazy lunatic to crack up and open the door, and they preferred the idea of voluntary imprisonment to mass poisoning.

Adam and Eve.

Rosalie released Max from the tension of her embrace. He was a little stunned.

"You want us to lock ourselves in?"

"Sure, why not? People will be forced to pretty soon anyway, if not this year, maybe the next. I was an environmental activist, I know how bad things are." Rosalie spoke quickly, as if fearful that having made her decision, she might, on reflection, change her mind. "Let's do it now, forget them all. There's only us, anyway. This is our world. Let's lock the universe out."

Max thought about it for a while.

"How long would you want to set it for?" he asked.

"I don't know, ten, maybe fifteen years. Just till our baby's grown. We can reassess the situation on the monitors then."

"Our baby?"

"That's right. Our baby."

"I didn't know we were going to have a baby."

"Well, we are, and I want it to live in a beautiful world."

Max looked at Rosalie, and he smiled, a great happy smile. It was dusk in the Claustrosphere, but that smile lit up Rosalie's whole universe.

"Okay," he said. "Let's do it."

Out of paradise.

They left the Claustrosphere for the first time since their honeymoon had begun. Max had one or two things that he wanted to put in order, and Rosalie had to telephone her grandparents. He knew they would be saddened at the collapse of her principles, but she did not care. They were in the past, her baby was the future. She had the chance to give her baby a childhood in paradise, and she was going to take it.

They went through the BioLock and up to the house. After weeks inside the pristine environment of the Claustrosphere it seemed to Max and Rosalie as if the world were already dead. The air stank, and the filtered sunlight was weak and watery.

Max made a few calls. Canceling his subscription to *Life* magazine. Putting all his money into high-yield long-term accounts and informing his astonished agent that he was retiring. Soon they were ready. Rosalie had only to make her call, and they could go back into their little private paradise and lock the Earth out behind them.

Then the front doorbell rang.

"Leave it," said Rosalie. "We don't live in this world anymore."

"Oh, come on, we might as well see who it is," said Max, and before Rosalie could stop him he had flipped on the video camera that covered his front door.

Judy was standing outside.

"I don't believe it!" Rosalie gasped. "It's that little bastard from the FBI."

"This is not good," said Max.

"Max." There was panic in Rosalie's voice. "Don't answer the door, let's go, now, into the Claustrosphere, leave him. We were going to go, let's go."

Max spoke gently. For the first time in their relationship, it was he who would have to be the sensible and realistic one.

305

"Rosalie, listen, you've got yourself thinking about that Claustrosphere as if it were a whole other world—"

"It is," said Rosalie.

The bell rang again.

"It isn't, Rosalie, it's a Claustrosphere. A building on a piece of real estate that exists in the real world. Now that man is an FBI agent, an agent who's already tried to arrest you once. The chances are he's come to do it properly this time. If we disappear, believe me the first thing they'll do is blast open the BioLock on the Claustrosphere. What you have to do is hide while I talk to him. Maybe I can get him to go away. Then we can plan our next move."

Suddenly Rosalie saw her dream idyll fading like the dream it was. Desperately she tried to save it.

"Let's kill him," she said.

Max looked at Rosalie, a little shocked.

"Now, I hope you said that because you're hormonally imbalanced, due to being pregnant," he said. "Quite apart from the fact that icing people is kind of dubious in a moral sense. Practically, it would be a no-win call. If you kill FBI agents, they send more, lots more. It's a rule they have. Now you get behind the two-way mirror, and I'll let the guy in."

"Two-way mirror?" said Rosalie, returning to the real world with a bump.

"Yeah . . . um . . . yeah, the guy who had the house before me was a porn king," said Max, and pushing Rosalie into a recess in the wall behind a mirror, he buzzed open the door and let Judy in.

"Come on up!" he called, and Judy nervously climbed the stairs.

"I nearly went off home," Judy said, arriving in the lounge area.

"Yeah, I was out back in the Claustrosphere. Nice to see you again, man, what's happening?" Max replied.

"Ms. Connolly not with you?" Judy inquired. "The way

you two seemed to be getting on in Ireland, I thought she might be here."

"No, she ain't here."

"It doesn't matter anyway," said Judy. "It's you I need to speak to."

"Me?" replied Max, full of suspicion. "What do you want with me, man?"

"I need your help to catch a ruthless, callous, immoral viper, a man with not a single shred of compassion or decency in his body, a man who cares nothing for anything or anybody but himself."

"Hey, man, this is Hollywood," said Max. "I know a lot of guys like that, you'll have to be more specific."

24

The sale of the century

Waiting for the drugs to warm up.

MAX HAD BEEN WITH PLASTIC TOLSTOY FOR ABOUT HALF AN
hour. He had requested a meeting under the pretext of
discussing the progress of the film project that Nathan had
been supposed to write, but really he was Judy's spy.

Tolstoy had readily agreed to the meeting and invited
Max up to his house. Busy though Plastic Tolstoy was,
Max was one of the most popular stars in the industry and
even as exalted a figure as Tolstoy still understood the
value of "the money."

They were talking in Plastic's office, Max having declined an invitation to go through to the Claustrosphere.
He was carrying a tiny transmitter, and he knew that
nothing, not even radio waves, escaped from a closed
Claustrosphere.

"I've just spent nearly a month in mine," Max said by
way of explanation. "A guy can get too much fresh air and
sunshine. I hate to feel that healthy."

"You've been in your Claustrosphere for a month?
How come?"

"As a matter of fact I've been working on the first fermentation from my vineyard. I brought a bottle with me, I'd appreciate your opinion."

Max had brought along a half bottle of red wine labeled "Wine to the Max."

"You brewed this inside your Claustrosphere? Wow! I don't have a vineyard in mine."

"Hey, you have to have a vineyard, Plastic. What can you do with a rain forest? Nothing, hunt iguanas maybe. A vineyard will keep you occupied as many years as you have to be in there. Try it."

"Nice. Very nice," said Plastic, taking a delicate little sip. "Lotta nose. I like a wine with a big schnozzle. . . . So this is what you've been up to then? I heard you'd gone underground."

Max wondered whether Tolstoy knew that he had been at Nathan's house on the night of Nathan's murder. Had the killers recognized him in his VR helmet? Had they reported it to Tolstoy? Max had to presume the worst, so he confessed.

"Yeah, I did hide out for a while there. To tell you the truth, Plastic, I was kind of shaken by something. . . . You know Nathan Hoddy? The guy who was going to write our film?"

"Yeah, I know, he died," said Plastic with apparent indifference.

"I was there the night he got it," said Max.

"No kidding? You were there?" Tolstoy certainly seemed genuinely surprised. "So who bumped the poor guy off, then?"

"That's the stupid point," Max replied. "I was there, but I didn't know who did it. We were playing a Virtual Reality game, and we were both inside the helmets when they killed him. I didn't see him die. Believe it or not, what I saw was his *thoughts* while he died, although of course I didn't know that was what they were until afterward. It was extremely weird."

"You saw his dying mind? Wow! Did you get a tape? I could sell something like that."

"No way, man. When I found him, I just ran. That's why I kind of disappeared, you know? Like, I didn't feel that was the wrong thing to do. . . . I had no information that could help the cops or anything. . . ."

"And you didn't want to get involved."

"In a murder investigation? No way! Would you? That kind of shit sticks. I can just hear what they'd say about me. 'Wild, tough Max Maximus . . . hear about him? He was in the room when his pal got wasted, and he didn't lift a finger. Says he was playing a game and didn't notice!' "

"Well I guess it's all blown over now, huh? The cops have got about another thousand unsolved murders to deal with since then," Plastic Tolstoy assured Max with a kindly slap on the shoulder. Max could not help but feel a tiny shiver at the man's touch. He hoped Plastic did not notice.

"Yeah," said Max, "I reckon that's history now, and so I was wondering what was happening about the film, you know? I mean, it's too bad about Nathan, obviously, but like, you know, the town's full of writers. You hear what I'm saying?"

"I certainly do, Max," said Plastic. "And let me tell you, I am still very interested in putting you into a picture about those Mother Earth assholes."

"Well, that's great, Plastic," Max said and he knew that he could put it off no longer. If the drug was going to work, it would have worked by now; it took only the tiniest amount, and its effects were virtually instantaneous. It was time to put it to the test.

"So Plastic," Max said casually, "I hear you like to watch girls go to the toilet, is that right?"

"Yeah, I like to do that," Plastic replied, without batting an eyelid.

Max's whole body relaxed. The drug was working; it had to be working. Emboldened, he gave it another test.

310

"So how the hell do you manage it? I mean, do you get them to bend over you or what?"

"I lie under that glass table, and they squat on top of it."

Tolstoy nodded toward the coffee table upon which Max's drink was standing. Max decided that he was no longer thirsty. He wanted to get the job over with, and get out. Very casually he asked his last and most dangerous test question.

"So, I guess you knew that Nathan would have to die the minute he worked out that you're the guy who pays for the green terrorists."

Baby's Mouth.

Max was smiling his gentlest, friendliest smile. Baby's Mouth was a subtle drug, and it worked better if the recipient was relaxed and unaware that it had been administered. It had been originally developed by psychoanalysts after their profession had been reduced to a laughingstock by daytime talk shows. These were the daily confessionals in which every possible type of loser was encouraged and indeed cajoled into describing in the most lurid detail just exactly how completely and utterly screwed up they were. The losers would then be confronted with other losers, who either had similar problems, had caused the problems, were the victims of the problems, or, as became increasingly common, were hoping to develop the problem. An expert psychiatrist would then tell the whole lot of them that they were not to worry because the thing was far more common than they imagined, and the studio audience gave everyone a great big round of applause for "sharing" the whole horrid business with thirty or forty million complete strangers. Now this type of TV had been fine for a while, while there were still some legitimate skeletons left in society's closet. Unfortunately, gloating over other people's private misfortune made such good television that the search for new problems and new victims very quickly became a network necessity.

"I'm not interested in decent ideas for comedy and drama," the network chief would shout. "Bring me more losers."

Teams of researchers scoured the countryside, encouraging people to think of something, anything, that might have rendered them dysfunctional. Large sections of the public racked its collective brain attempting to conjure up ever more interesting ways to glamorize their boring lives. The researcher's job was also to ensure that, no matter what problem people came up with, there was always an "expert" ready to assure the world that this was just the tip of the iceberg. The inevitable development was, of course, that those watching the shows began to feel a little inadequate. They began to wonder, since all these desperate family situations were apparently so common, what was wrong with them. Why were they not attempting to divorce their pets, blaming their mothers for making them fat, or trying to trace the parents who *would* have adopted them *if* their natural parents had chosen to give them up. Eventually, of course, these people also found their way on to the shows, in order to confess how dysfunctional they felt about not having anything to feel dysfunctional about. The resident psychiatrist soon put them right by assuring them that they were doubtless suppressing something absolutely fascinating, and they went away happy, promising to return the moment they had discovered what their problem was; and so the dreadful cycle continued.

One of the few desirable side effects of this broadcast voyeurism was that it temporarily popped the bubble of the analyst industry. An industry that had been growing unchecked for decades and was out of control. At one point, the prevalence of people seeing analysts, particularly among the middle class, had grown to such an extent that society was in danger of grinding to a halt because everybody was sitting in small rooms talking about themselves. All this changed with the introduction of saturation afternoon discussion TV, which rendered the analyst redundant. People began to ask themselves why they should spend enormous sums talking about themselves to just one person, when they could actually be paid an appearance fee to talk about themselves to millions of people. Eventually, however, the analysts rebuilt their fortunes by playing the snob card. Enticing people back to their couches by pointing out that important people had important problems, and should not be used merely as a source of entertainment for the masses. Unfortunately, when people did begin to drift back to their analysts, they found they had become so utterly immersed in the combined problems of just about everybody else that they had lost track of what, if anything, had happened to them that would be worth talking about in the first place.

The drug Baby's Mouth had been developed in order to enable people whose brains had been filled with crap to discover some genuine thoughts and emotions. It was a truth drug. It made the person who took it say, not what they thought others wanted to hear, nor indeed what they themselves thought they wanted to say, but the truth. The basic effect of Baby's Mouth was to suppress that part of the brain that is in charge of bullshit. This, of course, meant that some people were rendered completely dumb by the drug. Many politicians, game-show hosts, and a surprising number of poets all had the disconcerting experience of being rendered absolutely speechless after so much as a sniff of it. For most people, however, Baby's Mouth simply gave them the unusual sensation of genuinely expressing their true feelings, of actually saying what they thought.

The drug had, of course, been quickly banned. Its capacity to create mischief was far too great. People need their secrets, and in the brief period that Baby's Mouth was available, dinner parties ended in gunfights, marriages foundered, and even the most saintly politicians were found occasionally to harbor uncharitable thoughts about their constituents. No society can exist without some bull-shit. It was soon recognized that if everybody told the whole truth, the whole time, we would all be at each other's throats.

Lines of communication.

Baby's Mouth had been suppressed, but it remained a valuable weapon in the world of the secret service, and it was Judy who had supplied Max with the dose with which he had spiked Plastic Tolstoy's wine. Tolstoy had only taken a sip, but a sip was all that was required, and by the easy way Tolstoy had offered details of his sexual preferences, it seemed to be working. Max repeated his question about Nathan's death, this time a little more firmly. Judy had told him that those under the influence of the drug responded well to a firm hand.

"Like I said, I suppose you decided to have Nathan Hoddy killed, once he'd come up with the idea that you're the person who pays for Mother Earth?"

"It's an interesting question," said Tolstoy. "Now let me ask you this. Where the hell do you get off coming in here and trying to hit me with a shot of Baby's Mouth, huh? Is that nice, Max? Is that fair?"

In another part of the Beverly Hills Fortified Village, Judy and Rosalie exchanged nervous glances. They were in Max's living room, listening to the conversation taking place between Max and Tolstoy via the tiny radio transmitter that was hidden inside one of Max's buttons. The reception was excellent, and they could hear only too clearly that Judy's plan was not going well.

"You think when some guy asks me to taste their stupid wine right out of the blue, I don't smell a rat?" Judy and Rosalie heard Tolstoy saying. "What am I? An idiot? Like you, Max? Is that it? Am I as *stupid* as you? I only pretended to drink your wine, and now I wanna know just what you tried to stick me with. It was Baby's Mouth, wasn't it?"

"Yeah," said Max, rather weakly. Denial seemed futile. "Should I leave?"

"Leave? No way, Max, not until you've told me why you came."

"Because I want to know if the Claustrosphere Company is in the business of creating environmental catastrophe . . . you bastard!"

As the word *bastard* barked out of their earphones, Judy and Rosalie could hear a sudden rush of movement. Max had intended to grab the drugged wine and force it down Plastic Tolstoy's throat. Instead, he found himself facing a gun.

"Max, please. No physical stuff. I hate that," said Tolstoy calmly. "You know what I ought to do? I ought to have you drink that wine yourself, then I could find out who's put you up to all this. But I'm not going to. Guess why?"

"Because you're a nice man?"

"No, not that, not even my best friends, were I to have any, which I don't, would call me a nice man. No, I'm not going to force you to take the Baby's Mouth because I don't need to, that's why." Suddenly Plastic Tolstoy raised his voice. "Do I, *Mr. Schwartz!* You hear that, do you, *Judy?* I *know* who's pulling this dick's strings!" and Tolstoy laughed a loud, unpleasant, triumphant laugh.

Judy and Rosalie were nonplussed, particularly Judy. He was not an arrogant man, but he had taken some pride in the trail he had followed and the plans that he had laid to bring that trail to a conclusion. Now the sound of cruel laughter ringing in his earphones told him that somehow he had been completely trumped by the object of his investigations. What's more, he was being taunted about it over his own secret radio!

Tolstoy continued to gloat.

315

"Hey, Schwartz, you think when some guy starts delving into my business I don't *hear* about it? You think when some little punk Fed starts checking out where *I've* been placing *my* ads on *my* communications empire for the past thirty years, I don't *know!* How the hell do you think I got to *have* my own communications empire? By being a prick? Like you? Huh?"

Max was beginning to feel rather superfluous to requirements.

"Look, Plastic," he said, "you've clearly guessed I'm wired, so why don't I just leave you with the radio, and you can talk to Judy without my standing around looking stupid. Or maybe you could just phone him, you know who he is."

"You stay where you are, Max," said Tolstoy. "I want to know what gives with you. The FBI got something on you? Is that it? Is that why you did this for Schwartz? Is that why you agreed to come in here and abuse my trust? Abuse the privilege of my hospitality that I extend to so few?"

Max found himself staring at the floor in embarrassment.

"Why did you do it, Max? Let me guess again. Hah! I got it! It's a girl, isn't it? That's the only time a guy would be so stupid as to try and get the better of Plastic Tolstoy. For a girl! A *green* girl in this case, no doubt considering the outrageous nature of Schwartz's libelous theories. The girl, I would like to hazard a guess, who tried to kill me that time in my own Claustrosphere. Am I right, Max? Yes, I think I'm right." Tolstoy called out again, "You listening, girlie? I can't remember your name, I'm afraid, but . . . let me see, that's it, you had red hair, I remember."

Judy and Rosalie were ready to sink through the floor by this time. The man was positively clairvoyant.

"I have never felt so stupid in my entire life," Rosalie whispered.

"There's no need to whisper," Judy replied, "he can't hear us."

"He doesn't need to, does he?" Rosalie said angrily. "He seems to be able to read our minds."

"Okay," they could hear Tolstoy saying. "Give me the transmitter, and anything else metal you've got on you. This office carries a metal scanner, so I'll know if you try to cheat, and I won't be happy."

Back in Tolstoy's office Max handed over both the transmitters that Judy had supplied him with.

"Bye-bye, G-man," Tolstoy sneered. "You look after yourself now, and you look after Max's cute little girlfriend too. Because you both may just be hearing from my people."

Tolstoy smashed the little button-sized radios, and Judy and Rosalie heard no more. They looked at each other in despair.

"Maybe the phone will ring," said Judy.

They could only sit and wait.

Back in Tolstoy's office, Max emptied out his pockets, a notebook, a wallet, some cigarettes . . . a portable telephone.

"Thank you," said Tolstoy. "By the way, I don't have no metal scanner, who do you think I am, James Bond?"

Max smiled weakly, scarcely daring to hope that the trick that Judy had suggested he try if his transmitters were discovered would work. Tolstoy had been several jumps ahead of Judy on every point so far. It seemed unlikely that such a simple idea would fool him, but Max had to try.

"Are you going to kill me, Plastic?" he asked as he put his phone down on the table beside his other possessions. It was as dramatic an inquiry as he could muster, and Max made it in the hope that Plastic would not notice that as he put the phone down he had deftly pressed * 1, the preset automatic dialing code for his phone at home. Max used it occasionally when he was out and about in order to leave messages on his answering machine. He was hoping to leave a message now.

Back at Max's house the phone rang. Instinctively, Rosa-

317

lie nearly picked it up, but fortunately Judy stayed her hand. There were three rings, and then the machine clicked into action. First they heard Max's outgoing message. "Uh . . . Hi, yeah . . . Okay, it's the machine, right? But you knew that. Listen, um . . . leave a message, don't leave a message . . . live, die, it's all the same dream, right? . . . Bye."

Despite the tension of the situation, Rosalie grimaced slightly at what she considered to be a highly pretentious message. It did have one advantage, though: It was delivered in a lazy, quiet growl, which at the other end of the line Max was desperately hoping Tolstoy would not hear emanating from the phone.

"C'mon, man!" Max half shouted, timing it to coincide with the point when he guessed his message would be playing. "I asked if you were going to kill me!"

Tolstoy did not hear the message, and he did not spot the trick either, he had seen so many portable phones placed on desks in his time.

Tolstoy answered Max's question at the point at which, in Max's house, Max's answering machine began to record. The portable phone was a video phone, as indeed were all phones, barring the occasional chic antique one, and Max had contrived to place it with its tiny camera facing across the desk. Judy and Rosalie could not only hear Plastic Tolstoy, but also see him, and all the while he was, of course, being recorded.

The hard sell.

"Am I going to kill you?" Tolstoy said, reiterating Max's question. "I don't think so, no. You don't know shit, and your pal Schwartz knows less. That's why he sent you here, to try and truth-drug a confession out of me. I guess the last thing I need to do right now is to give credence to his libelous hypothesis by murdering his stool pigeon, right?"

"And about his hypothesis?" said Max, trying to hide his relief. "Is it true? Do you sink oil tankers to sell Claustrospheres?"

"What do you think?"

"I think if you can fund Mother Earth while it tries to kill you, you'd pretty much do anything to make a sale."

"You know you may not be so stupid after all, Max. How did you cotton on to the fact that I fund Mother Earth? . . . Oh, yeah, I remember now, you were with Nathan Hoddy, weren't you? That's right. I guess he told you the plot of his movie, huh?"

"That's right, and when he died for it, I guessed he must have unwittingly stumbled on the truth."

"Clever. No, really, clever. You sure the girl didn't work all that out for you? I never had you picked out as a brain boy."

"No, I figured it out all on my own. The girl's my wife now, by the way."

"Really? Congratulations. Like I could give a fuck about your domestic arrangements. I must confess to you, though, she looked eminently screwable, nice and natural. Although to be frank, armed women with too much attitude make my dick go limp."

Max was thinking hard, trying to conjure up the right words to suit his purpose. He knew that it was his job to coax some information out of Tolstoy about the secret Claustrosphere marketing strategy. He also knew that he was dealing with a far subtler and cleverer man than he was himself. But even clever people have weak spots; Max felt that he knew what Tolstoy's was. It was vanity.

"Plastic, does it ever bother you that what you do might be a little unethical?"

"Huh?" Tolstoy asked, as if he did not understand the question.

"I mean, I grant you it's *clever,* but . . ."

"No, Max, no *buts.* It's clever, just that."

Max congratulated himself. He felt that he had judged

his man well; he believed that he was drawing Tolstoy in, playing on the well-known fact that Tolstoy could not resist the sound of his own voice. Unfortunately for Max, this was not the case. Contrary to what he'd said earlier, Plastic had decided that Max would have to die that day. The Mother Earth girl and the FBI man, he was unconcerned about. One was a terrorist, the other Plastic knew to be held in contempt by his own colleagues and known in the Bureau as a paranoid conspiracy theorist. Without evidence, of which they clearly had none, their voice would not be heard. Max, however, was different. Here was a colossal star, a man whose every word was reported in the media. True, Tolstoy owned the lion's share of that media, and Max, like his comrades, had no evidence. Nonetheless, he was a figure of sufficient significance to be capable, in a single interview, of sparking public debate and rumor, which Tolstoy naturally wished to avoid.

Tolstoy had therefore decided to have Max killed immediately, before he had a chance to make his suspicions public. This was not a job that Plastic wanted carried out in his house, and so he had therefore decided to occupy Max for a few minutes, while summoning his killing people. They could then be instructed to dispatch the inconvenient film star, once he had driven a suitably non-incriminating distance from the Tolstoy mansion.

Tolstoy idly pressed a button on his intercom.

"Hey, Sugar," he said to his trusted assistant, "I'm busy with a pal right now. When the guys from dispatch arrive, just get them to wait at the main gate, will you?"

The guys from dispatch had not, in fact, up to that point, been summoned, but they had been now. Tolstoy turned back to Max with an easy smile. Max had been right about one thing, Tolstoy loved to show off, and confident that he would not be overheard, he was quite happy to occupy a condemned man's final minutes by demonstrating what a genius he was.

"What I do is not unethical at all," Plastic said.

"Maybe just a little bit," said Max, pleased with himself for being such a subtle interrogator.

"No, I don't accept that. It is not unethical."

"But you do deliberately sink oil tankers, cause nuclear leaks, and hole toxic waste convoys in the middle of big cities."

"I do that, yes. Or, at least, I have my people do it. My sabotage people."

"And this is not unethical?"

"I don't consider it unethical. Illegal, certainly. But not unethical."

"Look," said Max. "God knows, I realize you're busy, but I would love to know how you get from poisoning kids to not being unethical. I mean, genuinely, I'm fascinated. I know you're a brilliant guy, I bet you can make the leap."

"It ain't unethical, because all the things we do would happen anyway," Tolstoy said.

"I don't understand," said Max.

"Because you're stupid," Tolstoy replied, and commenced to explain what had to be the nastiest marketing campaign in history, and there had been some horrors.

"So the Second Great Green Scare is coming to an end, and we're trying to off-load the early-model Edens, right? Eden One, Eden Two, Eden Three. You wouldn't remember them because all this was before you were born, right? But the boom's over, and I'm feeling down, okay? Sure, we'd done great for a while there, sold a shitload of product, but things were dropping off. I was young and hungry, and I knew that with a surefire item like Claustrosphere, we could do better. You getting me?"

Max explained that, though he might not be Albert Einstein, he could follow a simple narrative. Tolstoy continued.

"My problem was that I could not use negative advertising; you know the kind of thing . . . 'Hey! The world's fucked! Save your ass! Buy a shelter!' "

"Why couldn't you do that?" Max inquired, to demonstrate how attentive he was being. "Seems to me that would have been your best shot."

"Yeah? Well, you're wrong. Popular research informed us that people felt guilty enough about the environment already. They took a very negative view toward a company gleefully embracing Earth death in order to make a profit from it. So I had to be clever, right? And believe me I was. I was young and I was clever. I had ideas then! Man, did I have ideas! I used Rodin's 'Thinker' as my principal symbol and that bit out of Shakespeare . . . you know, 'This fortress built by Nature,' etc."

" 'This sceptered isle, This earth of majesty . . . This other Eden,' " said Max, remembering how recently he had heard that very quote, and how happy he had been for a short while.

"You know it? Cute piece, am I right? And beautifully deployed, though I say it myself. I had a product that was basically an immoral, irresponsible, cowardly, cop-out, and I gave it *class*. If you give something class, then you make people think they're being clever. If you've done that, you can sell them anything. But not forever, right? You can only play the chess game for so long. Engaging a customer intellectually has never been a substitute for engaging them emotionally. What I really needed was scare tactics, and, like I say, I couldn't use them. So as the Second Green Scare dies down, so do my figures; plummeting would not be too depressing a word to describe the sales situation during this time. Sure, we had some good months, sometimes very good, but we were bumping along the bottom. Then I began to notice something, I noticed that those good months always coincided with—"

"Some terrible environmental catastrophe."

"Clever kid. That chick must be good for you, Max. Of course they did. You open a paper, you see there's some province of India where no one can breathe anymore. You think, hey, the future's looking kind of bleak, maybe I'd better start covering my ass here. Disaster was good for business. So I started to buy into news channels to make sure everybody got to hear about all the disasters. If Claustrosphere itself couldn't use scare tactics, then I'd get somebody else to do it."

"Cute," Max observed.

"Wasn't it?" Plastic Tolstoy agreed. "There I was, running these news channels that were getting awards and praise from greenies for prioritizing environmental news, and all the time I was just doing it to scare people into buying my product. Boy, it was funny! We had all these environmentally concerned journalists and researchers lining up to work on my channels. They thought, 'At last somebody's taking the fate of the planet seriously.' And I sure was! Claustrosphere was turning into a multibillion-dollar industry. To me, that is serious."

Tolstoy had leapt from his chair and was pacing about the room in a manner that Nathan would have recognized, had he not been dead.

Back at Max's place, this movement caused some concern.

"I wish he wouldn't do that," said Rosalie. "He keeps walking out of the shot."

"Don't worry," Judy replied, scarcely able to contain his excitement. "We've got enough of his smug mug, and the voice is coming over fine."

Indeed it was, and Plastic Tolstoy, blissfully ignorant of the phone trick, had scarcely stopped for breath.

"That's when I started to fund Natura and Mother Earth. They were my best advertisers of all. Anything environmentally conscious, I promoted it . . . secretly, of course. Protest concerts, documentaries, terrorism. I was the greenest guy on Earth, and all the while, I'm selling Claustrospheres. Ha ha ha! It was perfect. But I still got a problem."

"It all seems pretty straightforward to me," Max ventured.

"Straightforward! It was a nightmare! Everything depended on one nonconstant factor, and in manufacturing terms, if you're dependent on a nonconstant factor, that's your profit gone."

"Excuse me?" said Max, the eager pupil.

"A nonconstant factor! Which in this case was environmental disaster! Everyone was hanging around waiting for one. The manufacturer, the distributor, the retailer, the marketer, all waiting, and why? Because none of them could move without *the customer,* and the customer did not appear in any great numbers without the disaster. The tail was wagging the dog! You got Joe Soap, right? He runs a small-town Claustrosphere showroom, normal weeks he's selling one, maybe two units, right? Suddenly, there's a local disaster. The methane build-up in an old landfill that has since been built over goes pop, and wipes out half the suburbs. Bang! It's a wake-up call! A Pavlovian response. 'My God, Marjorie,' says every short-sighted little schmuck in town, 'the world's exploding, we'd better get a Claustrosphere.' Suddenly Joe Soap gets four, maybe five *hundred,* orders. But he doesn't have the stock, he's geared to selling one a week. 'I'll get 'em,' he cries and calls the factory, which starts a rush build. Three months later, five hundred units worth a billion dollars turns up in Nowheresville, by which time the explosion is forgotten, it's history, and everybody has spent the money on sending little Jimmy to college instead. A nightmare. Like I told you."

"It certainly sounds it," Max agreed, trying to look sympathetic.

"All the time the product was chasing the demand. You can't run a business like that; the *demand* has to chase the *product.* I knew then that I had to rationalize my principal sales strategy."

"Your principal sales strategy? That would be the environmental disasters, wouldn't it?" Max inquired.

"Exactly. I get to thinking, if only I knew *when* these terrible things were going to happen I could have the whole operation ready in place. The news teams ready to report, the stock ready to go, and above all the tasteful, classy, nonexploitative little Claustrosphere commercials to play in heavy rotation around the news breaks that reported the disaster. That's the connection your FBI pal made, and which he tried to prove with his pathetic little plan to drug me. The breakthrough was to get the *news to fit my commercials,* in fact, to make the news itself the commercial, and the actual commercial just the product placement."

"So you start creating disasters?" Max asked.

"Hey hey hey! Hold on!" Tolstoy replied, and for a moment Max thought he might be about to become cautious, but Tolstoy was waiting for his killing people and was happy to tell his story in his own time and in the right order.

"At first, I'm still trying to do it legitimately, right? Trying to work out when these genuine disasters will occur so I can be ready for them. So I get all these scientists together and ask them to predict what's going to happen next. Ask me how they did."

"How did they do?" asked Max obligingly.

"They did shit. Never picked one, not one! They'd say, *maybe* a tanker will go down off Alaska, *maybe* a Russian power station will blow. Well, of course they would! I knew that! What I didn't know was when! Now here is where we get to the point about what I did *not* being unethical."

"I just can't see how you're going to make that trick, Plastic," said Max, his face a picture of concentration.

"Watch me. So I'm telling you that me and my scientists know the stuff is going to happen, we just don't know when. They're giving me all these probability charts saying ten nuke disasters a year, fifty oil spills, tigers to be extinct sometime soon, all that stuff, and I'm thinking, well if it's *going* to happen *anyway,* then there's nothing wrong in my organizing it to happen in a disciplined manner. It's like carrying your own bomb onto a plane because the chances of there being two people with bombs on any one plane are basically zero."

"I'm not sure I follow that analogy, man," said Max.

"What are you, stupid? It's like crystal. I'm thinking, if my science guys say that two tankers will sink in the Panama Canal in the next three months, then why don't I sink 'em? It's the same damage, and there are huge national and international benefits to be achieved. The common good is well served."

"It is?"

"Well, of course it is! Have you any idea how many *jobs* are involved in Claustrosphere manufacturing? Also distribution and installation? Even then, we had a colossal work force, not to mention the associate industries. Maybe you think that millions of working men and women should be laid off while we all wait for some dumb rust-bucket to sink in the Panama Canal? A rust-bucket, I might remind you, that we all know is *going to sink anyway!* Then there's the huge investment involved. Even then anyone could see that Claustrosphere was going to be bigger than cars. In global economic terms Claustrosphere is the difference between boom and bust. If the wind goes out of our sales, bang, recession! I had a *duty* to make the Claustrosphere operation manageable. The issue was jobs and dollars in the heartlands! That is not something that can be left drifting on the vagaries of nonspecific probabilities."

"You mean chance?"

"Exactly, I mean chance."

"So you saw creating environmental disaster as a kind of moral thing, then?" Max really was fascinated. Tolstoy's sense of conviction was awesome.

"I saw creating a situation that was healthy for investors and employees alike as a moral thing, certainly, and if that meant creating environmental disaster, then so be it," said Tolstoy. "To me, encouraging growth and creating jobs is the only morality, which as it happens is fortunate, because I must admit to you, it turned out that my probabilities theory did not hold water."

"The one about if two tankers were going to sink anyway, you might as well be the person to sink them?"

"Yeah, what actually happened was that four tankers sank, our two and the two that were going to anyway."

"So the bomb on the plane theory's crap?"

"It's a cute theory. I still think it should work."

"But it doesn't?"

"Apparently not, no."

Plastic Tolstoy paused for the first time in a while. Max could not help but gape at the enormity of the horrors of which he had been told. Back at his house, Rosalie and Judy too were completely dumbfounded. The sheer scale of Tolstoy's crimes left them lost for words.

"Well, I guess tough decisions take tough guys," Max said finally.

"Exactly," Tolstoy replied. "Personally, I see myself as a global philanthropist."

Another job for the killing people.

Max decided it was time to leave. The danger he was in had suddenly dawned upon him. He remembered how Tolstoy had served Nathan for simply suggesting a screenplay idea. Now he, Max, knew the whole dreadful story.

"Thanks, Plastic, it's been real," he said and ran for the door. Unfortunately, the door of the office was locked. Max turned to face Plastic Tolstoy, who was playing with his gun.

"Max, you leaving without saying good-bye?" said Tolstoy.

"Are you going to kill me, Plastic?" Max inquired.

"Oh, yes, thanks for reminding me," said Plastic and fired at Max. When the noise died away, Max was still standing, if rather paler than before.

"Just kidding," said Plastic. "It's a hologram. Ha ha! Like I told you, I don't want dead movie stars cluttering up my house. Besides, Schwartz and your girl know you came here. If I kill you here, it might get complicated, even for a guy with my clout. See ya, kid. Be lucky."

Tolstoy pressed a button, the door sprang open, and Max turned and ran. He left everything behind, including the telephone. He just ran, out of the office, out of the house, into his car, and away.

Rosalie and Judy turned to each other in triumph. They had the whole confession on tape, this was dynamite indeed.

"We have to take it to the police," said Judy. "Now."

"No way!" Rosalie replied. "If we do that, sure we get Tolstoy, but the tape becomes evidence, prejudicial to the trial, then the appeal, then the appeal on the appeal. We need it now! People have to see it, they have to know what's been happening to the world, what we've all let happen. This tape could be the thing that finally turns the environmental argument around."

"I don't think so, Rosalie," said Judy. "Tolstoy owns the lion's share of the world's communication systems. You can't fight a propaganda war with him, even with that tape. His will be the loudest voice."

"Maybe, but there's one voice people still listen to. One voice that will always be heard, even if not one of Tolstoy's channels were to broadcast him. Jurgen Thor has the status to get the truth about Tolstoy into the public domain. I say we take the tape to him."

Rosalie had been galvanized back into action. All thoughts of retreating from the world had vanished from her mind. She no longer wanted to hide away in Max's Claustrosphere. She knew now that the end of the world was not inevitable, it was being manipulated, and she wanted to fight.

Just then, further discussion was cut short by the voice of Plastic Tolstoy. He was not speaking to them, but Rosalie and Judy could still see and hear him over Max's phone, which still lay, its open line, on Tolstoy's desk.

Plastic Tolstoy was speaking to his assistant on his intercom.

"Sugar, are the dispatch people at the gate? . . . Good. . . . Yes, Max Maximus the movie star will be emerging in a red Porsche. . . . Yes, tell them to make sure they do it well away from the house. The usual rules apply."

Rosalie and Judy both knew instantly what Tolstoy was saying. Rosalie grabbed the phone off the hook, thus finally ending the lengthy recording.

"Call it off, Tolstoy!!" she screamed down the phone, desperately trying to make the man at the other end hear. "We know what you're doing! We heard you! Killing Max will achieve nothing!"

But Tolstoy got up and left his office without hearing the tiny, tinny voice emanating from Max's phone.

"Tolstoy!" Rosalie screamed. "I'll kill you if you hurt him. I'll kill you!"

But she could hear the office door close, and knew that he was gone.

25

The Hollywood treatment

Foiling the hit.

"ROSALIE," JUDY PLEADED, COWERING BEHIND THE DASHBOARD, his knuckles translucent on the armrests of his seat. "If we get pulled for busting red lights we won't even get a chance to try and save Max."

"Nobody's going to pull me over," Rosalie responded tersely. Her whole body was hunched forward, willing the car to go faster, her chin nearly touching the steering wheel. "If we can get a few cops chasing us, all the better."

They were driving very fast through the quiet tree-lined streets of the Beverly Hills Fortified Village, in a desperate effort to intercept Max's red Porsche.

"They can't have got to him yet. They can't," Rosalie was repeating to herself as they hurtled across the exclusive residential area.

But they could, and they had.

Rosalie and Judy skidded around a sharp corner in a leafy little road to find Max's Porsche skidded into the middle of the highway and another car, full of what looked like common hoodlums, pumping bullets into it.

Much to Judy's dismay, this terrible sight caused Rosalie to accelerate forward, and she deliberately slammed her car into the side of the car occupied by the hoodlums.

"Get Max," Rosalie cried, as they came to rest, and their heads stopped whipping back and forth. "I'll cover you." It was only then that she remembered she did not actually have a gun. "Shit!" she said.

"Here, use mine," said Judy. "I'm not very good with it anyway," and he handed her his regulation-issue automatic.

By this time, the killers had regained some of their composure, and were thinking about finishing off the job that had been interrupted by the crash. They did not realize that what had happened was anything other than an ordinary accident on the public highway. They were therefore considerably surprised when the driver of the car began to shoot at them, killing one of their number almost immediately. This was not how the contract was supposed to go. There was not, as far as the killers were aware, supposed to be any resistance. Perhaps it was the cops? If it was not the cops, it would certainly not be long before the cops arrived. The killers took stock, and the situation was not to their liking. The police were coming, and some mad woman was firing at them for some reason, but what? Could it possibly be because she'd dented her car? The killers wondered if they should call it a day; their job seemed done, anyway. Max definitely looked dead. He was slumped in his car, completely covered in blood and bullet holes. Indeed, so much blood did there seem to be that, if the bullets hadn't killed him already, he would shortly drown. Feeling their professional obligations to have been fulfilled, the killers withdrew.

Talk to my agent.

Having got the dead, or at the very least, nearly dead, Max into the back of the car, Rosalie also accelerated away from the scene of the incident. She did not know where she was going, but she did know that she had to get away. Max was a celebrity, and if news of his being gunned down got out there would be a media circus, and it would be impossible to keep him hidden. Rosalie felt sure that if Max was alive Tolstoy would try to hit him again.

"Is he alive?" she shouted over her shoulder at Judy, who had got into the backseat and was attempting to tend to Max. "Please tell me he's alive!"

"I don't know, I think so. Yes, I think he is. He's twitching a little, although that could just be reflexes," Judy replied.

"Is his hand on his crotch?" Rosalie shouted back.

"No."

"Then it isn't his reflexes."

Rosalie, like most women who live with men, found the male habit of constantly rearranging their wedding tackle whenever an idle moment occurred most disconcerting. On the phone, reading a book, stirring the dinner, guys were always handling their privates, and Rosalie, who had just spent nearly a month alone with Max, felt certain that if Max were dead and his muscles were going through their final involuntary spasms, somehow or other, one of his hands would end up on his dick.

"Is he breathing?" she asked desperately.

"Yes, he is, but he's a mess, that's for sure. Most of his insides are on his outside. We have to get him to a hospital."

"We can't. If we do that, Tolstoy will find him for sure, and he won't screw it up twice. We have to stay undercover."

"Rosalie," Judy pleaded, "this is Hollywood, and a huge star has been terribly wounded, possibly fatally. This is not something we can keep quiet."

Max wasn't dead. His body was in total shock, but he could hear what they were saying. What's more, he knew how to deal with the problem under discussion—the same way you dealt with any problem. With a considerable effort Max managed to attract Judy's attention by tugging at his sleeve.

"Call my agent," Max whispered into Judy's ear and gave him the number.

"Of course," said Judy, "why didn't I think of that," and grabbed his phone.

Judy was not himself in that great biz called show, but he lived in Los Angeles, and he knew that when stars had problems, whatever those problems might be, they turned to their agents to sort them out.

"Koch Associates," said a steely voice over Judy's phone. A voice that implied by its very tone that unless you had already had a featured role in at least three shows, not to even think of seeking representation. Even Judy was momentarily intimidated. Then he remembered that he was not actually an aspiring actor and had no burning belief inside him that he could make it, if only he were given the chance, nor was he seeking representation. He therefore had nothing to fear from the armor-plated voice that answered the phones at Koch Associates.

Emboldened by this thought, he said, "Listen, my name is J. Schwartz, I'm an officer with the FBI. Max Maximus is in big trouble, and I have to speak to his agent."

There was a brief pause, and another voice came on the line, this time even steelier and more forbidding than the first.

"This is Geraldine Koch. If you're some actor trying to bluff your way through to me, get off the phone now, or I shall see to it that your next public appearance will be in a Salvation Army breadline!"

"Ms. Koch, this is J. Schwartz of the FBI. Now shut up and listen to me!" Geraldine was so unused to being addressed in this manner that, astonishingly, she did shut up, at least long enough for Judy to say, "Plastic Tolstoy has taken out a contract on Max."

"What!" Geraldine cried, panic cracking the steel of her

voice. "Max told me he was retiring! You say he has a contract with Plastic Tolstoy! That can't be, I do his deals, not the FBI!"

"Ms. Koch, will you be quiet," Judy shouted. "I am not talking about a film contract, I'm talking about a murder contract! They've already hit him once, and he's got about a hundred bullets in him. Now we know that Tolstoy will try to hit him again the moment he finds out where Max is. He needs hospital treatment in complete secrecy, and he needs it now."

Geraldine was calm again. Things were not quite as bad as she had thought; Max was only dying. For a moment she had thought that he had gone to another agent.

"Where are you?" she asked.

"We're in a car just coming onto Sunset at the Chateau Marmont."

"Head for 289043 Melrose," Geraldine said. "It's just past all the bondage gear shops, and don't ask me how I know that. It's a convent hospital called the Little Sisters of the Desperately Over Budget. There will be a medical team waiting."

Geraldine put the phone down and tried to concentrate. Max may not have left her, but the situation was still very serious. What could Max possibly have done to offend Tolstoy enough for Tolstoy to try to kill him? Trying to kill someone was a fairly radical step, even by the cutthroat standards of Hollywood. Geraldine wondered if this meant that the movie deal that she had been negotiating for Max with Tolstoy's people was off? It would at least be on hold, that was certain. Max's position was clearly a delicate one. When a producer took out a murder contract on an actor, the actor's agent knew that difficult negotiations lay ahead. Geraldine resolved not to panic. She had worked in a tough town for more years than her cosmetic surgeon cared to remember, and she had learned over those years that there were very few problems, if any, that saturation lunching could not eventually fix.

"Pixie Dawn," she snapped into her intercom. "Clear my diary. As of now, we are lunching for our lives."

Specialist treatment.

Rosalie pulled into 289043 Melrose to find a crack medical team on full alert. Max was whisked out of the car and onto an emergency trolley and taken straight into an intensive care operating room. Judy and Rosalie could only watch anxiously through the glass wall as Max's clothes were cut away, and the dedicated surgeons and doctors began their work.

"They look like they know their business," Judy said, attempting to comfort a tight-lipped Rosalie. Rosalie's hand stole to her stomach. She had only just become pregnant, so there was nothing to feel, but she nonetheless felt aware of some presence inside her.

"I want my child to know its father," she said quietly.

Judy had not realized that Rosalie was pregnant. He did not know what to say, so he said nothing.

After about ten minutes the head surgeon emerged from the operating room, looking very perplexed.

"Well, we can't find anything wrong with him, I'm afraid," he said, and there was a hint of irritation in his voice. He had been called in from a particularly tense game of VR golf against Jack Nicklaus, and he rather resented the intrusion.

"Can't find anything wrong!" Rosalie gasped.

"That's right. There's not a whiff of drugs about him. We've checked his genitals and his posterior, and all that's clean as a whistle. There's no overdose, no sexual disease, I've looked right up him, and there's definitely nothing wedged in his backside. To be quite frank, I've absolutely no idea why you've brought him here at all."

"Because he's dying! You stupid bastard!" Rosalie screamed in the man's face. "Look at him."

The surgeon turned and seemed to notice for the first

time that Max was riddled with bullet holes, and had virtually no blood left in him.

"You mean *that's* what you want us to look at?" he asked, very surprised.

The misunderstanding lay in the fact that the Little Sisters of the Desperately Over Budget was a private hospital, with the emphasis on private. It was not used to dealing with ailments that might be categorized as nonscandalous. People got riddled with bullets all the time in L.A. Death by gunfire was a perfectly socially acceptable way to go, it could happen to anyone and could not possibly be considered in any way embarrassing or necessitating expensive cover-ups. The Little Sisters was a hospital that specialized in such cover-ups, dealing as it did with things that people needed to be kept quiet. Drug overdoses, pubic lice, strange objects that had got themselves stuck up people's bottoms or in other orifices—vacuum cleaner nozzles, Coke bottles, small animals, etc. (Small animals were particularly common; in fact, the hospital boasted rather a fine menagerie of assorted gerbils, hamsters, and possums that had been rescued from the interior plumbing of various drugged-out movie stars.)

When the Little Sisters had received an urgent call from Max Maximus's agent, demanding an immediate admission, they had of course presumed that the ailment was of a scandalous nature, which is why they had spent so long probing one of the few holes in his body that had not been caused by a bullet.

Counsel.

While the doctors worked on Max, Judy and Rosalie considered a plan of action. Despite being understandably upset and anxious about Max, Rosalie was thinking clearly. She remained adamant that the only course of action was to take the evidence of Plastic Tolstoy's crimes to Jurgen Thor, the one person with the influence to get it properly before the public. Judy, on the other hand, still wanted to go to the police and have Tolstoy arrested.

"With what we've got on that tape, we could put him away for thirty years," Judy said. "I mean quite apart from all the environmental stuff, we have him commissioning an attempted murder."

But Rosalie was absolutely insistent.

"He's my husband, it's my tape, and we're taking it to Thor."

In her own mind Rosalie had rejoined Mother Earth. She was again a green activist, and Plastic Tolstoy's confessional tape was the most effective weapon the Environmental Movement had ever been given.

"If we can get this out to people, maybe we can stop the rot!" Rosalie said. "Maybe we can show people what's being done to their world while they twiddle their thumbs. It could be the Third Great Green Scare, something to really shock people into fighting back."

"I suppose it could," Judy conceded.

"Of course it could. We have to try, anyway, and that means getting this tape back to Europe. If we stay here we'll be dead anyway."

That reminded Judy of something. Plastic Tolstoy knew all about him. He was in as much danger as Max was, and so, in that case, were his loved ones. He called home. His husband, Roger, was very upset.

"Judy! Thank goodness it's you! You have to come home right now! The house has been ransacked. I just got back, everything is—"

"Roger!" Judy interrupted. "Are the police there?"

"Not yet. I called them, but—"

"Get your passport and get out now! Come to 289043 Melrose."

"Don't be stupid, Judy, the house is a bomb-site, I have salmon for—"

"Now, Roger! Get out now!"

Agent of conflict.

For a few hours Max's condition remained critical, but as it turned out Rosalie and Judy had interrupted the killers in time. By the afternoon he began to respond to treatment.

They knew they could not remain long at the hospital, though, reasoning that on hearing Max had been spirited away, Plastic Tolstoy would be anxious to ensure that he was dead.

"The first thing he's going to do is start checking the hospitals," said Judy. "We need to get Max out of town quickly and into some hiding place or other that Tolstoy can't figure out. That goes for me too, for that matter. Tolstoy's going to want to clean this whole thing up properly, and that includes me."

"Well, I really don't see how looking up old TV schedules could have got you into so much trouble," Roger observed, but Judy assured him that it had.

"The best place to go would be my granny's place in Ireland," said Rosalie. "Tolstoy doesn't know my name, so I doubt that he would find us there, and it gets me close to Jurgen Thor."

"That means an air ambulance," Judy replied, "also European visas. Those things are difficult to organize, and we could certainly never do it without sticking our necks out. If we wander around L.A. trying to get plane tickets and our passports stamped, Tolstoy will spot us for sure."

There was a gloomy silence. Every second they remained inactive brought Tolstoy's deadly shadow closer. Just then, the solution arrived in the unlikely figure of Max's agent, Geraldine, who burst through the door with flowers from her Claustrosphere.

"Okay," she said to Judy and Rosalie. "Thanks for getting him to the hospital, but I'll be taking charge from here on in."

"I don't think so," said Rosalie.

"Well, I'm sorry, miss, but I'm not interested in what

you think. What you think doesn't matter. All that matters is Max needs me, and I'm here for him. Excuse me." Geraldine turned her back on Rosalie and tapped a number into her phone. Rosalie and Judy were a little nonplussed. It was not so much what Geraldine had said, but the way that she had said it. No one can put people down the way an agent can, particularly an important Hollywood agent.

It is probably not that they particularly enjoy being rude. Being rude just happens to be the principal function of their professional existence. To an agent there are two types of actor, those who are happening and those who are not. Hence there are two kinds of rudeness. There is the rudeness that is directed at those who are not happening, and the rudeness that is directed at others *on behalf* of and for the benefit of those who are happening. The rudeness directed at the unhappening is not normally very rude. In fact, it is really no more than the understandable brusqueness that any decent agent must develop in a world where there are a thousand actors seeking every job. The rudeness directed downward is often tinged with affection and understanding, for agents are human beings too, and it would soften any heart to be constantly surrounded by so much frustrated ambition.

Where the rudeness gets nasty is when it is delivered on behalf of a star. This is because of the great agent's dilemma, the terrible cross that all agents have to bear, that which turns young, starry-eyed enthusiasts who "love this business" into hardened, chain-smoking attack animals.

The agent's dilemma is this: No matter how hard they work, they can never succeed. The success or failure of their clients only means failure to them. For an agent will never be loved or appreciated by those on whose behalf they labor. Never. Agents were born to be resented.

It starts at the bottom. When an actor is out of work, and it is three months since they were even invited up for an audition, they become obsessed with the notion that their agent is crap.

"No, seriously, I really am thinking of changing my agent," the actor will assure his or her friends. "I mean she just hasn't got me a thing. Not a fucking thing! I mean, I wouldn't mind, but I'm actually *really fucking good.*"

A subtle variation of this whine is the conviction that the agent is actually capable of getting work, but for some reason does not care to do so for them. Actors conceive this latter prejudice if anybody else on the agent's books happens to have landed an audition for a soap commercial in the previous five years.

Sometimes, not often, but sometimes, a glint of hope peeks into the actor's life. After making two hundred calls, the agent lands the actor an audition, and astonishingly, the actor gets the job. At this point there is a brief moment when the agent may bask in a thimbleful of the actor's affection. They will lunch together to celebrate the start of a great career, and the agent will order good California chardonnay. Even as the glasses clink, however, the actor will secretly be thinking that his or her success in getting a job was really no thanks to the agent at all. It was, in fact, entirely due to the brilliant way that he or she handled the audition. Anyone, after all, can make a phone call.

If this brief moment of glory is a one-shot and the actor fails to capitalize on it, he or she will soon return to the conviction that the agent is either crap, or uninterested in them. However, if the actor's career takes off and they find themselves in demand, then the agent will have to swallow a bitter pill indeed. For the actor will now be thinking that work is available to them anyway, so what does the agent do? What skill, they ask themselves, does it require to find work for somebody whom everybody already wants?

"I really don't know," the actor will tell their friends, "what I'm paying my ten percent for."

It is this terrible betrayal that truly leads agents to their joyless life of rudeness. Because they become obsessed with demonstrating to their star clients what it is that the star clients are paying their ten percents for.

"You will not *believe* what the studio's opening offer was," the agent will assure the star. "No, I'm not even going to tell you. It was an insult and an offense, and you should not even have to hear about it, but let me tell you, it was a disgrace. I just told them to stuff it, shove it, and take a hike, and believe me, I wasn't that restrained. Anyway, they've come back with a figure that is at least located on planet Earth."

The agent's job is to make themselves appear indispensable. What they are saying to their clients is this, "You are too important and famous to have to deal with any shit, anytime, anywhere. I will take the shit away from you. Trust me. *I will be rude for you.*"

The agent creates the impression that the star is surrounded by people who are hell-bent on ripping them off, taking advantage of them, demeaning them, and generally laying shit on them (shit, which, of course, the star *does not need right now!*). The suggestion being that without the agent endlessly being rude on their behalf, the star would live a life no better than that of a sewer rat.

"You mean they flew you on a *scheduled flight?* Booked you a suite with no *spa bath?* Put you in worse seats than *so and so?* The car was *how many* seconds late? . . . I don't believe it! This is simply unacceptable! Don't you worry about it, though, leave it to me. You do not need this shit! You should not have to *deal with this shit!*"

It is not just the agents, of course, who act in this way. The life of a star is filled with people making complaints and being rude on the star's behalf, for which they receive a percentage of the star's earnings. If many stars turn eventually into ego-monsters, they are certainly given plenty of encouragement.

Power struggle.

Geraldine, having turned her back on Judy and Rosalie, was speaking on the phone.

"Yes, thank you, I should like to speak to Plastic Tolstoy's office. Yes, now! My name is Geraldine Koch, and I represent . . ."

Geraldine got no further because at that point Rosalie knocked the phone from her hand and ground it under her heel.

"Phone calls can be traced, you know, Miss Koch. I thought we'd told you. Tolstoy is trying to kill Max."

Geraldine could not believe what had just happened. Somebody had touched her phone! In fact, not just touched it, destroyed it! That was a personal violation. Her phone was the medium of her artistry. To destroy it was like taking an artist's brush, or breaking a musician's instrument. Fortunately, she was carrying eight more. Geraldine turned on Rosalie.

"Now, listen to me, young lady, I don't know who the hell you are, but I am Max's agent—"

"And I am his wife!"

This stopped Geraldine in her tracks. Wives were tricky things. They could poison the air between agent and star, or they could sweeten it. You had to keep on the right side of wives. On the other hand, you didn't want to get too close to them because it left you in a very tricky position when the star dumped the wife and married the nanny. If the new wife felt that the agent was too chummy with the old wife, then the agent's life would become hell until they had ingratiated themselves with the new wife. Unfortunately, by the time they had done this, the new wife could easily be an old wife. Wives certainly were tricky things. In the long run, it was kids that were the determining factor in an agent's attitude. If there were kids, the wife had to be taken very seriously indeed.

"Well, congratulations, my dear," said Geraldine, testing

the water, "and may one ask if we can expect to hear the patter of tiny feet?"

Rosalie was a little taken aback by the question, but she saw no reason to deny it.

"Yes, as a matter of fact, we are expecting."

"But, my *darling,* that's *wonderful,*" said Geraldine, thinking to herself, Damn, some waitress has trapped Max with a pregnancy, and now we're stuck with the little bitch.

"If there's anything I can do. Anything at all," Geraldine said.

"Well, as a matter of fact, there is," said Rosalie. "Max wants to recuperate discreetly in Europe. So what we need is an air ambulance and four false passports with Euro visas in them."

Geraldine was delighted. Nothing pleases an agent more than to sort out difficult things for their clients' spouses, especially if those things are slightly risky. It puts the spouse in the agent's debt. Geraldine reckoned that obtaining false visas would provide her with a good deal of leverage with Max in the future. Little did poor Geraldine know that there was in fact not a great deal of future left.

26

Debauchery and murder

Caligula's palace.

JURGEN THOR WAS IN THE MIDDLE OF AN ORGY WHEN ROSALIE called him. His once pristine bedroom, which had been so stylishly furnished with its single enormous bed and a few floor cushions, was now a mass of naked bodies, water couches, bondage gear, and various other sexual paraphernalia. There was booze and drugs aplenty, and Jurgen was a little drunk when he picked up the phone.

"Jurgen Thor? It's me, Rosalie Connolly," the soft Irish voice said. "I came to see you a few weeks back, I was with Max Maximus. Do you remember?"

Did he remember? Rosalie could not know it, but Jurgen Thor could never forget that night. It haunted his dreams. Scarcely a night went by now when he did not awake in a sweat with the vision of a dead girl screaming at him from the bottom of a deep, dark chasm.

"Yes, I remember everything. I heard you had left us, Rosalie."

"Well, I haven't and I need to see you again, urgently."

Jurgen may have been drunk, but not so much that he

was immune to the memory of those flashing green eyes and the pale skin. The beautiful voice brought it all back to him very clearly. The earlier part of that terrible evening, the pleasanter part, when he had still been in control, and girls had still done what he told them to without having to be murdered first. Yes, that bit had been fun in its way, showing off to the lovely young woman, *soiling* her with the knowledge of her compromise. That soft voice also brought a more distant night back to Jurgen's mind. A night when it had been just him and Rosalie, alone. Now that had been a truly wonderful night. She had been weaker then, and he stronger. Then she had really been his possession. But that was in a different time, when he had still been at the height of his powers, not like now. Even so, it was fun to look back. Yes, Jurgen had fond memories of Rosalie. How nice, he thought in his alcoholic haze, it would be to see her again. He was wrong.

"You need to see me, huh, baby doll?" Jurgen breathed into the phone, trying to sound sexy, but in fact merely giving Rosalie the impression that he had a cold. "Well, come on over to my place. Hey, girl! We're having a party!"

Rosalie put the phone down feeling a little puzzled. Jurgen had sounded strange. Could he have been drunk? It seemed unlikely; his capacity to hold his booze had always been legendary. Rosalie was not, of course, to know just how many Jurgen Thor had been letting himself go of late. The man was slowly giving up. The process had begun even before he had found himself forced to murder poor Scout. He was weighed down with the knowledge of doom. The end was coming, and he wished that it would hurry up and come. He was fed up with waiting and fed up with lying.

Scout's death had accelerated this process. Once she started returning each night to interrupt his sleep, Jurgen began to sag. It was as if a ball that had been firm and strong with tension for so long had finally been punctured.

It only takes a little hole, and all the air soon rushes out, leaving the ball looking much the same, but useless for all that.

In an effort to regain his former aggressive joie de vivre, Jurgen had started to party, in fact, to orgy. He had jettisoned the sexual habits he had practiced for decades in favor of a wild free-for-all. No more for him the private one-on-one seduction, of which he had been the master for so long. He could no longer do it. Private sex reminded him of Scout, and he had enough of Scout to contend with in his dreams without seeing her in the faces of the women he screwed. Jurgen had never imagined that such a little murder would affect him so. He had lived a rough life and seen and done many terrible things, and yet he simply could not shake the death of this one innocent from his mind. He supposed it was because she had died to protect a lie. He had killed her to defend the indefensible, and now he was paying the price. He could not even make love to a woman if he was alone with her; he had to have a crowd around him. Jurgen was scared of the dark.

Latecomer.

All the lights in the mountain home were blazing as Rosalie guided her little monocopter down through the darkness and onto Jurgen's rooftop helipad. She was surprised to see a number of aircraft already parked, their blades folded down to make more space. Despite this evidence that Jurgen had company, it was all strangely quiet. No one had come up onto the roof to meet her, which was very much a break with Jurgen Thor's old ways. In the past he had been extremely security-conscious, never allowing people to land on his roof unchallenged.

There was no bell to ring; none had ever been needed, because the occupants of the house always heard any approaching aircraft from miles away. Rosalie was forced to bang and kick upon the door in an effort to attract attention. For a while she got nowhere and began to wonder if she would ever succeed in gaining access to Jurgen's lair. There was music playing somewhere, but she could hear no talk or laughter. She became alarmed. Had some terrible gas leak or something occurred? Were they all dead?

Finally she heard footsteps on the stairs within, and the door was opened by a dreamy-looking young woman, completely naked, with quite the largest breasts and the biggest pupils that Rosalie had ever seen.

"Hi," said the very stoned woman. "Aren't the stars amazing. People never take time to look at things, do they? I mean, *really* look at them. Come on in."

Rosalie followed the girl down the spiral staircase and found herself yet again in Jurgen Thor's bedroom. How different it was from the other two occasions on which she had seen it. Then it had been a chic and elegant palace of seduction; now it looked like Sodom and Gomorrah must have looked on the days when the populace had decided to stop being so prissy, throw inhibition to the wind, and get properly naughty.

There must have been thirty naked bodies in the room. Jurgen never had any problem assembling a decent guest list for his orgies. People were thrilled to be invited to his legendary and, until recently, totally exclusive private home. Jurgen was one of the most important and respected people in the world, everybody wanted to know him. Society beauties flocked around, as did free-spirited Natura hippie girls . . . they always had. Jurgen was never shy of making the most of this popularity for the purpose of sexual conquest; these days he just did it in bulk, that was all.

For a nice Catholic girl the whole outrageous scene was something of a shock, and as she looked around the room, Rosalie might have thought that she was dreaming, except that these were not the sort of dreams that she had.

"What on earth have you all been doing?" Rosalie asked, perhaps rather stupidly.

"We've been making good thoughts and feelings," the large-breasted girl replied. "They'll emanate out from this place and make the whole world beautiful again." Which was not a bad excuse for getting shit-faced drunk and fucking a lot of virtual strangers.

The girl drifted away, leaving Rosalie alone on the stairs. Most of the company were asleep, or unconscious more like, to judge from their unnatural positions. A few couples, however, were still lazily making love in a distant, soporific kind of way. One or two others were drinking and smoking, staring trancelike into the middle distance and nodding sagely, as if in agreement with some brilliant point, even though no one had actually said anything. Jurgen Thor himself lay in the center of it all, unconscious upon his great bed, prostrate among no fewer than four women, one of whom was still half awake and sleepily blowing Jurgen's sleepy member.

Jurgen was still a magnificent figure of a man, but Rosalie could not help but feel a bit queasy, contemplating the state he was in. She liked a party as much as the next girl, but to be so off your head that you could have somebody going down on you and not even notice was slightly sickmaking, in Rosalie's opinion. However, she was not there to moralize, she had a desperately important job to do, and she needed Jurgen Thor.

Rosalie picked her way across the prostrate bodies stranded on the floor.

"Excuse me . . . I'm awfully sorry . . . Oh, my God! Did I just tread on your thing? Sorry," she mumbled to the sleeping forms as she made her way to the bed.

"Jurgen," she said, gently shaking the great man's shoulder. "Jurgen?"

She got no further because at that moment her attention was distracted somewhat. She was standing beside the bed, and the girl who had been concentrating on Jurgen's loins had reached out a hand, and was now using it to massage the inside of Rosalie's leg.

"Would you not do that, please?" Rosalie said to the spaced-out girl.

"Hey, come on," the girl replied, looking up from the parts that she had been nibbling. "Jurgen's rules, right? Everybody has to party. So get naked, lady, no spectators allowed." With that, the girl moved her hand up to the top of Rosalie's inner leg, with the clear intention of unzipping her trousers.

"I said, would you not do that, please," said Rosalie, and pointed her gun into the girl's face.

"Wow! Are you the cops?" the girl asked, quickly removing her hand. But Rosalie had no wish to converse with this rampant space cadet any further. She shook Jurgen by the shoulder and loudly demanded that he wake up. He did so with a scream that briefly roused the room.

"She's falling!" he shouted, before coming slowly around and focusing on Rosalie. "Welcome to ancient Rome, yes, baby. My name is Caligula, and the world is coming to an end. You have been designated my latest concubine." He made a lunge at Rosalie, but she backed away.

"Let's get out of here, Jurgen, I have to talk to you."

But Jurgen had already drifted back into fitful unconsciousness, and Rosalie was forced to try to rouse him further.

"Jurgen, it's urgent! It's Mother Earth business!" she said, shaking him again. "You have to get out of bed and talk to me."

"If you haven't come to party, don't bother knocking on my door." Jurgen giggled and again made a grab at Rosalie. This time he found his mark and roughly took hold of one of her breasts. She hit him in the face, hard, and with a clenched fist. His hand dropped away, but apart from that he scarcely seemed to notice. He certainly registered no pain, his eyes just rolled a little, and he laughed again.

Rosalie could see that no sense would be got out of Jurgen for a few hours yet, and that she would have to wait.

She retreated to the kitchen, which was mercifully empty of naked bodies, and made herself a cup of coffee. Jurgen's condition had shocked her deeply. True, she had long since jettisoned the adolescent hero-worship that she had felt for him as a girl; and, of course, recently his image had been further tarnished in her eyes by the revelations of who paid for his house and all the luxuries that he enjoyed so much. But he was still Jurgen Thor, the most important and inspirational green activist there was. The Green God, the last sane man on Earth. To see him like this, a debauched and giggling wretch, was a hard sight indeed for Rosalie, particularly coming as it did on top of all the other shocking truths that she had had to accept of late.

She did not feel angry with Jurgen Thor, she felt sorry for him. Clearly the colossal burdens that he had carried for so long had finally got the better of him. The mighty and inspirational idealogue who had become an embittered pragmatist had finally taken refuge in the hollow pleasures of the dilettante. Jurgen Thor had given up, and who could blame him? Rosalie had given up herself only a few days earlier. In fact, thinking about it, drinking her coffee in that silent house, Rosalie realized that Jurgen's orgies were no more desperate or irresponsible than her own decision to hide away with Max in his Claustrosphere. She too had been planning to fiddle while Rome burned. Planning to luxuriate in the pleasures of the senses while the doomed world died. It had only been the knowledge of Plastic Tolstoy's marketing strategy that had galvanized her to return to the real world and take up arms again. Rosalie believed that the same thing would happen with Jurgen. He too would see that all was not lost, that once Tolstoy's taped confession was placed before the public, a new age of protest would dawn, and that Jurgen Thor would lead it.

All that would have to wait, though. For the time being, Rosalie would have to leave Jurgen to sleep it off among his concubines. But how strange he had looked. The mighty Thor turned into an insensitive, groping drunk. He had certainly surprised her. He was going to surprise her a great deal more before the night was over.

Another penny drops.

Before setting out to enlist Jurgen Thor, Rosalie had left Judy, Roger, and Max in the care of her grandparents at their little cottage in Western Ireland. On that first evening after Rosalie had left, and with Max lying in bed under sedation, Judy explained to Ruth and Sean (and indeed Roger, who was still very much catching up with things) the sequence of events that had brought them all to the current position.

"You're trying to tell us, young man, that environmental protest is basically an arm of Claustrosphere's marketing policy," said Ruth as she produced a delicious-looking Yorkshire pudding, which she served up with a thick vegetable casserole.

"That's right," said Judy. "Neat, isn't it?"

"And they actually create disasters to fit in with their ads?"

"It's unbelievable," said Roger. "Just so crisp and light."

"What?" said Judy.

"This pudding, it's the best I've ever seen."

"Roger," Judy said, "we're talking about Claustrosphere."

"Well, I don't know why you're so surprised. The world's run on dirty tricks, isn't it? Nothing shocks me. I think the rot set in for America when the FBI killed Kennedy."

"The FBI did *not* kill Kennedy!" Judy said firmly.

"Oh, you are so naive, Judy," said Roger. "But please, let's not discuss it, I could not *bear* another Kennedy discussion."

One of the more surprising facts about social intercourse as the twenty-first century plodded its weary course was the fact that the number of people discussing how JFK had died was actually increasing. Elvis had peaked long before, but the Kennedys went from strength to strength.

"I'll tell you what is unbelievable," said Roger, sticking to his preferred subject. "This ratatouille, Ruth, is quite simply gastronomically orgasmic, and, let me tell you, I know. Oral orgasm is my specialty."

There was a slightly uncomfortable pause.

"Roger's a chef," said Judy, feeling some sort of explanation was necessary.

"Well, I thought he must be," said Ruth disingenuously.

"You know what surprises me?" Sean said, looking up from his pipe. "That you're still alive, Judy, after accusing Rosalie of spreading that toxic waste all over Brussels. I'm surprised she didn't kill you there and then."

"I think she wanted to, but we had to run away from all the poison. I still can't figure out how I got that so wrong. I was so sure, you see. It all fitted."

"Well, we can't be a genius the whole time, can we?" said Roger. "This is called a Yorkshire pudding, isn't it, Ruth? We make pudding in the States, but it's usually much heavier. How in heaven do you get it so fluffy?"

"The most important element is the fat, dear. The fat has got to be absolutely smoking hot. Also, the mix has to stand for at lest an hour."

"Well, it's yummy," Roger assured Ruth. "Would you like me to do this for you sometimes, Judy? ... Judy, please don't daydream at the table, we're guests here."

But Judy was not daydreaming. He was thinking very hard. Yet again rehearsing in his mind the circumstances that had led him to the conclusion that Mother Earth was provoking its own disasters.

"Natura was always there, you see. It was as if it knew where and when the disasters would occur. That's why I thought Mother Earth was causing them and tipping Natura off."

"Yes, you've *said* that, dear! But it wasn't, was it?" Roger reiterated wearily. "You were wrong. Plastic Tolstoy was doing it, which is why we've had to flee America like criminals."

"But that doesn't change the fact that Natura is always there! Somehow it gets sent into areas where the disasters occur. If Mother Earth isn't pointing them in the right direction, then it must be Tolstoy. He's causing the disasters, and he's the one who profits most from Natura protest. He's giving the orders."

"But Tolstoy isn't the leader of Natura," said Sean.

"No," Judy replied, and he was suddenly very afraid. "Jurgen Thor is."

There was a pause. Sean wondered if Judy could truly be hinting at what he seemed to be hinting at.

"What about Brussels?" Sean said hurriedly. "We know why Natura were there on that occasion, to cover the Mother Earth protest, not because they were expecting a disaster."

"That's right," said Judy. "But the disaster occurred anyway. Tolstoy had sabotaged the tankers, which means . . ."

"That he knew the action was going to take place," said Ruth.

"So Natura gets told to go where Tolstoy is sinking boats, and Tolstoy gets told where Mother Earth is creating opportunities for high-profile sabotage. It seems to me that there is a rather unhealthy level of cooperation here," Roger observed.

"Who authorizes Mother Earth actions?" said Judy.

"The Number One Equal Person, of course," Ruth replied.

"And the Number One Equal Person is—?" asked Judy, but of course he already knew the answer.

"Jurgen Thor," said Sean.

"They're partners," Judy said quietly, as if trying to diminish the enormity of his suspicion. *"Tolstoy and Thor are partners."* He leapt to his feet. "Rosalie is in terrible danger. She's only been gone a couple of hours, it may not be too late. Is there anyone you can call who has access to a helicopter? One of Rosalie's colleagues, for instance? One we can trust."

Ruth crossed to the dresser, and opening the bread bin, she took out a tiny two-way radio.

"Rosalie's old unit are back in the Partry Mountains. They have a new commander. Sean and I have known him for years. He's a good fighter, and loyal to Rosalie, although she never liked him. The poor fellow was terribly injured, and it's made him rather moody."

Judy feared the worst.

"This guy's name . . . it wouldn't by any chance be Saunders, would it?"

Rude awakening.

Rosalie must have fallen asleep, because she woke up with a start to find Jurgen Thor standing beside her, gently running his fingers through her hair. He was still stark naked, and it was quite clear that he was pleased to see her. Rosalie had slumped forward in her chair and had been resting her head on her arms on the table. Hence Jurgen's erection was the first thing she saw when she opened her eyes.

"Congratulations, Jurgen. If I had a medal I'd hang one on it; now put it away. I have something quite incredible to talk to you about."

"I don't want to talk, babe, okay?" Jurgen replied, his words still slightly slurred with sleep, booze, and pills. "I want to make love."

"Jurgen, this idiocy has gone far enough," Rosalie said firmly, "I have to talk to you about Plastic Tolstoy."

Jurgen Thor looked at Rosalie for a moment, and even in that moment his eyes became a little clearer. He took up a robe that had been dropped upon the kitchen floor and covered himself. He did not reply until he had made himself a cup of coffee and cleared his head a little.

"What about Plastic Tolstoy?" he said finally. "I hope you're not thinking of bringing up that stuff about the funding again, okay? If you don't like what you hear, then you shouldn't ask questions. We discussed it, right? It's a secret we can never tell, and the subject is closed."

"No, it's not about the funding, Jurgen. Something much, much nastier than that. Believe me, Plastic Tolstoy's pragmatism goes a deal further than funding a few greenies. That man will do anything, and I mean quite literally anything, to sell a Claustrosphere."

"And what do you mean by that?" Jurgen asked.

"I mean that Plastic Tolstoy has been wreaking his own private environmental holocaust, Jurgen, and I have proof."

Jurgen stared at Rosalie. She was so young and pretty. Just as Scout had been. It seemed that now there would be two beautiful innocents to deny him rest and haunt his dreams.

"This sounds most fascinating, baby," Jurgen said. "We should not discuss it here, anyone might come in. They are fools, but even fools can tell tales. Come down to my study."

"The dead menagerie?" said Rosalie, recalling all the animal heads.

"Yes, that's right. The dead menagerie."

And, taking Rosalie gently by the arm, Jurgen Thor led her out of the kitchen and down the stairs into the bottom floor of the house, to his study, with its stuffed animals, antler chairs, and its trapdoor.

Unlikely comrades.

Even above the sound of the helicopter blades beating at the air, Judy could hear the sound of grinding teeth emanating from inside the bag that Saunders was, of course, wearing over his head.

"I don't mind telling you," said Saunders, finally giving his teeth a rest. "When I walked in and found out that it was you that I was supposed to help, I nearly shot you there and then. In fact, it was only out of deference to Rosalie's gran that I didn't."

Saunders, it must be remembered, was a Liverpudlian, and there are certain codes on Merseyside, one of which is to try to avoid upsetting people's grannies.

"That was very nice of you," Judy said, attempting to sound ingratiating. Even though Saunders appeared to have accepted Judy's story, he still made Judy nervous.

"It's a pretty incredible theory, Schwartz," Saunders said. "If it's the truth, then everything's shit, you know that, don't you? The whole world's pointless, and we might as well give up because it's all a fucking joke."

"Yes, I suppose that's true," Judy admitted.

"Well, I just hope you're right, that's all, because this is the unit helicopter, and let me tell you, I'm breaking a lot of rules just taking it like this."

Judy found Saunders's attitude strange, but he did not say so. He found most things about Saunders strange, and if he had started mentioning them all he would have been at it all night. Besides, Judy was too anxious to want to make conversation. It had taken two hours for Ruth to get hold of Saunders and another one and a half for Saunders to get to the cottage. What with the start Rosalie had on them in the first place, that put her about six hours ahead. Judy could only hope that somehow she had got delayed, or had put off confiding in Jurgen for some reason. If she had not, then she was probably already dead, and the vital Ansafone tape, which was their only proof against Plastic Tolstoy, lost forever. There was no copy, the recording was contained within a microchip inside the machine, not the easiest thing to reproduce. Judy had been hoping to make a copy of sorts at Ruth and Sean's by playing back the message and videotaping the playback, but to his amazement Ruth and Sean had no video. Rosalie had said that she would make a copy of the tape at Jurgen Thor's place.

The message is murder.

"I think we should make a copy of this right now," said Rosalie to Jurgen. "Do you have a video camera?"

"What? Oh, yes . . . Of course I have."

Jurgen was distracted. He was more than distracted, he was stunned. Taped evidence of Plastic Tolstoy confessing to poisoning seas. Taped evidence of Tolstoy attempting to organize a film star's murder. This was dynamite indeed. Jurgen had expected nothing so spectacularly damning when Rosalie set up Max's little answering machine. Indeed, for a moment, he thought that the whole thing must be a joke.

"This is the most important bit of recording you will ever see in your life," Rosalie said with deadly earnestness. "It's the ultimate smoking gun."

She pressed playback, and immediately a very beautiful woman in a tiny, skintight minidress had appeared on the screen.

"Max. Haven't seen you in a while. Call me," the stunning beauty said, adding, "I had the hammock repaired, by the way."

Jurgen looked at Rosalie and grinned. She, of course, colored bright red.

"Hang on a minute," she said, "this isn't it."

A second and third girl appeared on the little screen, wearing similarly minimal clothing and leaving similarly seductive messages. Then Geraldine, Max's agent, popped up.

"Max? Are you back yet? You will not believe the *shit* I've been fielding for you while you've been away, but you don't need to hear about that. Leave it to me, okay?"

There were more girls, one even wearing a bikini, de-spite clearly being indoors. Jurgen grunted appreciatively; Rosalie chewed her lower lip. The bikini girl pouted that she had heard about Max's divorce from Krystal and guessed he must be lonely.

"How about dinner?" she breathed over her cleavage. "I haven't had a really good nibble for ages." She then began to move her video phone all around her body, offering close-ups of her artificially tanned flesh. Just as she was about to drop the phone down into the bottom of her swimsuit, Rosalie got up and hit fast-forward.

"It's obviously further down the tape than I'd realized," Rosalie said crossly. Of course Max could hardly help who phoned him, but those girls seemed awfully familiar, and, what's more, he must at some point have given them his number. It is never any fun for a husband or wife to bump into evidence of their partner's past. Rosalie felt particu-larly hot under the collar, since her own past consisted of exactly two affairs (not counting Jurgen). If Max ever came across an old Ansafone tape of hers, he could play it at the next Sunday School picnic, a fact that Rosalie found herself resenting.

"I was enjoying that," Jurgen Thor complained as the tape whizzed on.

"Never mind that, Jurgen," Rosalie assured him. "This will really grab your interest."

And of course it did. Although not in the manner that Rosalie had presumed.

Having watched the tape, Rosalie suggested that they video-record it, as that was the only means they had at present of producing a copy. Jurgen pondered a moment and then agreed.

"Certainly we must video-record it, baby," he said. "I have a camera here in my desk. Would you be so kind as to carry the machine over to that far wall; the light is better there, and there are no distractions in the background. Just put it on the floor."

Somehow Jurgen felt easier about it this time. Yes, this girl was young, and she was innocent, but not like Scout had been. Nor was she so naive. This girl was a tough fighter, just like he was. She knew the stakes and had voluntarily chosen to bring the battle to him.

Jurgen Thor did not think that he would cry this time.

Rosalie picked up her husband's Ansafone and began to cross the floor with it. Walking the same condemned walk that Scout had walked before her.

27

The End

The trapdoor opens.

JUDY AND SAUNDERS DID NOT HAVE QUITE SO LONG TO WAIT UP on the roof as Rosalie. Most of the party-goers in Jurgen's bedroom had roused themselves by the time the two men arrived, and a single knock had solicited a response. It was morning, and the girl that opened the door for them had donned a sarong.

"Hi. You're just in time for breakfast," she said. "Hot croissant and drugs, want some?" The girl did not say so, but she felt that Jurgen had rather let the side down with these two. It was just presumed that anybody coming to one of these functions would be beautiful, and the two men on the roof were most definitely not. At least the nerd wasn't, and the other one had a bag over his head, which did not bode well at all. The beautiful girl in the sarong made a mental note not to get stuck anywhere near either of them if things began to get going again, which they just might, once the breakfast drugs had kicked in.

"Where's Jurgen Thor?" asked Judy, as he and Saunders pushed their way past the girl and into the house.

Standing at the top of the spiral staircase, the scene that greeted them was slightly less decadent than the one that Rosalie had encountered on the previous evening. However, slightly less decadent than that still meant pretty decadent, especially to the likes of Judy and Saunders. They were momentarily lost for words, finding themselves faced with a room full of half-naked people nibbling at drugs, drink, breakfast, and each other in an extremely spaced-out manner. Trying not to stare, Judy cast his eyes around the room. Neither Rosalie nor Jurgen were anywhere to be seen.

"Um, excuse me, everybody," Judy mumbled, "sorry to burst in on you like this, but does anybody know where Jurgen Thor is?"

"He was here a few minutes ago," said the girl in the sarong.

"Yeah." A voice came from the bed. It was the girl who had tried to feel up Rosalie in the night. "He went off to find that uptight redhead chick. I don't think he'll get very far there."

The suggestion that Rosalie had possibly been alive as late as a few minutes ago spurred Judy on, and followed by Saunders, he ran down the spiral staircase, past the bedroom, and farther into the house. They passed the ablutions floor, where jolly squeals of glee were to be heard emanating through the steam of the spa baths and power showers. They passed the kitchen, where a couple of slightly more together souls were making coffee.

"That's Rosalie's coat!" Saunders shouted, spotting the combat jacket that was hanging over a chair.

A floor below them, in the study, Rosalie herself had crossed the floor and was now standing on the trap door, the answering machine in her arms.

"Where do you want me to put it?" she inquired.

"I want you to take it with you, baby. *Ciao,* good-looking," Jurgen replied, and his hand moved toward the deadly lever.

Just then, the door of the study burst open, and Judy stood in the doorway with Saunders behind him. Jurgen paused, his hand hovering over the switch that would consign Rosalie to the chasm below.

"Rosalie!" Judy said. "Thank God, you're alive!"

"Of course I'm alive, you fool," Rosalie replied. "Why wouldn't I be? More to the point, what are you doing here?"

"That bastard there is Plastic Tolstoy's partner!"

Rosalie looked at Jurgen. His face showed it all. Judy was right. Then she saw his hand move. A warning bell rang inside her. Somehow with that hand Jurgen Thor was attacking her, she knew it. Her whole body knew it. Every muscle suddenly tensed as she instinctively readied herself for the attack that she knew was coming. That attack, whatever it might be, that Jurgen's hand was somehow initiating.

That moment of knowledge saved her. When the attack came, the tension in her body gave her the power with which to reach for safety. As the floor dropped away beneath her feet, Rosalie's arms shot out like bolts from a sprung lock. Indeed, her whole body seemed to twist in midair as she lunged for the edge of the bottomless tomb that Jurgen Thor had attempted to consign her to. The Ansafone, of course, leapt from her grasp and fell away into the darkness, but Rosalie found a grip and hung on, her fingertips all that remained visible from inside the room.

During her Mother Earth training days, Rosalie had been taught to rock climb, a sport in which the last joints on the fingers are the most crucial part of the body. The climber is instructed to exercise these joints constantly, and the preferred method for doing this is to perform chin-ups, while suspending yourself from the tops of door frames. Rosalie had never lost the habit and seldom went through a door at home without pulling a couple of fingertip chin-ups on the frame. Her granny had often lamented the damage done to her door frames as they slowly cracked and pulled away from the wall, not having been built to withstand the hanging weight of an adult person, even a small one like Rosalie. Had Ruth been able to see her granddaughter now, she would have counted those door frames cheap and a million more like them. For Rosalie was hanging on, quite literally by her fingertips, while hundreds of feet below her, inside the terrible granite jaws of the chasm, poor Scout's rotting corpse lay awaiting company.

All this had, of course, happened in one stunning moment. Nearly as stunning for Judy and Saunders as it had been for Rosalie, since they had not expected to see their comrade suddenly drop through the floor. Jurgen Thor was able to capitalize upon this second or two of shock to produce a gun from his desk, fit a silencer to its muzzle out of deference to his guests upstairs, and level it at the two men.

Keeping the gun trained firmly upon Judy and Saunders, Jurgen walked around his desk and toward the hole in the floor where the eight white points of Rosalie's fingertips were flattened on the edge. It was clear what his intention was. He was going to stamp on Rosalie's fingers.

"Please remain exactly where you are, okay, guys, yes?" Jurgen said. "Once I have said farewell to Rosalie, I should like to know how you came upon the wild idea that I hang out with Plastic Tolstoy, okay?"

It was Saunders who acted. He had a plan, not a very good one as it turned out, at least not for him, but it saved Rosalie's life anyway. Also it meant that Saunders got to die the way he had always wanted, in the defense of the planet, so perhaps it wasn't such a bad plan.

Saunders's plan was to remove his bag. The idea being that the shock effect of his gruesome visage upon Jurgen Thor would be enough to make Jurgen throw up his arms in horror, thus giving Saunders the crucial split second in which to rush him and, if possible, hurl him down into the chasm.

"Aaargh!" shouted Saunders and tore off his bag, revealing, as he had done so many times at parties, his absence of face. Sadly for Saunders, Jurgen was a big boy and had seen many horrid sights in his time. He remained unmoved, and as Saunders leapt toward him, Jurgen fired, killing poor Saunders with a single shot to the head, or what there was of the head anyway. Saunders hit the ground with a thud.

Judy now had to face Jurgen Thor alone, but not for long. Hanging in midair as she was, Rosalie heard the commotion of Saunders's lunge and subsequent death. She did not know what these noises signified, but since her strength was already ebbing, she judged it a good time to attempt a chin-up and try to scramble to safety. She hauled her head above the edge and managed to slide one elbow over onto the floor before the sound of her movements made Jurgen turn. Seeing Rosalie clawing her way back into the land of the living, he launched a huge kick at her, catching her full in the face. Had he been wearing shoes, that would have been the end of the matter, but Jurgen was of course barefoot, and despite the pain, Rosalie was able not only to hang on, but also to grab hold of his foot.

In order to avoid being toppled forward into the trap, Jurgen was forced to throw himself backward to the floor, dropping the gun as he did so. He was about to try to kick Rosalie away with his free leg, when Judy made a lunge for the gun. Reaching backward, Jurgen was able to grab Judy by the trousers, and despite being flat on his back with a desperate woman using one of his legs as a climbing rope, he easily pulled Judy over. The little agent crashed down on top of Jurgen and bravely started trying to bang Jurgen's head on the floor. It was a futile gesture, considering Jurgen's physical superiority, but Judy did at least distract the prostrate giant for a moment while Rosalie, still pulling on Jurgen's leg, was able to drag her chest up over the edge of the precipice. That was all the breathing space she had, for Jurgen, quickly tiring of having Judy on top of him, hurled a mighty hammerlike fist at the side of

Judy's chest, thus punching him away and also breaking most of his ribs and knocking all the wind out of his small body.

As Judy lay in agony, retching beside him, Jurgen turned his attention back to Rosalie, raising his free leg in order to kick her back down into the chasm once and for all. But the respite caused by Judy's tiny attack had been enough. Rosalie had her other elbow up over the edge, thus momentarily freeing the arm with which she had been hanging onto Jurgen's leg. As Jurgen raised his other leg to kick her down, Rosalie's opportunity lay stretched out before her. Jurgen was, of course, wearing only a robe, and by raising one leg to kick Rosalie, he revealed his meat and two veggies to her in all their glory. Rosalie threw her free arm forward and grabbed Jurgen's mighty dick.

"Don't kick me off, Jurgen!" she shouted. "I swear I'll never let go of it, no matter how hard you kick. If I go, it goes."

Jurgen looked down at Rosalie in amazement. This was not a development that he had expected. In fact, he was at a loss to work out how in such a short space of time he had managed to move from being in complete control, to lying on the edge of the precipice from which his enemy was climbing, using his prick as a rope.

At that moment, the door of the study opened, and one of Jurgen's guests poked their head in.

"There's been a monsoon warning, Jurgen. People are thinking about heading off before—" The visitor stopped midsentence and took in the scene: Judy retching, Jurgen prostrate on his back, his robe thrown open while a girl hung on to his dick halfway out through the door. "Well, excuse *me*," she said. "Wow, you people are *wild! Ciao*, Jurgen baby, thanks for a great party."

The woman left, shutting the door behind her. Rosalie got a leg up over the edge and, leaving hold of Jurgen's penis, lunged up and over him, trying to make it to the gun. Jurgen was too quick for her, though, and grabbing

Rosalie in his mighty arms, he rolled over on top of her, his hands upon her throat.

"Now I will finish the job," he shouted. "It seems that I must kill you before I throw you into the precipice, depriving you of the final exhilaration of terminal free-fall. So be it, Rosalie. Bye-bye, baby, bye-bye!"

He began to throttle her with his huge hands. So big indeed were they, and so small was Rosalie's neck, that Jurgen could probably have choked her with only one of them. Within seconds Rosalie began to lose the plot, his grip was crushing the life out of her before she even had a chance to suffocate. Her legs flailed about, her arms flailed about, she was helpless. Judy, who could see what was happening, tried to come to her aid, but he could move only very slowly in case his broken ribs punctured his lungs. He was helpless, knowing that Rosalie would be dead long before he reached the gun.

Her face was turning blue, her limbs were now twitching more than flailing. She was definitely dying. One of her hands fell upon the pocket of Jurgen's gown. She could feel herself gripping something, the only item in the pocket. She recognized it; something stirred the memory in her fast-darkening brain. . . . That was it! She knew what she was holding. What else would she find in the pocket of a bathrobe at an orgy but a condom spray?

At this point, Rosalie probably only had one voluntary act left in her, but it was a beauty. With one movement she swung her arm upward, the spray in her hand, and let Jurgen have it full in the face. Within seconds his head was completely laminated. Now it was Jurgen Thor who was suffocating. His grip relaxed almost instantly as he realized the danger he was in. There was no solvent in the pockets of the robe; he had to get to the bathroom. He staggered to his feet, leaving Rosalie on the floor gasping life back into her desperate body. Blinded, for he had on reflex shut his eyes as the liquid rubber hit him, Jurgen bumbled his way across the room and felt his way to the study door, bursting through it as Rosalie was beginning to drag herself to her feet behind him.

Staggering up the stairs, naked but for the open robe, Jurgen presented a shocking sight to those guests who had not yet ascended to the helipad, his head encased in rubber, the black hole of his mouth tugging at the merciless laminate stretched across it. A great heaving and wheezing was emanating from his mighty chest. Behind him came a girl, a wild, dangerous-looking girl. She too was staggering, her chest was also heaving with the pain of breathing. She was still blue in the face, and the livid marks of strangulation were yet bright red upon her neck. In her hand was a gun. The remaining guests mumbled their apologies and retreated upward. This was rough stuff indeed. Much too rough for them. What they liked was to take designer drugs and make love to people who were as beautiful as they were. Indeed, the simple fact of being beautiful was the biggest buzz, and this was not beautiful, this was positively horrid. Pain, strangulation, guns, and rubber were things that they wanted no part of. If Jurgen was pushing the party that way, then they were definitely leaving.

Jurgen kicked open the bathroom door as the last of his guests jumped out of the spa bath and slipped past him. He crashed up against a basin and, hurling open the cupboard above it, groped blindly among various creams and lotions, spraying his face with various scents and aftershaves before, finally, he found what he was looking for . . . the solvent. Turning it on himself he sprayed and sprayed, gasping and retching with relief as the tight-as-a-drum skin that had enveloped his mouth dissolved, and he was at last able to suck in great gusts of air. Collapsing to his knees, he coughed and burped as little bits of melting rubber found their way into his lungs. He scarcely noticed, though, for he was breathing again . . . that was all that mattered. It did not even matter very much that Rosalie was standing at the bathroom door, leaning against the wall and pointing the gun at him. For the moment, Jurgen was simply happy to be alive.

Rosalie stared at him for a long time. That once mighty man, a man who had been an inspiration to a generation, and was now revealed for what he really was and had been all along, a contemptible, double-crossing wretch. Rosalie stared and stared, trying to recognize in this low figure the hero of old, but she could not. Instead she asked a question, a single word, in fact.

"Why?"

Death of a salesman.

"Why?" Jurgen spoke not to Rosalie, but to the basin that he still held on to for support. "Because I may be many things, Rosalie, you dig? But I am not a jerk, okay? The world is dying, and nobody can stop it."

"That's not true," said Rosalie.

"It is bloody true!" Jurgen replied hoarsely. "It's always been dying, ever since man began to take from it more than he needed. *This planet is a finite quantity; logic dictates that it cannot be consumed indefinitely.* I tell you, Rosalie, Earth as we know it is finished, because man rules it, and man is incapable of acting responsibly! Of thinking in anything other than the short term."

"That's just a pathetic generalization to justify your—"

"Is it, Rosalie? Is it? Let me ask you this. What politician, facing an election next year, would be prepared to make laws, the benefit of which would not be felt until the following year! I will tell you. None. There is no *profit* to be had today in protecting tomorrow."

Jurgen Thor had said his piece. He sat down on the floor, brushing aside the various toiletries that had fallen from the bathroom cabinet. He took another great breath and leaned back against the plinth of the marble washbasin. He was still coughing from the rubber in his throat, and there were great strands of semidissolved latex hanging from his eyelashes, hair, and nose. He looked like one of the living dead . . . which in many ways was what he was.

"So you've always known what Plastic Tolstoy has been doing?" Rosalie asked.

"Not always, but nearly always. I joined the board of Claustrosphere as Tolstoy's number two about a year after I founded Natura."

"But that's nearly thirty years ago! You've been on the board of Claustrosphere for thirty years?" Rosalie gasped.

"Yes, my attitude changed very quickly," Jurgen replied. "Like any good greenie, I could see the way the wind was blowing. The industrialized world's blind obsession with 'growth' meant death, that much was obvious. The human race was going to self-destruct and take the planet with it. That would happen whatever anybody did, despite me, despite Tolstoy, despite Claustrosphere. I knew that then, and I know it now. At least Claustrosphere offers people some kind of future."

"Have you got one?" Rosalie inquired.

"Of course. I am not a fool. My Claustrosphere covers the whole of a small Pacific atoll. It is very beautiful."

"How come they tried to kill you with that bomb?"

It was Judy who asked this question. He had collected himself sufficiently to slowly follow Rosalie up to the bathroom and had heard most of what Jurgen Thor had said.

"Believe me, man," Jurgen said. "If they'd wanted to kill me they would have succeeded. It was just a marketing strategy. Claustrosphere sales have been down for a while, Plastic was planning a relaunch, and I volunteered to be a part of it."

"That was good of you," said Rosalie bitterly.

"Get real, baby, I'm no philanthropist. I have nearly as many shares as Tolstoy does, it's my profits too. I must admit to you, though, I was pretty annoyed that my dick got blown off. The blast was only supposed to singe my hair. Our sabotage people said there must have been other bombs planted in the building that ours set off. That's European democracy for you, for every delegate, an assassin."

They made a strange triumvirate. Judy was on his hands and knees, the only position he could sustain without fainting. Jurgen sat against the basin among the broken bottles. Only Rosalie was on her feet, and she was mightily bruised about the head and neck. It was a sorry scene, but a fitting one in which to learn how careful and meticulous was the marketing of the end of the world.

"You seem kind of happy to talk about all this. You've kept your secret carefully up until now," Judy gasped between breaths.

"I once promised myself that if I could, I would one day tell pretty little Rosalie here the whole truth. The whole truth about her life and her world. Crueler than killing you, eh, baby? Don't you think? Your tape of Tolstoy's confession has long since vanished into the depths of my mountain. The only evidence you possess now is your word, and let me tell you, okay? Dead people speak neither truth nor lies."

"Dead people?" Rosalie inquired.

"Yes, I'm afraid so, baby. I know Plastic Tolstoy, you see, and if you attempt to tell your story, you will be dead almost before you have uttered the first sentence."

Jurgen spoke no further. He could not, for he himself was dead. Rosalie shot him through the head. She did not plan to do it, she just did it, without even saying goodbye. The world's second best Claustrosphere salesman was no more.

The end of the world.

Shortly after which, the Rat Run started.

It began quite slowly. One morning, about a week after the incidents described above, all the news bulletins were suddenly full of stories describing the Claustrospheres of the rich and famous. Also detailed reports about the preparations that those people were making for their own personal Rat Runs.

"These days, I have a chopper on permanent standby wherever I go, man. Hey, you're looking at one mother who ain't gonna get left out with the garbage."

There was nothing new in stories like this, except that the reports seemed to indicate a slightly disturbing sense of urgency about the preparations being made. Almost as if the elite were in possession of information that was denied to the general public.

On the second day, these dark hints had become the top story, gaining weight with each repetition. Was there something that the people did not know? Had the pestilence and hunger so long predicted in fact arrived, and were those in authority refusing to admit it for fear of mass panic? By late that afternoon there were widespread reports that a large, unspecified number of important people had *already* retreated into their Claustrospheres. The bulletins reported that the U.S. President and the Chairperson of the European Federation could not be contacted for comment, the scarcely veiled suggestion being that their staff did not actually know where they were. Both the White House and the Palace of Peace and Profit quickly issued detailed statements about the whereabouts of the two key figures, but these were only sparsely reported. The suspicion had been planted, and it was widely rumored that the leaders were jumping ship. These rumors were of course immediately picked up and re-reported, gaining credibility as they did so.

"Is government on auto pilot? Who's driving the bus? I'm Dan Bland coming to you live, as it happens."

The story had become self-perpetuating. Those channels that had not run with the original rumors soon found themselves reporting the fact that the rumors had been reported.

By now fear had gripped the world community. Those people who found themselves away from home began to try to get back. Flights were booked up, roads were clogged. Footage of packed airports and colossal traffic jams played heavily on the news media, causing more people to rush to the airports and jump into their cars. Every official denial that there was a problem served only to heighten the suspicion that there really was one. If not, why were they denying it? Smoke was being wafted about, and everybody was looking for the fire.

The rumors were turning to fact.

The President of the U.S.A. announced that he would make an emergency statement on television. This he did, appearing dressed in a chunky cardigan, standing in front of a fire, and assuring America and the world that there was no need for panic. The exercise backfired badly. The statement was broadcast, but so, almost simultaneously, was the news that the majority of people considered it a hoax. They felt that the President looked younger, his hair shorter, his teeth whiter than had been the case of late. The idea that the broadcast had been recorded a year or more earlier quickly gained ground.

Panic now set in in earnest. People spoke of nothing else. Everybody knew someone who knew someone who had already retreated to their Claustrosphere. Ships were returning to port. Airlines and other transport services faltered as staff took time off in order to avoid traveling too far away from their place in a shelter.

The question was no longer if, but when, and for how long?

"If we must go," People asked each other in anguish, "how long must we set our timers for? When will we be released?"

The answer was forty years. Nobody knew quite how it came about, but that figure was suddenly on everybody's lips. It seemed that some scientist or other on the news had been pressed to take a guess, and scarcely before the words had left his lips, it had become the truth.

"We're hearing forty years," reporters endlessly asked experts. "How accurate do you think that is?"

"That certainly seems to be the figure we're hearing."

"Four decades!" The cry went around the world, and with every repetition the accuracy of the prediction became more inalienable.

Then it happened. The panic dam burst. Ten billion television sets seemed to broadcast the bad news simultaneously. The Rat Run had started. People had decided that the Earth was giving up. It was being reported that the planet could not and would not support the human race any longer. "Don't drink the water!" the TVs said. "Don't breathe the air! Get in your Claustrospheres and set your timers for forty years! Everybody else is."

And everybody was. They all ran at once. Newscasters turned around, having read their last bulletin, to discover that they were sitting alone in empty studios. Their colleagues had already gone.

As people rushed for their shelters, it was almost as if they were embracing the Rat Run, as if it was in some way a relief to be done with the Earth at last. To be done with the waiting and the uncertainty. To be done with the guilt, and that constant, nagging feeling that you really ought to be *doing* something, and never really knowing what. Now there was nothing to be done. It was over and nobody had to worry about it anymore.

There were, of course, doubters, those who wondered for a moment if what they were hearing could be true, but they did not wonder for long. The panic was its own proof. People needed no further evidence that eco-Armageddon was truly upon them than to see their neighbors disappearing into their Claustrospheres. There was no question of holding back, once others had begun to run, particularly for the majority of people who were destined to spend their remaining years in communal shelters. The prospect of being left outside once the BioLocks had been closed and the timers set was too horrible to contemplate.

It was all over in a day. The human race simply disappeared. Not quite all of it, of course. There were those in the poverty nations who had no access to Claustrospheres. They remained outside, scratching away at the dust upon which they lived. Perhaps not even noticing that anything had happened, except that from that moment on, their lives began slowly to improve. To all intents and purposes, however, people just vanished, the only evidence that they still existed at all being the millions and millions of geodesic domes that dotted what had up until recently been the industrialized world. The human race was hiding from its own nightmare.

This Other Eden.

Plastic Tolstoy had saved the Earth, and ironies do not come any more ironic than that. Judy pieced together the sequence of events as he sat outside Ruth and Sean's cottage, peeling the potatoes with which Roger had promised to make a shepherd's pie.

It had happened this way.

Judy and Rosalie had returned from Jurgen Thor's mausoleum to discover Max sufficiently recovered to inform them that he did not, for God's sake, possess only *one* Ansafone. There were, in fact, machines in every room of his mansion and on every one would be a copy of Plastic Tolstoy's confession.

"I'm a big star, you know?" he had whispered from his sick bed. "I get a lot of important messages."

Rosalie decided to wait until Max had recovered a little before telling him that she had seen the type of messages that he received, and that he'd better never receive any more. Meanwhile, Sean paid his first and only trip to Hollywood, collecting all of the incriminating tapes from Max's Beverly Hills home.

Judy sent one tape to the FBI, one to the L.A. Police Department, one to the U.S. President, and one to Plastic Tolstoy.

That was the day that the Rat Run started. Tolstoy, faced with the certainty of ending his life in a cell, had chosen instead to serve out his sentence inside his fabulous Claustrosphere. It was not difficult to arrange. Panic is an easy thing to provoke, particularly if you own a large percentage of the world's media. In order to escape the justice of the law, Plastic Tolstoy used his power to sentence the rest of the world to serve time with him.

The extraordinary side effect of this entirely selfish act was that Plastic Tolstoy ended his wicked life by saving the world. For the Earth, cured temporarily of people, soon began to recover. Free from the exploitative, parasitic human virus that had infected it for so long, the planet was able to cleanse itself. With no further poisons being produced and no further natural resources being destroyed, the process of renewal actually began with the Rat Run; and when, forty years later, the human race reappeared, it was to a fresh start and a whole new view of the planet. For as far as this new generation were concerned, the Rat Run had been for real. A genuine response to a genuine global emergency, which of course in many ways it had been. Only a strange little group of aged, weather-beaten people in the west of Ireland knew the truth, and they would never tell. It was better that the people who emerged from the Claustrospheres believed that the lonely exile of the human race had been a necessary punishment for its sins, that they had survived the flood and it was time to start afresh, resolving never again to practice the selfish planetary vandalism that had led their forefathers and mothers to the day of the Rat Run.

Of course, some Claustrospheres were destined never to open again, those into which only the old or the lonely had gone. One such shelter stood silent in California, and inside it, under a false sky at the foot of a mountain on the edge of a rain forest, lay a slowly decomposing body. Lasting proof of the fact that while the planet may survive, all people, no matter how powerful, must surely die.